OXFORD READINGS IN PHILOSOPHY

FREE WILL

Also published in this series

The Philosophy of Law, edited by Ronald M. Dworkin
Moral Concepts, edited by Joel Feinberg
Theories of Ethics, edited by Philippa Foot
The Philosophy of History, edited by Patrick Gardiner
The Philosophy of Mind, edited by Jonathan Glover
Knowledge and Belief, edited by A. Phillips Griffiths
Scientific Revolutions, edited by Ian Hacking
Philosophy and Economic Theory, edited by Frank Hahn and Martin Hollis
Divine Commands and Morality, edited by Paul Helm
Reference and Modality, edited by Leonard Linsky
The Philosophy of Religion, edited by Basil Mitchell
The Philosophy of Science, edited by P. H. Nidditch
Aesthetics, edited by Harold Osborne.
The Theory of Meaning, edited by G. H. R. Parkinson
The Philosophy of Education, edited by R. S. Peters
Political Philosophy, edited by Anthony Quinton
Practical Reasoning, edited by Joseph Raz
The Philosophy of Social Explanation, edited by Alan Ryan
The Philosophy of Language, edited by J. R. Searle
Semantic Syntax, edited by Pieter A. M. Seuren
Causation and Conditionals, edited by Ernest Sosa
Philosophical Logic, edited by P. F. Strawson
The Justification of Induction, edited by Richard Swinburne
Locke on Human Understanding, edited by I. C. Tipton
Kant on Pure Reason, edited by Ralph C. S. Walker
The Philosophy of Perception, edited by G. J. Warnock
The Philosophy of Action, edited by Alan R. White
Leibniz: Metaphysics and Philosophy of Science, edited by R. S. Woolhouse

Other volumes are in preparation

FREE WILL

Edited by
GARY WATSON

OXFORD UNIVERSITY PRESS
1982

Oxford University Press, Walton Street, Oxford OX2 6DP

LONDON GLASGOW NEW YORK TORONTO
DELHI BOMBAY CALCUTTA MADRAS KARACHI
KUALA LUMPUR SINGAPORE HONG KONG TOKYO
NAIROBI DAR ES SALAAM CAPE TOWN
MELBOURNE AUCKLAND

AND ASSOCIATE COMPANIES IN
BEIRUT BERLIN IBADAN MEXICO CITY

Published in the United States by Oxford University Press, New York

British Library Cataloguing in Publication Data
Free will.—(Oxford readings in philosophy)
1. Free will and determinism
I. Watson, Gary
123 B105.F/

ISBN 0–19–875054–4

Library of Congress Cataloging in Publication Data
Main entry under title:
Free will.
(Oxford readings in philosophy)
Bibliography: p.
Includes index.
1. Free will and determinism—Addresses, essays, lectures. I. Watson, Gary, 1943– II. Series.
BJ1461.F75 123′.5 82–3576
ISBN 0–19–87054–4 (pbk.) AACR2

Typeset by CCC in Great Britain by
William Clowes (Beccles) Limited, Beccles and London
Printed in the United States of America

CONTENTS

INTRODUCTION*

1. THE PROBLEM OF FREE WILL

IN practical life, our concern with freedom normally focuses on more or less obvious impediments: on technical and physical restrictions, or on political and social sanctions. But now and then we encounter, in ourselves and others, less conspicuous constraints—for instance, when we come up against severe phobias, addictions, neurosis, or 'brainwashing'. Here subtler kinds of freedom are at stake. Sometimes we call these 'free will'.[1]

In the sense suggested by these examples, some people have free will and others do not. But free will is a general philosophical problem only because of the more *global* doubts that this concept provokes. We are sometimes struck (and some of us chronically) by the disquieting thought that free will is an *illusion*, that freedom of this kind eludes us quite generally. Not that all of us are thoroughly phobic, or addicted, or brainwashed, in the literal sense, but that the difference between those conditions and the 'normal' predicament is of little significance.

This troubling thought takes different forms. We may seem like puppets or machines; in a different simile, our behaviour is like the 'falling rain'. Casy the preacher, in Steinbeck's *The Grapes of Wrath*, awoke one night, to say out loud: 'There ain't no sin and there ain't no virtue. There's just stuff people do. It's all part of the same thing. And some of the things people do is nice, and some ain't so nice, but that's as far as any man got a right to say'. It is tempting to dismiss such thoughts as confused or worse, but that response will seem unsatisfying and disingenuous so long as we remain susceptible to their grip.

Like other varieties of scepticism, these global doubts prove both hard to

*For philosophical and editorial advice, I am grateful to Roy Bauer, K. Jenni, Greg Kavka, Edwin McCann, Susan Wolf and the advisers to the Oxford University Press; Eddie Yeghiayan compiled the Index of Names and provided valuable bibliographical information.

[1] The use of this phrase should not prejudice the questions of whether there is a *single* kind of freedom in question in such cases, and of whether the concept of will is ultimately helpful to our understanding of them.

define and hard to exorcise. It is part of the sceptical thought that the elusive freedom *matters* a great deal, that in particular the values of autonomy and moral responsibility are at stake. Consequently, scepticism should transform our lives. But in what way? The appropriate changes can seem alternately oppressive and liberating. Does the denial of free will demean humanity, or liberate us from the suffering and hostility that is pervasively condoned in its name?

Apparently, the belief in free will presumes for human beings a special and puzzling status in the natural world, one that is central to our moral outlook. A convincing treatment of the problem of free will must give an account of the values in question, as well as of this presumed status. For this reason, free will is as much a problem in moral philosophy as in metaphysics. Our view of what free will is depends on our view of what matters. The essays in this volume illuminate a number of the issues, moral and metaphysical, into which the general problem fragments. In the remainder of this introduction, I will say something about what these issues are and what needs to be done.

2. FREE WILL AND DETERMINISM

Free will is problematic to many philosophers because of its controversial relation to determinism: the view, roughly, that every event and state of affairs is 'causally necessitated' by preceding events and states of affairs.[2] The issue is whether the existence of free will is compatible with this view. Those who think not usually reason as follows:

(1) If determinism is true, then every human action is causally necessitated by events and states of affairs that occurred or obtained prior to its agent's existence.
(2) If every action is causally necessitated in this way, no one could ever have acted otherwise.
(3) One has free will only if one could at least sometimes have acted otherwise.
(4) Therefore, if determinism is true, no one has free will.

Some incompatibilists go on to add that determinism threatens moral responsibility for the same reason. For they believe that if we are unable to do otherwise, we cannot be properly held morally responsible for what we do. (For doubts about this, see Frankfurt's contribution to this volume.)

A common reply to this reasoning is that it involves a misunderstanding

[2] For more precise formulations, see David Wiggins, 'Towards a Reasonable Libertarianism' (for publication details not given in the Introduction, consult the Bibliography), and the essay by van Inwagen below.

of what it is to be able to do otherwise. What I can do is what is up to me, and what is up to me is what depends on my choice or preference. So to say that I can lift my arm is to say that whether or not I do so depends on my choice (or preference): that *if* I choose (or prefer) to do so, I will do so. And to say that I could have acted otherwise (than lift my arm) is to say that if I had chosen (or preferred), I would have done so.

On these grounds, many would challenge premiss (2) of the above argument. They conclude that free will and determinism are compatible because, even in a deterministic world, sometimes people would have done otherwise if they had chosen. Some of our actions would after all be up to us, in this important sense.

But the hypothetical interpretation of 'can' has been strenuously contested. The fact that I would raise my arm if I chose or preferred would not show that I *am* able to raise my arm, it would seem, unless I am able to choose or prefer to do so. For in general, if my doing x depends on my doing y, I am not able to do x unless I am able to do y. (See Chisholm's essay below for objections of this kind.) Therefore, the compatibilist will have to show that the ability to choose or prefer otherwise is compatible with determinism, and for this the hypothetical interpretation will not help.

In 'Cans and Ifs', this and other criticisms of the hypothetical interpretation are debated by Bruce Aune and Keith Lehrer. Aune argues that this criticism in particular trades on ambiguities in 'can' and 'possible', and contends that a similar criticism by Lehrer begs the question. He concludes that the hypothetical interpretation adequately expresses the sense of 'can' that is relevant to human freedom. In his reply, Lehrer defends his criticism against Aune's contention.[3]

Peter van Inwagen tightens the case for incompatibilism in his closely argued paper, 'The Incompatibility of Free Will and Determinism'. Van Inwagen presents an argument for incompatibilism that he thinks avoids the debate over the hypothetical interpretation.[4] If determinism is true, the

[3] Aune replies to Lehrer in 'Free Will, "Can", and Ethics: A Reply to Lehrer'. For further discussion of Lehrer's criticism, see G. E. M. Anscombe, 'Soft Determinism'.

[4] But in his defence of his premisses, van Inwagen appeals to a principle that seems to him analytically true: 'If S can render R false, and if Q entails R, then S can render Q false.' This principle will not be acceptable on the hypothetical interpretation. Whether this counts against the principle or the interpretation depends upon whether the principle seems unquestionably true.

It would be profitable to investigate the parallels between arguments of this type and arguments for the incompatibility of divine foreknowledge and free will, which employ similar principles. (See for example, 'Divine Omniscience and Voluntary Action', Nelson Pike, *Philosophical Review*, 1965, 27–46' and a reply by Alvin Plantinga, *God, Freedom, and Evil* (New York: Harper Torchbooks, 1974), 66–72.) In these, God's essential omniscience plays the role of the laws of nature and the antecedent conditions that are inaccessible to human agency. For a critical discussion of such principles in the theological context, see J. Hoffman and G. Rosenkrantz, 'On Divine Foreknowledge and Human Freedom', *Philosophical Studies*, 289–96.

laws of nature, together with a statement of the conditions of the universe before my birth, entail every true statement about my physical movements. Therefore, van Inwagen concludes, I could have refrained from making those movements only if I could have falsified the laws of nature or altered those conditions. But even on the hypothetical interpretation I could have done neither of these things.

3. INCOMPATIBILISM AS THE BEST EXPLANATION

Whatever the fate of the hypothetical interpretation, one may well be suspicious of these incompatibilist arguments on quite different grounds. According to these arguments, we are all totally *helpless* if determinism is true. But we have definite criteria for deciding when people are helpless in some respect, and the incompatibilist reasoning is suspiciously remote from these. No doubt I am able to remove my clothes now, though I prefer not to. They are not glued on, I possess the relevant skills of co-ordination, no one will stop me, I am unbound, awake, and so on. Such facts as these ground my certainty, and these have no bearing on the laws of nature or the condition of the universe prior to my birth. And these ordinary criteria are the ones that are relevant in contexts of moral appraisal. If I were a member of a nudist club, and subject to censure for remaining clothed at the dinner table, it would be a joke to come to my defence by invoking the doctrine of determinism. Quite generally, there is splendid evidence that we are not all 'helpless'. But this evidence does not disconfirm determinism. Therefore, the incompatibilist reasoning must be unsound, because it employs an irrelevant sense of 'can'.[5] So the incompatibilists must show the relevance to our ordinary thought and practice of the sense of 'can' they exploit. In response, they may argue as follows. Of course, the attempt to excuse someone by invoking determinism would be ludicrous in this context, but only because of its absurd presumption to knowledge. We must consider what we would say if someone produced an *actual* deterministic explanation.

For example, suppose it were shown that I remained clothed only because of a *phobia* about self-exposure. Then we *would* doubt that I was able then and there to undress. So the 'criteria' mentioned earlier are very incomplete. And incompatibilists may say that their view explains why phobias are relevant: what we discover is that my behaviour (or omission) was causally necessitated by factors over which I have no control. Where we find

[5] Compare Keith Lehrer, 'An Empirical Proof of Determinism?' Lehrer defends compatibilism in this way even though he rejects the hypothetical interpretation. Lehrer's argument is similar but not identical to 'paradigm case' arguments popularized by Anthony Flew's 'Divine Omniscience and Human Freedom', in *New Essays in Philosophical Theology*, ed. Flew and A. J. MacIntyre (London: SCM Press, 1955). See van Inwagen's response to Flew's argument below.

explanations of this kind, we deny freedom. Incompatibilism is then presented as simply a generalization of this ordinary response; if determinism were true, all behaviour would be so explainable.

4. FREEDOM AND RESENTMENT

This exchange shifts our attention in a fruitful way to the nature of the concepts that are involved in our actual practices. Incompatibilists claim that, in practice, whenever we find some particular deterministic explanation, we regard it as inconsistent with freedom and responsibility. This claim is hard to assess, however, since we have few if any instances of genuine explanations of this kind. That our responses to phobias and similar phenomena are evidence for incompatibilism is far from clear. It is doubtful, first, that these are even examples of deterministic explanations in any strict sense, and, second, that their allegedly deterministic character is what is relevant to our responses. Incompatibilism may rest on hasty induction from a very few samples, sketchily described.[6] In 'Freedom and Resentment', Peter Strawson submits that we never in fact cease to see others as responsible beings simply as a result of accepting deterministic explanations, but only when we see them as 'incapacitated in some or all respects for ordinary personal relationships'. In Strawson's view, the concepts of freedom and responsibility are rooted in a 'complicated web of attitudes and feelings which form an essential part of the moral life as we know it'. The prominent strands of this web are 'participant' or 'reactive' attitudes and responses of gratitude, resentment, love, and hurt feelings, as well as asking and granting forgiveness, moral indignation, and approbation. These responses and attitudes are natural expressions of the human concern for 'whether the actions of other people . . . reflect . . . goodwill, affection, or esteem, . . . contempt, indifference, or malevolence . . .'.

Such attitudes are affected by the ordinary excuses ('She didn't realize you were there', 'He lost his balance'), and also by the extent to which others are not (yet) capable of real involvement in the general range of adult impersonal relationships (small children, the deranged, the sociopathic). Toward the latter we tend to take up 'objective' attitudes characterized by a concern for treatment and consequences. But determinism does not entail that no one is capable of involvement in the moral community, that no one is 'normal'. It

[6] Such hasty induction is evident in John Hospers' well-known article, 'Meaning and Free Will'. After a convincing deployment of examples in which certain psychoanalytic explanations conflict with freedom and responsibility, Hospers leaps to the conclusion that the behaviour is unfree because determined. He thereby abstracts from what I should have thought were the essential features of the psychoanalytic cases, namely, that one's motivation is deeply inaccessible to one's consciousness. Moreover, it is doubtful that such explanations *are* deterministic in any precise sense.

is thus silent about the propriety of the 'participant' attitudes that constitute our conceptions of ourselves as free and responsible.

Strawson rejects the idea that we *should* give up the participant attitudes if we accept determinism, on the ground that this idea falsely assumes the existence of an intelligible external standpoint from which this form of life can be assessed. The relevant criteria of rationality are internal to our forms of life: 'the existence of the general framework of attitudes itself is something we are given with the fact of human society. As a whole, it neither calls for, nor permits, an external "rational" justification.' This 'network of attitudes' does not rest on any theoretical or metaphysical commitments at all, beyond what is relevant to the basic human concern for the quality of the attitudes manifested in interpersonal affairs.[7]

5. COMPATIBILISM REFINED

Strawson's response to the incompatibilist interpretation of our practices can be reinforced by recent explorations of the phenomenon of compulsive behaviour. Consider A. J. Ayer's remarks in 'Freedom and Necessity':

> A kleptomaniac is not a free agent, in respect of his stealing, because he does not go through any process of deciding whether or not to steal. Or rather, if he does . . . it is irrelevant to his behaviour. Whatever he resolved to do, he would steal all the same. And it is this that distinguishes him from the ordinary thief.

Here the idea, roughly, is that the kleptomaniac's capacity for practical

[7] Strawson's essay is an interesting combination of Wittgensteinian and Kantian points: it is illicit to demand an external justification of our moral framework, and this general framework is a presupposition of a coherent concept of human moral community. (For a rejection of the idea that incompatibilism arises from such an illicit demand, see Nagel's essay below.)

I am not sure how far the Kantian point is really in the essay. The question is troublesome in view of Strawson's claim that 'the preparedness to acquiesce in the infliction of suffering on the offender' is 'all of a piece with [the reactive] attitudes . . .'. One might well hope to challenge the propriety of retributive attitudes without giving up the concept of responsibility, or the other 'participant' attitudes. (For this, see Lawrence Stern, 'Freedom, Blame, and Moral Community'.) But it is not so clear what content the claim that a criminal was morally responsible would have if it were denied that any retributive attitudes were appropriate toward him. Surely to blame someone is more than to express the belief that he voluntarily did what he shouldn't. What is needed here is a discussion of the possibility of retribution without hostility.

It is also not clear that all retributive attitudes involve viewing the other as morally responsible. Recently I viewed a TV documentary on an American Nazi. My attitude toward him was very participant and reactive indeed: I loathed the man and would gladly see him dead. Such attitudes are appropriate here if anywhere. I did not see him as a member of the moral community, or as a potential moral interlocuter; I suspect that he was quite 'beyond the pale' and all the more detestable for that. (Was he responsible for his present moral corruption? Even so, I hate the man he *is* now.) There is a tension here in our (my?) thought about responsibility: between the idea that moral responsibility requires potential responsiveness to moral criticism and dialogue, and the idea that morally evil character and conduct is pre-eminently worthy of blame.

For extended discussion of Strawson's paper, see also Jonathan Bennett, 'Accountability', and Susan Wolf, 'The Importance of Free Will'.

deliberation is impaired. This, rather than the alleged fact that his behaviour is deterministically explicable, is what diminishes his free will.

This line is developed by Harry Frankfurt in his influential essay, 'Freedom of the Will and the Concept of a Person'. Frankfurt construes free will as the capacity to form effective second-order 'volitions', that is, desires that some particular (first-order) desire lead one to action. (This capacity is a condition of personhood, according to Frankfurt.) Presumably, it is lacking altogether in non-human beings, and perhaps in some *homo sapiens* as well, who are moved indifferently by their strongest inclinations. These Frankfurt calls *wantons*. Most people have this capacity to some extent, but like the kleptomaniac, are sometimes moved contrary to (or at least independently of) their higher-order 'volitions'. In these respects we lack free will. At least many of the examples the incompatibilist appeals to can be understood in this way. Just as we can distinguish ordinary thieves from kleptomaniacs without benefit of indetermination, so we can distinguish persons from wantons.[8]

While this kind of dependency of our motivation upon our higher-order attitudes is undoubtedly an important part of our conception of freedom, it is not, as Frankfurt suggests, all that we might intelligibly want to have by way of free will. Frankfurt's distinctions illuminate the problem of compulsive desires, but fail to cope with problems about the genesis of one's second-order attitudes. For example, might not the citizens of the Brave New World have effective second-order volitions? Phenomena such as 'brainwashing' and 'indoctrination' seem to require a different treatment from compulsive desires.[9] Moreover, the notion of second-order motivation is arguably not rich enough to capture Frankfurt's important notion of a wanton; it merely elevates wantonness to higher motivational levels. Higher-order motivation precludes wantonness only if one also cares about that motivation. Frankfurt wishes to explain 'identification' and its contrary in terms of higher-order desires, but the explanatory primacy appears to be the other way around. Higher-order desires are simply further desires, with no special 'authority', unless one 'identifies' with these in turn.[10]

[8] For accounts along these lines, see also Gerald Dworkin, 'Acting Freely', Wright Neely, 'Freedom and Desire', Joel Feinberg, 'What's So Special about Mental Illness?', Jonathan Glover, *Responsibility*, and L. H. Davis, *Theory of Action* (Englewood Cliffs: Prentice-Hall, 1979), ch. 6.

Frankfurt's notion of a person is apparently more inclusive than Strawson's notion of those with the capacity for involvement in normal adult interpersonal relationships. Frankfurt places no restrictions on the *content* of second-order volitions, so persons in his sense need share no framework for significant interpersonal discourse, nor have any of the participant attitudes Strawson emphasizes.

[9] On this point, see Michael Slote, 'Understanding Free Will'. It applies equally to the editor's own contribution to this volume.

[10] Frankfurt reconsiders this kind of problem in 'Identification and Externality'.

So I argue in 'Free Agency'. I suggest that human freedom cannot be understood independently of the notion of practical reason or judgement, and that this notion is bound up with a distinction between desiring and *valuing*. Reasons for action derive from one's conception of *a good way to live*; motivation that arises independently of that conception does not, contrary to Hume, give one reasons for doing what one wants. The significance of higher-order volitions is that they characteristically derive from one's conception of how to live; when one wants to do something as a result of one's valuations, one will want that 'desire' to be effective in action.

A focus on the concept of evaluation may help as well with the problems posed by the example of the Brave New World. Free will involves the capacity to reflect critically upon one's values according to relevant criteria of practical thought and to change one's values and actions in the process. To be free is to have the capacity to effect, by unimpaired practical thought, the determinants of one's actions. So viewed, free will is not something we simply have or lack, but is an achievement, that admits of degrees. The theme of critical evaluation, among others, is explored with insight by Charles Taylor, in 'Responsibility for Self'. Whatever is involved in this capacity, it is plausible to suggest that its radical impairment is what is bothersome about indoctrination and brainwashing.[11]

We regard the significant impairment of these capacities as particularly degrading, and this underlies our sense of the importance of free will. The same capacities are clearly relevant to moral responsibility as well. Moral blame, for example, may be understood as, in part, a form of moral criticism that presupposes the capacity of its subjects to respond in appropriate ways to the claims of 'practical reason'.[12]

6. LIBERTARIANISM AND SCEPTICISM

These attempts to answer the incompatibilist have refined our understanding of the freedom in question: it is the freedom that is relevant to our conceptions of ourselves and others as moral beings, with the capacities for meaningful endeavour and critical evaluation, for moral dialogue and interpersonal relationships of a certain character. Does the possibility of deterministic explanation threaten the possession of such capacities? That would seem to depend on the content of such explanations. And the incompatibilist arguments we have considered so far have nothing to say

[11] For discussions of conditioning and indoctrination, see Gerald Dworkin, 'Autonomy and Bahavior Control', and Robert Young, 'Compatibilism and Conditioning'. P. S. Greenspan takes a different approach in 'Behaviour Control and Freedom of Action'.

[12] But the doubts raised in the middle part of note 5 pertain here as well.

about this. For all they have shown, determinism is consistent with the explanation of human behaviour in terms of the exercise of the unimpared faculty of practical deliberation, and therefore with the activities of free and morally responsible men and women.[13]

On the other hand, the notion of practical thought remains dark. Here issues about the nature of practical reason interlock with the problem of free will. Without an adequate grasp of this notion, we cannot pretend to be clear about the distinction between indoctrination (or 'brainwashing') and other ways of acquiring beliefs and values. Here is a source of scepticism about free will that has been insufficiently explored. We will consider a related point in the next section.

Now we should pause to consider why the issue of compatibilism has so preoccupied discussions of free will. After all, the issue would seem urgent only to the extent to which determinism is a credible doctrine. But its credibility is arguably very low. (Does the notion of a *law* of nature have clear sense; is the idea of a *complete* description of the world at a moment a coherent one?[14]) Indeed, the agnostics or disbelievers include many compatibilists. Why do they worry so, instead of turning to other matters?

The answer is that they fear that incompatibility leads ultimately to scepticism about freedom and responsibility, not because determinism is probably true, but because they suspect that incompatibilist requirements for freedom cannot be met. Their worry may be expressed as follows. We would lack free will in a deterministic world, incompatibilists think, because there we would not determine our own behaviour—we would lack *self*-determination. But the denial of determinism does not ensure, by itself, that *we* determine anything. So an incompatibilist who affirms freedom—conventionally called a *libertarian*—must say what more is needed besides the absence of causal determination to get 'self-determination'. The compatibilist (or indeed the sceptic) suspects that the freedom demanded by the incompatibilist—a 'self-determination' that could not obtain in a deterministic world—obtains in no possible world.

The compatibilist or the sceptic challenges the libertarian to develop an account of human agency that satisfies the following conditions:

(a) The account must explain how we can be morally responsible agents of events that are deterministically explainable.

Equally important:

[13] The provocative thesis that freedom is consistent with 'being determined to be good' but inconsistent with 'being determined to be bad' is argued by Susan Wolf, 'Asymmetrical Freedom'.

[14] See Wiggins, op. cit., for a helpful discussion of this.

(b) The account must explain why we cannot be morally responsible agents of events that *are* deterministically explainable.

This challenge, as it turns out, is not so easy to meet. Some libertarians try to do so by distinguishing two kinds of 'causation': causation by events and causation by agents. in 'Human Freedom and the Self', Roderick Chisholm admits that, if there were only event-causation, then uncaused events could never be attributed to responsible agents—these would be mere 'accidents'. But some events are caused, Chisholm insists, not by other events, but by the *agents themselves*. This is causation of a unique kind. While the denial of determinism implies that some events are uncaused by other events, some of these may be caused in a very different manner (sense?)—by a human being who is thereby a responsible agent of that event.

Chisholm's answer has the right form to meet the challenge (indeed, it seems tailor-made for doing so), but its content remains obscure. Chisholm emphasizes that agent-causation is unanalysable. All we know of this relation is that it holds between an agent and an event when that agent is the responsible agent of that event, and the event is uncaused by other events. That is, agent-causation meets conditions (a) and (b) by stipulation. But the challenge is to say what this relation amounts to in such a way as to give some reason for thinking it to be empirically possible. 'Agent-causation' simply labels, not illuminates, what the libertarian needs.[15]

Compatibilists have often argued that condition (a) cannot be met because events that cannot be deterministically explained will be 'accidental', 'random', 'chance', or 'fortuitous' in a sense that precludes ascriptions of responsible agency. (See Ayer's essay for this argument.) But this complaint begs the question by simply assuming that all explanations are deterministic; the libertarian insists, after all, that free actions *are* open to explanations of a different kind. While talk of agent-causation may be, as such, unhelpful, David Wiggins has recently offered a different candidate.[16] All the libertarian needs, Wiggins suggests, is that our biographies unfold 'non-deterministically but intelligibly' in terms of our purposes, ends, or

[15] Chisholm protests, first, that agent-causation is no worse off than event-causation for being unanalysable, and, second, that we are acquainted, in any case, with our own causal efficacy as we act. While the latter claim is no doubt true, it may surely be doubtful whether the object of our acquaintance meets the conditions of the challenge.

[16] Op. cit. Wiggins wants to avoid a 'metaphysical self' of a kind that provokes Strawson's charge of 'panic' and 'obscurity', and Frankfurt's remark that free action for Chisholm would be 'miraculous'. But it is not clear to me that Chisholm's 'agent-causation' commits him to anything more empirically dubious than the idea that some events have a kind of non-deterministic explanation in which a reference to the agent, *qua* agent, is essential. Wiggins's own candidate may be seen as a further specification of just such an idea, and therefore not as a rival to agent-causation.

choices, that our behaviour be 'coherent and intelligible in the low-level terms of practical deliberation'. Thus Wiggins' candidate for condition (a) is *teleological* intelligibility of this kind.

This point seems to me correct and important.[17] The failure of deterministic explanation does not imply that an action is unintelligible from the agent's practical viewpoint. And such intelligibility is plainly pertinent to moral responsibility. But the status of condition (b) is less clear. For compatibilists might well exploit the idea of teleological intelligibility for their own cause. (After all, that's what we did in effect in the last section.) If the introduction of such intelligibility into an indeterministic world transforms it from a world of mere happening, without meaning, into a world of moral significance, in which moral responsibility and autonomy have a secure place, it is hard to see how its presence in a deterministic world would fail to have the same import. While teleological intelligibility may warrant ascriptions of responsibility for undetermined events (condition (a)), it does not help incompatibilism unless nothing could be intelligible in this way in a deterministic world.

7. A NEW VERSION OF INCOMPATIBILISM

We have taken libertarianism to be searching for a 'positive' condition in addition to the absence of causal determination. Instead, perhaps, we should view the condition in question as sufficient both for responsible agency and for the negative condition. It is not that behaviour must be undetermined and *in addition* teleologically intelligible; rather it must be undetermined *in order to be* so intelligible. But why think that this is so?

In 'The Conceivability of Mechanism', Norman Malcolm argues that teleological ('purposive') explanations are at odds with what he calls 'mechanistic' explanations—that is, deterministic explanations that do not employ such 'purposive' concepts as intentions, desires, and purposes. (For example, explanations solely in neurophysiological terms.)

The argument for the conflict is very roughly this. When we say that a person drank some whisky in order to drown her sorrows, that explanation generally has counterfactual implications—for example, that if she had not wanted to, she would not have drunk it. In the context, this also implies that without that purpose, her arm would not have moved in such a way as to contact and elevate the flask to her lips. But a mechanistic explanation of

[17] It is anticipated by Philippa Foot, 'Free Will as Involving Determinism'. For a challenge to the idea that causal explanation must be deterministic, see G. E. M. Anscombe, 'Causality and Determination', Inaugural Lecture, (Cambridge University Press, 1971). Of course, to be adequate to the problems of compulsive desire and indoctrination, 'teleological intelligibility' will have to be fleshed out.

these movements would not support this implication. Indeed, a comprehensive explanation of this kind would suggest that this counter-factual was false, since it would give all the relevant explanatory conditions, and the woman's desire would not be among them. (Malcolm rejects the thesis that her purpose or intention might be *identical* with some set of neurophysiological conditions.)

Now if ascriptions of responsible agency require seeing behaviour as teleologically intelligible, then if no teleological explanations are valid, no one is free and responsible. If Malcolm is right, then, mechanism (the view that all behaviour is subject to mechanistic explanations) is incompatible with freedom and responsibility.

This reasoning supports only a restricted incompatibilism, since it says nothing about deterministic explanations that are formulated in 'purposive' terms. But many philosophers believe that the concepts of intention, choice, and so on are unsuited for employment in deterministic laws, that any such laws are bound to be 'mechanistic'.[18] In that case, Malcolm's conclusion implies the unrestricted thesis that determinism is incompatible with teleological intelligibility. And this is what the libertarian wants: both conditions (a) and (b) are satisfied.

This version of incompatibilism differs significantly from the standard brand. The question of compatibility has shifted from the compatibility of determinism with being able to do otherwise to the compatibility of determinism with teleological ways of understanding human behaviour. On this approach, determinism is threatening because it belongs to a way of viewing people that allows no room for genuine explanations in terms of values, purposes, and choices. Determinism entails explanations that *compete* with our usual explanatory scheme. The success of determinism would force us to discard the concept of human agency that is inherent in this scheme, in the same way as advances in science cast to the wayside such concepts as vital force, ether, and phlogiston. (Malcolm argues that such a development is in an important sense inconceivable.) Let us call this version *explanatory incompatibilism*, and the older version *modal incompatibilism*.

Explanatory incompatibilism (or the idea that 'mechanism displaces the purposive') is explored at length by Daniel Dennett in 'Mechanism and Responsibility'. Dennett usefully distinguishes three explanatory 'stances'. The 'Intentional' stance is associated with what we've been calling teleological intelligibility. The Intentional stance is governed by an assumption of rationality. In practice, mechanistic explanations are

[18] The arguments here are many and complex. Readers may consult A. I. Melden, *Free Action*, Donald Davidson, 'Mental Events', Anthony Kenny, 'Freedom, Spontaneity, and Indifference', A. C. MacIntyre, 'Determinism', and Stuart Hampshire, *Freedom of the Individual*, ch. 4.

forthcoming only when the assumption of rationality seems fruitless. None the less, Dennett claims, mechanistic explanations are not inconsistent with this assumption. For 'the absence of a presupposition of rationality is not the same as a presupposition of non-rationality'. So there is no theoretical conflict between mechanistic and Intentional 'stances'. Mechanistic explanations have a wider scope, since they explain the 'breakdowns' of Intentional systems. But they do not impugn the credentials of the Intentional stance, which may remain enormously useful and practically indispensable.[19]

Whether or not explanatory incompatibilism is finally defensible, it casts a new light on the problem of free will. It illuminates something that is obscured or distorted by the modal version. Incompatibilism is presented by that version as a generalization of our ordinary excusing conditions. Determinism is said to imply that certain criteria internal to our moral framework are never satisfied, for example, that we are all *excused* for our misconduct because not being able to do otherwise is an excuse. As I have tried to bring out, this account of the effect of determinism is not fully convincing. Explanatory incompatibilism explains why: it is not that determinism implies the omnipresence of the usual excusing conditions, but that it calls into question the whole framework in which talk of exculpation makes sense. Our conduct would then have the status of natural forces. The reason these are not morally responsible agents is not that they couldn't have done otherwise; it is that they are not teleological agents.[20]

Since it is doubtful that mechanistic explanations need to be deterministic (see Dennett's essay for this point), we may go a step further. A fruitful and comprehensive explanatory scheme that was both mechanistic and inherently probabilistic would tend just as much (or little) to displace teleological accounts. (Consider the claims made by B. F. Skinner for scientific behaviourism.) For this reason, teleological intelligibility, not indetermination, is the crucial issue. Determinism is relevant only if it implies mechanism.

Let us return to the sceptical thoughts we considered in the opening section. Certain prospective and actual explanations prompt us to think: 'If that's our world, we are like puppets or machines', or 'Our behaviour is like

[19] For another important response to Malcolm, see Alvin I. Goldman, 'The Compatibility of Mechanism and Purpose'.

[20] But compare: 'I cannot hold it against the corkscrew that it did what it did, because that was all it could have done'. (Ted Honderich, 'One Determinism', *Essays on Freedom of Action*, 208.) As though it would matter in the least whether its malfunctions were random. Surely what matters is that it cannot be seen as up to anything, as (in Dennett's term) an Intentional system.

In this paragraph, I have benefited from discussions with Roy Bauer of his interesting ideas on the problem of free will.

the falling rain'. As explanatory incompatibilism suggests, what prompts such thoughts may not be the deterministic character of the envisaged explanations (they may not have precisely that character), but their mechanistic character. The bothersome explanations seem to show that our behaviour is not intelligible in the way we ordinarily suppose. The guiding image of the puppet metaphor may not be that our behaviour is the ineluctable consequence of external forces, but (ineluctable or not), it is not ours, not 'self-directed', where the 'self' is conceived as a being responsive to the relevant norms of practical rationality. Like marionettes and machines, the image suggests, we have no 'insides': we are in the relevant sense 'empty'.[21]

Seen in this way, the problem of free will is another instance of a general difficulty in bringing together our views of ourselves both as moral beings and as creatures of nature. As Thomas Nagel suggests in 'Moral Luck', the problem arises from an apparent clash between an 'internal' 'subjective' view of ourselves, as agents, unified centres and sources of activity, and an 'external', 'objective' view from which one's behaviour appears as 'part of the course of events'. In Nagel's words, 'the self which acts and is the object of moral judgement is threatened with dissolution by the absorption of its acts and impulses into the class of events'. To adopt a mechanistic stance (whether deterministic or not) would be to take a standpoint from which one's agency is indiscernible. The problem of free will is part of the problem of finding room in the world for ourselves.

[21] Compare Charles Taylor, *The Explanation of Behaviour* (London: Routledge & Kegan Paul, 1964), 57–8: '. . . systems to whom action can be attributed have a special status, in that they are considered *loci* of responsibility, centres from which behaviour is directed. The notion "centre" seems very strongly rooted in our ordinary view . . . and it gives rise to a deep-seated and pervasive metaphor, that of the "inside". Beings who can act are thought of as having an inner core from which their overt action flows . . . What is essential to the notion of an inside . . . is the notion of . . . intentionality.'

I

FREEDOM AND NECESSITY

A. J. AYER

WHEN I am said to have done something of my own free will it is implied that I could have acted otherwise; and it is only when it is believed that I could have acted otherwise that I am held to be morally responsible for what I have done. For a man is not thought to be morally responsible for an action that it was not in his power to avoid. But if human behaviour is entirely governed by causal laws, it is not clear how any action that is done could ever have been avoided. It may be said of the agent that he would have acted otherwise if the causes of his action had been different, but they being what they were, it seems to follow that he was bound to act as he did. Now it is commonly assumed both that men are capable of acting freely, in the sense that is required to make them morally responsible, and that human behaviour is entirely governed by causal laws: and it is the apparent conflict between these two assumptions that gives rise to the philosophical problem of the freedom of the will.

Contronted with this problem, many people will be inclined to agree with Dr. Johnson: 'Sir, we *know* our will is free, and *there's* an end on't.' But, while this does very well for those who accept Dr. Johnson's premiss, it would hardly convince anyone who denied the freedom of the will. Certainly, if we do know that our wills are free, it follows that they are so. But the logical reply to this might be that since our wills are not free, it follows that no one can know that they are: so that if anyone claims, like Dr. Johnson, to know that they are, he must be mistaken. What is evident, indeed, is that people often believe themselves to be acting freely; and it is to this 'feeling' of freedom that some philosophers appeal when they wish, in the supposed interests of morality, to prove that not all human action is causally

From *Philosophical Essays* by Professor Sir Alfred Ayer (1954, pp. 271–84). Reprinted by permission of Macmillan, London and Basingstoke.

determined. But if these philosophers are right in their assumption that a man cannot be acting freely if his action is causally determined, then the fact that someone feels free to do, or not to do, a certain action does not prove that he really is so. It may prove that the agent does not himself know what it is that makes him act in one way rather than another: but from the fact that a man is unaware of the causes of his action, it does not follow that no such causes exist.

So much may be allowed to the determinist; but his belief that all human actions are subservient to causal laws still remains to be justified. If, indeed, it is necessary that every event should have a cause, then the rule must apply to human behaviour as much as to anything else. But why should it be supposed that every event must have a cause? The contrary is not unthinkable. Nor is the law of universal causation a necessary presupposition of scientific thought. The scientist may try to discover causal laws, and in many cases he succeeds; but sometimes he has to be content with statistical laws, and sometimes he comes upon events which, in the present state of his knowledge, he is not able to subsume under any law at all. In the case of these events he assumes that if he knew more he would be able to discover some law, whether causal or statistical, which would enable him to account for them. And this assumption cannot be disproved. For however far he may have carried his investigation, it is always open to him to carry it further; and it is always conceivable that if he carried it further he would discover the connection which had hitherto escaped him. Nevertheless, it is also conceivable that the events with which he is concerned are not systematically connected with any others: so that the reason why he does not discover the sort of laws that he requires is simply that they do not obtain.

Now in the case of human conduct the search for explanations has not in fact been altogether fruitless. Certain scientific laws have been established; and with the help of these laws we do make a number of successful predictions about the ways in which different people will behave. But these predictions do not always cover every detail. We may be able to predict that in certain circumstances a particular man will be angry, without being able to prescribe the precise form that the expression of his anger will take. We may be reasonably sure that he will shout, but not sure how loud his shout will be, or exactly what words he will use. And it is only a small proportion of human actions that we are able to forecast even so precisely as this. But that, it may be said, is because we have not carried our investigations very far. The science of psychology is still in its infancy and, as it is developed, not only will more human actions be explained, but the explanations will go into greater detail. The ideal of complete explanation may never in fact be attained: but it is theoretically attainable. Well, this may be so: and certainly it is impossible to show *a priori* that it is not so: but equally it cannot be shown that it is. This will not, however, discourage the scientist who, in the field of human behaviour, as elsewhere, will continue to formulate theories and test them by the facts. And in this he is justified. For since he has no reason *a priori* to admit that there is a limit to what he can discover, the fact that he also cannot be sure that there is no limit does not make it unreasonable for him to devise theories, nor, having devised them, to try constantly to improve them.

But now suppose it to be claimed that, so far as men's actions are concerned, there is a limit: and that this limit is set by the fact of human freedom. An obvious objection is that in many cases in which a person feels himself to be free to do, or not to do, a certain action, we are even now able to explain, in causal terms, why it is that he acts as he does. But it might be argued that even if men are sometimes mistaken in believing that they act freely, it does not follow that they are always so mistaken. For it is not always the case that when a man believes that he has acted freely we are in fact able to account for his action in causal terms. A determinist would say that we should be able to account for it if we had more knowledge of the circumstances, and had been able to discover the appropriate natural laws. But until those discoveries have been made, this remains only a pious hope. And may it not be true that, in some cases at least, the reason why we can give no causal explanation is that no causal explanation is available; and that this is because the agent's choice was literally free, as he himself felt it to be?

The answer is that this may indeed be true, inasmuch as it is open to anyone to hold that no explanation is possible until some explanation is actually found. But even so it does not give the moralist what he wants. For he is anxious to show that men are capable of acting freely in order to infer that they can be morally responsible for what they do. But if it is a matter of pure chance that a man should act in one way rather than another, he may be free but can hardly be responsible. And indeed when a man's actions seem to us quite unpredictable, when, as we say, there is no knowing what he will do, we do not look upon him as a moral agent. We look upon him as a lunatic.

To this it may be objected that we are not dealing fairly with the moralist. For when he makes it a condition of my being morally responsible that I should act freely, he does not wish to imply that it is purely a matter of chance that I act as I do. What he wishes to imply is that my actions are the result of my own free choice: and it is because they are the result of my own free choice that I am held to be morally responsible for them.

But now we must ask how it is that I come to make my choice. Either it is an accident that I choose to act as I do or it is not. If it is a accident, then it is merely a matter of chance that I did not choose otherwise; and if it is merely a matter of chance that I did not choose otherwise, it is surely irrational to hold me morally responsible for choosing as I did. But if it is not an accident that I choose to do one thing rather than another, then presumably there is some causal explanation of my choice: and in that case we are led back to determinism.

Again, the objection may be raised that we are not doing justice to the moralist's case. His view is not that it is a matter of chance that I choose to act as I do, but rather that my choice depends upon my character. Nevetheless he holds that I can still be free in the sense that he requires; for it is I who am responsible for my character. But in what way am I responsible for my character? Only, surely, in the sense that there is a causal connection between what I do now and what I have done in the past. It is only this that justifies the statement that I have made myself what I am: and even so this is an over-simplification, since it takes no account of the external influences to which I have been subjected. But, ignoring the external influences, let us assume that it is in fact the case that I have made myself what I am. Then it is still legitimate to ask how it is that I have come to make myself one sort of person rather than another. And if it be answered that it is a matter of my strength of will, we can put the same question in another form by asking how it is that my will has the strength that it has and not some other degree of strength. Once more, either it is an accident or it is not. If it is an accident, then by the same argument as before, I am not morally responsible, and if it is not an accident we are led back to determinism.

Furthermore, to say that my actions proceed from my character or, more colloquially, that I act in character, is to say that my behaviour is consistent and to that extent predictable: and since it is, above all, for the actions that I perform in character that I am held to be morally responsible, it looks as if the admission of moral responsibility, so far from being incompatible with determinism, tends rather to presuppose it. But how can this be so if it is a necessary condition of moral responsibility that the person who is held responsible should have acted freely? It seems that if we are to retain this idea of moral responsibility, we must either show that men can be held responsible for actions which they do not do freely, or else find some way of reconciling determinism with the freedom of the will.

It is no doubt with the object of effecting this reconciliation that some philosophers have defined freedom as the consciousness of necessity. And by so doing they are able to say not only that a man can be acting freely when his action is causally determined, but even that his action must be causally determined for it to be possible for him to be acting freely. Nevertheless this definition has the serious disadvantage that it gives to the word 'freedom' a meaning quite different from any that it ordinarily bears. It is indeed obvious that if we are allowed to give the word 'freedom' any meaning that we please, we can find a meaning that will reconcile it with determinism: but this is no more a solution of our present problem than the fact that the word 'horse' could be arbitrarily used to mean what is ordinarily meant by 'sparrow' is a proof that horses have wings. For suppose that I am compelled by another person to do something 'against my will'. In that case, as the word 'freedom' is ordinarily used, I should not be said to be acting freely: and the fact that I am fully aware of the constraint to which I am subjected makes no difference to the matter. I do not become free by becoming conscious that I am not. It may, indeed, be possible to show that my being aware that my action is causally determined is not incompatible with my acting freely: but it by no means follows that it is in this that my freedom consists. Moreover, I suspect that one of the reasons why people are inclined to define freedom as the consciousness of necessity is that they think that if one is conscious of necessity one may somehow be able to master it. But this is a fallacy. It is like someone's saying that he wishes he could see into the future, because if he did he would know what calamities lay in wait for him and so would be able to avoid them. But if he avoids the calamities then they don't lie in the future and it is not true that he foresees them. And similarly if I am able to master necessity, in the sense of escaping the operation of a necessary law, then the law in question is not necessary. And if the law is not necessary, then neither my freedom nor anything else can consist in my knowing that it is.

Let it be granted, then, when we speak of reconciling freedom with determination we are using the word 'freedom' in an ordinary sense. It still remains for us to make this usage clear: and perhaps the best way to make it clear is to show what it is that freedom, in this sense, is contrasted with. Now we began with the assumption that freedom is contrasted with causality: so that a man cannot be said to be acting freely if his action is causally determined. But this assumption has led us into difficulties and I now wish to suggest that it is mistaken. For it is not, I think, causality that freedom is to be contrasted with, but constraint. And while it is true that being constrained to do an action entails being caused to do it, I shall try to show that the converse does not hold. I shall try to show that from the fact that my action is causally determined it does not necessarily follow that I am constrained to do it: and this is equivalent to saying that it does not necessarily follow that I am not free.

If I am constrained, I do not act freely. But in what circumstances can I legitimately be said to be constrained? An obvious instance is the case in which I am compelled by another person to do what he wants. In a case of this sort the compulsion need not be such as to deprive one of the power of choice. It is not required that the other person should have hypnotized me, or that he should make it physically impossible for me to go against his will. It is enough that he should induce me to do what he wants by making it clear to me that, if I do not, he will bring about some situation that I regard as even more undesirable than the consequences of the action that he wishes me to do. Thus, if the man points a pistol at my head I may still choose to disobey him: but this does not prevent its being true that if I do fall in with his wishes he can legitimately be said to have compelled me. And if the circumstances are such that no reasonable person would be expected to choose the other alternative, then the action that I am made to do is not one for which I am held to be morally responsible.

A similar, but still somewhat different, case is that in which another person has obtained an habitual ascendancy over me. Where this is so, there may be no question of my being induced to act as the other person wishes by being confronted with a still more disagreeable alternative: for if I am sufficiently under his influence this special stimulus will not be necessary. Nevertheless I do not act freely, for the reason that I have been deprived of the power of choice. And this means that I have acquired so strong a habit of obedience that I no longer go through any process of deciding whether or not to do what the other person wants. About other matters I may still deliberate; but as regards the fulfilment of this other person's wishes, my own deliberations have ceased to be a causal factor in my behaviour. And it is in this sense that I may be said to be constrained. It is not, however, necessary that such constraint should take the form of subservience to another person. A kleptomaniac is not a free agent, in respect of his stealing, because he does not go through any process of deciding whether or not to steal. Or rather, if he does go through such a process, it is irrelevant to his behaviour. Whatever he resolved to do, he would steal all the same. And it is this that distinguishes him from the ordinary thief.

But now it may be asked whether there is any essential difference between these cases and those in which the agent is commonly thought to be free. No doubt the ordinary thief does go through a process of deciding whether or not to steal, and no doubt it does affect his behaviour. If he resolved to refrain from stealing, he could carry his resolution out. But if it be allowed that his making or not making this resolution is causally determined, then how can he be any more free than the kleptomaniac? It may be true that unlike the kleptomaniac he could refrain from stealing if he chose: but if there is a cause, or set of causes, which necessitate his choosing as he does, how can he be said to have the power of choice? Again, it may be true that no one now compels me to get up and walk across the room: but if my doing so can be causally explained in terms of my history or my environment, or whatever it may be, then how am I any more free than if some other person had compelled me? I do not have the feeling of constraint that I have when a pistol is manifestly pointed at my head; but the chains of causation by which I am bound are no less effective for being invisible.

The answer to this is that the cases I have mentioned as examples of constraint do differ from the others: and they differ just in the ways that I have tried to bring out. If I suffered from a compulsion neurosis, so that I got up and walked across the room, whether I wanted to or not, or if I did so because somebody else compelled me, then I should not be acting freely. But if I do it now, I shall be acting freely, just because these conditions do not obtain; and the fact that my action may nevertheless have a cause is, from this point of view, irrelevant. For it is not when my action has any cause at all, but only when it has a special sort of cause, that it is reckoned not to be free.

But here it may be objected that, even if this distinction corresponds to ordinary usage, it is still very irrational. For why should we distinguish, with regard to a person's freedom, between the operations of one sort of cause and those of another? Do not all causes equally necessitate? And is it not therefore arbitrary to say that a person is free when he is necessitated in one fashion but not when he is necessitated in another?

That all causes equally necessitate is indeed a tautology, if the word 'necessitate' is taken merely as equivalent to 'cause': but if, as the objection requires, it is taken as equivalent to 'constrain' or 'compel', then I do not think that this proposition is true. For all that is needed for one event to be the cause of another is that, in the given circumstances, the event which is said to be the effect would not have occurred if it had not been for the occurrence of the event which is said to be the cause, or vice versa, according as causes are interpreted as necessary, or sufficient, conditions: and this fact is usually deducible from some causal law which states that whenever an event of the one kind occurs then, given suitable conditions, an event of the other kind will occur in a certain temporal or spatio-temporal relationship to it. In short, there is an invariable concomitance between the two classes of events; but there is no compulsion, in any but a metaphorical sense. Suppose, for example, that a psycho-analyst is able to account for some aspect of my behaviour by referring it to some lesion that I suffered in my childhood. In that case, it may be said that my childhood experience, together with certain other events, necessitates my behaving as I do. But all that this involves is that it is found to be true in general that when people have had certain experiences as children, they subsequently behave in certain specifiable ways; and my case is just another instance of this general law. It is in this way indeed that my behaviour is explained. But from the fact that my behaviour is capable of being explained, in the sense that it can be subsumed under some natural law, it does not follow that I am acting under constraint.

If this is correct, to say that I could have acted otherwise is to say, first, that I should have acted otherwise if I had so chosen; secondly, that my action was voluntary in the sense in which the actions, say, of the kleptomaniac are not; and thirdly, that nobody compelled me to choose as I did: and these three conditions may very well be fulfilled. When they are fulfilled, I may be said to have acted freely. But this is not to say that it was a matter of chance that I acted as I did, or, in other words, that my action could not be explained. And that my actions should be capable of being explained is all that is required by the postulate of determinism.

If more than this seems to be required it is, I think, because the use of the very word 'determinism' is in some degree misleading. For it tends to suggest that one event is somehow in the power of another, whereas the truth is merely that they are factually correlated. And the same applies to the use, in this context, of the word 'necessity' and even of the word 'cause' itself. Moreover, there are various reasons for this. One is the tendency to confuse causal with logical necessitation, and so to infer mistakenly that the effect is contained in the cause. Another is the uncritical use of a concept of force which is derived from primitive experiences of pushing and striking. A third is the survival of an animistic conception of causality, in which all causal relationships are modelled on the example of one person's exercising authority over another. As a result we tend to form an imaginative picture of an unhappy effect trying vainly to escape from the clutches of an overmastering cause. But, I repeat, the fact is simply that when an event of one type occurs, an event of another type occurs also, in a certain temporal or spatio-temporal relation to the first. The rest is only metaphor. And it is because of the metaphor, and not because of the fact, that we come to think that there is an antithesis between causality and freedom.

Nevertheless, it may be said, if the postulate of determinism is valid, then the future can be explained in terms of the past: and this means that if one knew enough about the past one would be able to predict the future. But in that case what will happen in the future is already decided. And how then can I be said to be free? What is going to happen is going to happen and nothing that I do can prevent it. If the determinist is right, I am the helpless prisoner of fate.

But what is meant by saying that the future course of events is already decided? If the implication is that some person has arranged it, then the proposition is false. But if all that is meant is that it is possible, in principle, to deduce it from a set of particular facts about the past, together with the appropriate general laws, then, even if this is true, it does not in the least entail that I am the helpless prisoner of fate. It does not even entail that my actions make no difference to the future: for they are causes as well as effects; so that if they were different their consequences would be different also. What it does entail is that my behaviour can be predicted: but to say that my behaviour can be predicted is not to say that I am acting under constraint. It is indeed true that I cannot escape my destiny if this is taken to mean no more than that I shall do what I shall do. But this is a tautology, just as it is a tautology that what is going to happen is going to happen. And such tautologies as these prove nothing whatsoever about the freedom of the will.

II
HUMAN FREEDOM AND THE SELF
RODERICK M. CHISHOLM

'A staff moves a stone, and is moved by a hand, which is moved by a man.' Aristotle, *Physics*, 256a.

1. THE metaphysical problem of human freedom might be summarized in the following way: Human beings are responsible agents; but this fact appears to conflict with a deterministic view of human action (the view that every event that is involved in an act is caused by some other event); and it *also* appears to conflict with an indeterministic view of human action (the view that the act, or some event that is essential to the act, is not caused at all.) To solve the problem, I believe, we must make somewhat far-reaching assumptions about the self or the agent—about the man who performs the act.

Perhaps it is needless to remark that, in all likelihood, it is impossible to say anything significant about this ancient problem that has not been said before.[1]

2. Let us consider some deed, or misdeed, that may be attributed to a responsible agent: one man, say, shot another. If the man *was* responsible for what he did, then, I would urge, what was to happen at the time of the shooting was something that was entirely up to the man himself. There was a moment at which it was true, both that he could have fired the shot and

[1] The general position to be presented here is suggested in the following writings, among others: Aristotle, *Eudemian Ethics*, bk. ii ch. 6; *Nicomachean Ethics*, bk. iii, ch. 1–5; Thomas Reid, *Essays on the Active Powers of Man*; C. A. Campbell, 'Is "Free Will" a Pseudo-Problem?' *Mind*, 1951, 441–65; Roderick M. Chisholm, 'Responsibility and Avoidability', and Richard Taylor, 'Determination and the Theory of Agency', in *Determinism and Freedom in the Age of Modern Science*, ed. Sidney Hook (New York, 1958).

also that he could have refrained from firing it. And if this is so, then, even though he did fire it, he could have done something else instead. (He didn't find himself firing the shot 'against his will', as we say.) I think we can say, more generally, then, that if a man is responsible for a certain event or a certain state of affairs (in our example, the shooting of another man), then that event or state of affairs was brought about by some act of his, and the act was something that was in his power either to perform or not to perform.

But now if the act which he *did* perform was an act that was also in his power *not* to perform, then it could not have been caused or determined by any event that was not itself within his power either to bring about or not to bring about. For example, if what we say he did was really something that was brought about by a second man, one who forced his hand upon the trigger, say, or who, by means of hypnosis, compelled him to perform the act, then since the act was caused by the *second* man it was nothing that was within the power of the *first* man to prevent. And precisely the same thing is true, I think, if instead of referring to a second man who compelled the first one, we speak instead of the *desires* and *beliefs* which the first man happens to have had. For if what we say he did was really something that was brought about by his own beliefs and desires, if these beliefs and desires in the particular situation in which he happened to have found himself caused him to do just what it was that we say he did do, then, since *they* caused it, *he* was unable to do anything other than just what it was that he did do. It makes no difference whether the cause of the deed was internal or external; if the cause was some state or event for which the man himself was not responsible, then he was not responsible for what we have been mistakenly calling his act. If a flood caused the poorly constructed dam to break, then, given the flood and the constitution of the dam, the break, we may say, *had* to occur and nothing could have happened in its place. And if the flood of desire caused the weak-willed man to give in, then he, too, had to do just what it was that he did do and he was no more responsible than was the dam for the results that followed. (It is true, of course, that if the man is responsible for the beliefs and desires that he happens to have, then he may also be responsible for the things they lead him to do. But the question now becomes: *is* he responsible for the beliefs and desires he happens to have? If he is, then there was a time when they were within his power either to acquire or not to acquire, and we are left, therefore, with our general point.)

One may object: But surely if there were such a thing as a man who is really *good,* then he would be responsible for things that he would do; yet, he would be unable to do anything other than just what it is that he does do, since, being good, he will always choose to do what is best. The answer, I think, is suggested by a comment that Thomas Reid makes upon an ancient author. The author had said of Cato, 'He was good because he could not be otherwise', and Reid observes: 'This saying, if understood literally and strictly, is not the praise of Cato, but of his constitution, which was no more the work of Cato than his existence'.[2] If Cato was himself responsible for the good things that he did, then Cato, as Reid suggests, was such that, although he had the power to do what was not good, he exercised his power only for that which was good.

All of this, if it is true, may give a certain amount of comfort to those who are tender-minded. But we should remind them that it also conflicts with a familiar view about the nature of God—with the view that St. Thomas Aquinas expresses by saying that 'every movement both of the will and of nature proceeds from God as the Prime Mover'.[3] If the act of the sinner *did* proceed from God as the Prime Mover, then God was in the position of the second agent we just discussed—the man who forced the trigger finger, or the hypnotist—and the sinner, so-called, was *not* responsible for what he did. (This may be a bold assertion, in view of the history of western theology, but I must say that I have never encountered a single good reason for denying it.)

There is one standard objection to all of this and we should consider it briefly.

3. The objection takes the form of a stratagem—one designed to show that determinism (and divine providence) is consistent with human responsibility. The stratagem is one that was used by Jonathan Edwards and by many philosophers in the present century, most notably, G. E. Moore.[4]

One proceeds as follows: The expression

(a) He could have done otherwise,

it is argued, means no more nor less than

(b) If he had chosen to do otherwise, then he would have done otherwise.

(In place of 'chosen', one might say 'tried', 'set out', 'decided', 'undertaken', or 'willed'.) The truth of statement (b), it is then pointed out, is consistent with determinism (and with divine providence); for even if all of the man's actions were causally determined, the man could still be such that, *if* he had

[2] Thomas Reid, *Essays on the Active Powers of Man*, essay iv, ch. 4 (*Works*, 600).

[3] *Summa Theologica*, First Part of the Second Part, qu. vi ('On the Voluntary and Involuntary').

[4] Jonathan Edwards, *Freedom of the Will* (New Haven, 1957); G. E. Moore, *Ethics* (Home University Library, 1912), ch. 6.

chosen otherwise, then he would have done otherwise. What the murderers saw, let us suppose, along with his beliefs and desires, *caused* him to fire the shot; yet he was such that *if*, just then, he had chosen or decided *not* to fire the shot, then he would not have fired it. All of this is certainly possible. Similarly, we could say, of the dam, that the flood caused it to break and also that the dam was such that, *if* there had been no flood or any similar pressure, then the dam would have remained intact. And therefore, the argument proceeds, if (b) is consistent with determinism, and if (a) and (b) say the same thing, then (a) is also consistent with determinism; hence we can say that the agent *could* have done otherwise even though he was caused to do what he did do; and therefore determinism and moral responsibility are compatible.

Is the argument sound? The conclusion follows from the premises, but the catch, I think, lies in the first premiss—the one saying that statement (a) tells us no more nor less than what statement (b) tells us. For (b), it would seem, could be true while (a) is false. That is to say, our man might be such that, if he had chosen to do otherwise, then he would have done otherwise, and yet *also* such that he could not have done otherwise. Suppose, after all, that our murderer could not have *chosen*, or could not have *decided*, to do otherwise. Then the fact that he happens also to be a man such that, if he had chosen not to shoot he would not have shot, would make no difference. For if he could *not* have chosen *not* to shoot, then he could not have done anything other than just what it was that he did do. In a word: from our statement (b) above ('If he had chosen to do otherwise, then he would have done otherwise'), we cannot make an inference to (a) above ('He could have done otherwise') unless we can *also* assert:

(c) He could have chosen to do otherwise.

And therefore, if we must reject this third statement (c), then, even though we may be justified in asserting (b), we are not justified in asserting (a). If the man could not have chosen to do otherwise, then he would not have done otherwise—*even if* he was such that, if he *had* chosen to do otherwise, then he would have done otherwise.

The stratagem in question, then, seems to me not to work, and I would say, therefore, that the ascription of responsibility conflicts with a deterministic view of action.

4. Perhaps there is less need to argue that the ascription of responsibility also conflicts with an indeterministic view of action—with the view that the act, or some event that is essential to the act, is not caused at all. If the act—the firing of the shot—was not caused at all, if it was fortuitous or capricious,

happening so to speak out of the blue, then, presumably, no one—and nothing—was responsible for the act. Our conception of action, therefore, should be neither deterministic nor indeterministic. Is there any other possibility?

5. We must not say that every event involved in the act is caused by some other event; and we must not say that the act is something that is not caused at all. The possibility that remains, therefore, is this: We should say that at least one of the events that are involved in the act is caused, not by any other events, but by something else instead. And this something else can only be the agent—the man. If there is an event that is caused, not by other events, but by the man, then there are some events involved in the act that are not caused by other events. But if the event in question is caused by the man then it *is* caused and we are not committed to saying that there is something involved in the act that is not caused at all.

But this, of course, is a large consequence, implying something of considerable importance about the nature of the agent or the man.

6. If we consider only inanimate natural objects, we may say that causation, if it occurs, is a relation between *events* or *states of affairs*. The dam's breaking was an event that was caused by a set of other events—the dam being weak, the flood being strong, and so on. But if a man is responsible for a particular deed, then, if what I have said is true, there is some event, or set of events, that is caused, *not* by other events or states of affairs, but by the agent, whatever he may be.

I shall borrow a pair of medieval terms, using them, perhaps, in a way that is slightly different from that for which they were originally intended. I shall say that when one event or state of affairs (or set of events or states of affairs) causes some other event or state of affairs, then we have an instance of *transeunt* causation. And I shall say that when an *agent,* as distinguished from an event, causes an event or state of affairs, then we have an instance of *immanent* causation.

The nature of what is intended by the expression 'immanent causation' may be illustrated by this sentence from Aristotle's *Physics*: 'Thus, a staff moves a stone, and is moved by a hand, which is moved by a man.' (VII, 5, 256a, 6-8) If the man was responsible, then we have in this illustration a number of instances of causation—most of them transeunt but at least one of them immanent. What the staff did to the stone was an instance of transeunt causation, and thus we may describe it as a relation between events: 'the motion of the staff caused the motion of the stone.' And similarly for what the hand did to the staff: 'the motion of the hand caused the motion of the staff'. And, as we know from physiology, there are still other events which caused the motion of the hand. Hence we need not introduce the agent at this particular point, as Aristotle does—we *need* not, though we *may*. We *may* say that the hand was moved by the man, but we may *also* say that the motion of the hand was caused by the motion of certain muscles; and we may say that the motion of the muscles was caused by certain events that took place within the brain. But some event, and presumably one of those that took place within the brain, was caused by the agent and not by any other events.

There are, of course, objections to this way of putting the matter; I shall consider the two that seem to me to be most important.

7. One may object, firstly: 'If the *man* does anything, then, as Aristotle's remark suggests, what he does is to move the *hand*. But he certainly does not *do* anything to his brain—he may not even know that he *has* a brain. And if he doesn't do anything to the brain, and if the motion of the hand was caused by something that happened within the brain, then there is no point in appealing to "immanent causation" as being something incompatible with "transeunt causation"—for the whole thing, after all, is a matter of causal relations among events or states of affairs.'

The answer to this objection, I think, is this: It is true that the agent does not *do* anything with his brain, or to his brain, in the sense in which he *does* something with his hand and does something to the staff. But from this it does not follow that the agent was not the immanent cause of something that happened within his brain.

We should note a useful distinction that has been proposed by Professor A. I. Melden—namely, the distinction between 'making something A happen' and 'doing A'.[5] If I reach for the staff and pick it up, then one of the things that I *do* is just that—reach for the staff and pick it up. And if it is something that I do, then there is a very clear sense in which it may be said to be something that I know that I do. If you ask me, 'Are you doing something, or trying to do something, with the staff?', I will have no difficulty in finding an answer. But in doing something with the staff, I also make various things happen which are not in this same sense things that I do: I will make various air-particles move; I will free a number of blades of grass from the pressure that had been upon them; and I may cause a shadow to move from one place to another. If these are merely things that I make happen, as distinguished from things that I do, then I may know nothing whatever about them; I may not have the slightest idea that, in moving the

[5] A. I. Melden, *Free Action* (London, 1961), especially ch. 3. Mr. Meldern's own views, however, are quite the contrary of those that are proposed here.

staff, I am bringing about any such thing as the motion of air-particles, shadows, and blades of grass.

We may say, in answer to the first objection, therefore, that it is true that our agent does nothing to his brain or with his brain; but from this it does not follow that the agent is not the immanent cause of some event within his brain; for the brain event may be something which, like the motion of the air-particles, he made happen in picking up the staff. The only difference between the two cases is this: in each case, he made something happen when he picked up the staff; but in the one case—the motion of the air-particles or of the shadows—it was the motion of the staff that caused the event to happen; and in the other case—the event that took place in the brain—it was this event that caused the motion of the staff.

The point is, in a word, that whenever a man does something A, then (by 'immanent causation') he makes a certain cerebral event happen, and this cerebral event (by 'transeunt causation') makes A happen.

8. The second objection is more difficult and concerns the very concept of 'immanent causation', or causation by an agent, as this concept is to be interpreted here. The concept is subject to a difficulty which has long been associated with that of the prime mover unmoved. We have said that there must be some event A, presumably some cerebral event, which is caused not by any other event, but by the agent. Since A was not caused by any other event, then the agent himself cannot be said to have undergone any change or produced any other event (such as 'an act of will' or the like) which brought A about. But if, when the agent made A happen, there was no event involved other than A itself, no event which could be described as *making* A happen, what did the agent's causation consist of? What, for example, is the difference between A's just happening, and the agents' *causing* A to happen? We cannot attribute the difference to any event that took place within the agent. And so far as the event A itself is concerned, there would seem to be no discernible difference. Thus Aristotle said that the activity of the prime mover is nothing in addition to the motion that it produces, and Suarez said that 'the action is in reality nothing but the effect as it flows from the agent'.[6] Must we conclude, then, that there is no more to the man's action in causing event A than there is to the event A's happening by itself? Here we would seem to have a distinction without a difference—in which case we have failed to find a *via media* between a deterministic and an indeterministic view of action.

[6] Aristotle, *Physics*, bk. iii, ch. 3; Suarez, *Disputations Metaphysicae*, Disputation 18, s. 10.

The only answer, I think, can be this: that the difference between the man's causing A, on the one hand, and the event A just happening, on the other, lies in the fact that, in the first case but not the second, the event A *was* caused and was caused by the man. There was a brain event A; the agent did, in fact, cause the brain event; but there was nothing that he did to cause it.

This answer may not entirely satisfy and it will be likely to provoke the following question: 'But what are you really *adding* to the assertion that A happened when you utter the words "The agent *caused* A to happen"?' As soon as we have put the question this way, we see, I think, that whatever difficulty we may have encountered is one that may be traced to the concept of causation generally—whether 'immanent' or 'transeunt'. The problem, in other words, is not a problem that is peculiar to our conception of human action. It is a problem that must be faced by anyone who makes use of the concept of causation at all; and therefore, I would say, it is a problem for everyone but the complete indeterminist.

For the problem, as we put it, referring just to 'immanent causation', or causation by an agent, was this: 'What is the difference between saying, of an event A, that A just happened and saying that someone caused A to happen?' The analogous problem, which holds for 'transeunt causation', or causation by an event, is this: 'What is the difference between saying, of two events A and B, that B happened and then A happened, and saying that B's happening was the *cause* of A's happening?' And the only answer that one can give is this—that in the one case the agent was the cause of A's happening and in the other case event B was the cause of A's happening. The nature of transeunt causation is no more clear than is that of immanent causation.

9. But we may plausibly say—and there is a respectable philosophical tradition to which we may appeal—that the notion of immanent causation, or causation by an agent, is in fact more clear than that of transeunt causation, or causation by an event, and that it is only by understanding our own causal efficacy, as agents, that we can grasp the concept of *cause* at all. Hume may be said to have shown that we do not derive the concept of *cause* from what we perceive of external things. How, then, do we derive it? The most plausible suggestion, it seems to me, is that of Reid, once again: namely that 'the conception of an efficient cause may very probably be derived from the experience we have had . . . of our own power to produce certain effects'.[7] If we did not understand the concept of immanent causation, we would not understand that of transeunt causation.

[7] Reid, *Works*. 524.

10. It may have been noted that I have avoided the term 'free will' in all of this. For even if there is such a faculty as 'the will', which somehow sets our acts agoing, the question of freedom, as John Locke said, is not the question '*whether the will be free*'; it is the question '*whether a man be free*'.[8] For if there is a 'will', as a moving faculty, the question is whether the man is free to will to do these things that he does will to do—and also whether he is free *not* to will any of those things that he does will to do, and, again, whether he is free to will any of those things that he does not will to do. Jonathan Edwards tried to restrict himself to the question—'Is the man free to do what it is that he wills?'—but the answer to this question will not tell us whether the man is responsible for what it is that he *does* will to do. Using still another pair of medieval terms, we may say that the metaphysical problem of freedom does not concern the *actus imperatus*; it does not concern the question whether we are free to accomplish whatever it is that we will or set out to do; it concerns the *actus elicitus*, the question whether we are free to will or to set out to do those things that we do will or set out to do.

11. If we are responsible, and if what I have been trying to say is true, then we have a prerogative which some would attribute only to God: each of us, when we act, is a prime mover unmoved. In doing what we do, we cause certain events to happen, and nothing—or no one—causes us to cause those events to happen.

12. If we are thus prime movers unmoved and if our actions, or those for which we are responsible, are not causally determined, then they are not causally determined by our *desires*. And this means that the relation between what we want or what we desire, on the one hand, and what it is that we do, on the other, is not as simple as most philosophers would have it.

We may distinguish between what we might call the 'Hobbist approach' and what we might call the 'Kantian approach' to this question. The Hobbist approach is the one that is generally accepted at the present time, but the Kantian approach, I believe, is the one that is true. According to Hobbism, if we *know*, of some man, what his beliefs and desires happen to be and how strong they are, if we know what he feels certain of, what he desires more than anything else, and if we know the state of his body and what stimuli he is being subjected to, then we may *deduce*, logically, just what it is that he will do—or, more accurately, just what it is that he will try, set out, or undertake to do. Thus Professor Melden has said that 'the

[8] *Essay concerning Human Understanding*, bk. ii, ch. 21.

connection between wanting and doing is logical'.[9] But according to the Kantian approach to our problem, and this is the one that I would take, there is no such logical connection between wanting and doing, nor need there even be a causal connection. No set of statements about a man's desires, beliefs, and stimulus situation at any time implies any statement telling us what the man will try, set out, or undertake to do at that time. As Reid put it, though we may 'reason from men's motives to their actions and, in many cases, with great probability', we can never do so 'with absolute certainty'.[10]

This means that, in one very strict sense of the terms, there can be no science of man. If we think of science as a matter of finding out what laws happen to hold, and if the statement of a law tells us what kinds of events are caused by what other kinds of events, then there will be human actions which we cannot explain by subsuming them under any laws. We cannot say, 'It is causally necessary that, given such and such desires and beliefs, and being subject to such and such stimuli, the agent will do so and so'. For at times the agent, if he chooses, may rise above his desires and do something else instead.

But all of this is consistent with saying that, perhaps more often than not, our desires do exist under conditions such that those conditions necessitate us to act. And we may also say, with Leibniz, that at other times our desires may 'incline without necessitating'.

13. Leibniz's phrase presents us with our final philosophical problem. What does it mean to say that a desire, or a motive, might 'incline without necessitating'? There is a temptation, certainly, to say that 'to incline' means to cause and that 'not to necessitate' means not to cause, but obviously we cannot have it both ways.

Nor will Leibniz's own solution do. In his letter to Coste, he puts the problem as follows: 'When a choice is proposed, for example to go out or not to go out, it is a question whether, with all the circumstances, internal and external, motives, perceptions, dispositions, impressions, passions, inclinations taken together, I am still in a contingent state, or whether I am necessitated to make the choice, for example, to go out; that is to say, whether this proposition true and determined in fact, *In all these circumstances taken together I shall choose to go out*, is contingent or necessary.'[11] Leibniz's answer might be put as follows: in one sense of the

[9] Melden, 166.

[10] Reid, *Works*, 608, 612.

[11] 'Lettre à Mr. Coste de la Nécessité et de la Contingence' (1707) in *Opera Philosophica*, ed. Erdmann, 447–9.

terms 'necessary' and 'contingent', the proposition 'In all these circumstances taken together I shall choose to go out', may be said to be contingent and not necessary, and in another sense of these terms, it may be said to be necessary and not contingent. But the sense in which the proposition may be said to be contingent, according to Leibniz, is only this: there is no logical contradiction involved in denying the proposition. And the sense in which it may be said to be necessary is this: since 'nothing ever occurs without cause or determining reason', the proposition is causally necessary. 'Whenever all the circumstances taken together are such that the balance of deliberation is heavier on one side than on the other, it is certain and infallible that that is the side that is going to win out'. But if what we have been saying is true, the proposition 'In all these circumstances taken together I shall choose to go out', may be causally as well as logically contingent. Hence we must find another interpretation for Leibniz's statement that our motives and desires may incline us, or influence us, to choose without thereby necessitating us to choose.

Let us consider a public official who has some moral scruples but who also, as one says, could be had. Because of the scruples that he does have, he would never take any positive steps to receive a bribe—he would not actively solicit one. But his morality has its limits and he is also such that, if we were to confront him with a *fait accompli* or to let him see what is about to happen ($10,000 in cash is being deposited behind the garage), then he would succumb and be unable to resist. The general situation is a familiar one and this is one reason that people pray to be delivered from temptation. (It also justifies Kant's remark: 'And how many there are who may have led a long blameless life, who are only *fortunate* in having escaped so many temptations'.[12] Our relation to the misdeed that we contemplate may not be a matter simply of being able to bring it about or not to bring it about. As St. Anselm noted, there are at least four possibilities. We may illustrate them by reference to our public official and the event which is his receiving the bribe, in the following way: (i) he may be able to bring the event about himself (*facere esse*), in which case he would actively cause himself to receive the bribe; (ii) he may be able to refrain from bringing it about himself (*non facere esse*), in which case he would not himself do anything to insure that he receive the bribe; (iii) he may be able to do something to prevent the event from occurring (*facere non esse*), in which case he would make sure that the $10,000 was *not* left behind the garage; or (iv) he may be unable to do anything to prevent the event from occurring (*non facere non esse*), in which case, though he may not solicit the bribe, he would allow

[12] In the Preface to the *Metaphysical Elements of Ethics*, in *Kant's Critique of Practical Reason and Other Works on the Theory of Ethics*, ed. T. K. Abbott (London, 1959), 303.

himself to keep it.[13] We have envisaged our official as a man who can resist the temptation to (i) but cannot resist the temptation to (iv): he can refrain from bringing the event about himself, but he cannot bring himself to do anything to prevent it.

Let us think of 'inclination without necessitation', then, in such terms as these. First we may contrast the two propositions:

(1) He can resist the temptation to do something in order to make A happen;

(2) He can resist the temptation to allow A to happen (i.e. to do nothing to prevent A from happening).

We may suppose that the man has some desire to have A happen and thus has a motive for making A happen. His motive for making A happen, I suggest, is one that *necessitates* provided that, because of the motive, (1) is false; he cannot resist the temptation to do something in order to make A happen. His motive for making A happen is one that *inclines* provided that, because of the motive, (2) is false; like our public official, he cannot bring himself to do anything to prevent A from happening. And therefore we can say that this motive for making A happen is one that *inclines but does not necessitate* provided that, because of the motive, (1) is true and (2) is false; he can resist the temptation to make it happen but he cannot resist the temptation to allow it to happen.

[13] Cf. D. P. Henry, 'Saint Anselm's *De "Grammatico"*', *Philosophical Quarterly*, x (1960), 115–26. St. Anselm noted that (i) and (iii), respectively, may be thought of as forming the upper left and the upper right corners of a square of opposition, and (ii) and (iv) the lower left and the lower right.

III

CANS AND IFS: AN EXCHANGE

(i)

HYPOTHETICALS AND 'CAN': ANOTHER LOOK*

BRUCE AUNE

A familiar strategy for philosophers wishing to reconcile freedom and determinism is to follow G. E. Moore and insist that the relevant sense in which a free agent could have done other than what he did do is given by the equivalence:

(1) *S* could have done other than *A* = *S* would have done other than *A* if he had willed to do so.[1]

Although this equivalence has a strong initial plausibility, it has seemed to many that J. L. Austin's famous 'Ifs and Cans' (*Philosophical Papers,* 153–80) provides a decisive refutation of it. Very recent discussion of Austin's paper has shown, however, that Austin did not succeed in his attempted refutation; yet his critics have formulated new objections, which purport to lay (1) to rest for good.[2] The aim of this paper is to show that these new objections are really no better than the old ones, and that a decisive objection to Moore's equivalence has yet to be formulated.

In his admirable review of Austin's *Philosophical Papers* R. M. Chisholm

From *Analysis* **27** (6 June 1967), pp. 191–5. Reprinted by permission of Basil Blackwell, Publisher.

*I wish to thank my colleague John Robison for helpful discussion on the topics treated in this paper.

[1] See G. E. Moore, *Ethics* (London, 1911), ch. 6. Although this analysis can obviously be refined in various ways (for example, mention can be made of the specific circumstances under which the action might occur), I shall ignore such complications in this paper.

[2] See Roderick M. Chisholm 'J. L. Austin's *Philosophical Papers*', *Mind*, 1964, 20–5, and Keith Lehrer, 'An Empirical Disproof of Determinism?' in *Freedom and Determinism*, ed. K. Lehrer (New York, 1966), 175–202.

suggested a line of objection to (1) that he later developed more fully in his paper 'Freedom and Action' (in Lehrer, 11–44). This new line of objection is very general, applying to the entire family of analyses that might be generated from (1) by replacing the verb 'willed' in the 'if' clause by some other verb such as 'chosen' or 'undertaken', which might seem more promising. Although I myself believe that 'willed' is actually the most satisfactory verb, I shall follow Chisholm and use 'chosen' instead.

As he formulated his objection, Chisholm unfortunately misstated his case. A corrected form of his objection (communicated to me in private correspondence) may be stated as follows. Suppose that a man *S* was such that, at a certain time *t*, (i) he did *A*, (ii) he would have done other than *A* if he had so chosen, (iii) he would not have done otherwise if he had not so chosen, and (iv) he could not have so chosen. Under these suppositions we may conclude, according to Chisholm, that *S* could not have done other than *A* even though he would have done other than *a* if he had so chosen. To draw this conclusion is obviously to reject the proposed analysis of '*S* could have done otherwise'.

It will be useful to set out Chisholm's argument somewhat formally, so that the structure of his reasoning is clear. The proposed analysis of 'could have done otherwise' may be represented as follows, where *B* is any action other than *A*:

(2) *S* could have done *B* = df *S* would have done *B* if *S* had so chosen.

The relevant suppositions about *S* are then:

(3) *S* would have done *B* if *S* had so chosen.

(4) If *S* had not so chosen, *S* would not have done *B*.

(5) *S* could not have so chosen.

Taking (4) as equivalent to 'If *S* had done *B, S* would have so chosen', Chisholm's claim is a dual one: first, that (3), (4) and (5) are consistent; and second, that (4) and (5) imply that *S* could not have done *B*. Given the sound modal principle that if *P*, *Q*, and *R* are consistent, and if *Q* and *R* entail not-*S*, then *P* is not logically equivalent to *S*, it follows that if Chisholm's claims are acceptable, the proposed equivalence must be erroneous.

To anyone familiar with the ins and outs of the free will debate, Chisholm's claim that (4) and (5) imply that *S* could not have done *B*—that is, other than what he did do—will immediately appear suspicious. It is easily granted, of course, that there may be *some* sense of 'could' for which this inference holds. There is, after all, the familiar modal principle that if *P* entails *Q* and it is impossible that *Q*, then it is impossible that *P*. Assuming that 'could not' may mean 'it was impossible', this principle may thus warrant the inference that if *S*'s choosing *B* is in some way necessary for *S* to do *B* and if *S* cannot, in some sense, choose to do *B*, then, in that same sense of 'cannot', *S* cannot do *B* either. But what is highly questionable about Chisholm's claim is the assumption that the sense of 'cannot do otherwise' *relevant to the question of a man's freedom* might be involved in this inference.

The point is this. Since the time of Moore, philosophers have generally agreed that not every sense in which a man *cannot* do something is equally relevant to the question of his freedom. If, for example, a man's willing or choosing to do something (for example, holding his breath) is causally sufficient for his doing it, then, given that he wills to do such a thing, any other action on his part will be *relatively* impossible. But the fact that a man cannot, in this sense, do other than what he does do is in no sense a limitation on his freedom. On the contrary, it is by exercising his presumed freedom that he rules out the possibility (in *this* sense) of his doing other than what he does do.

Now, for most philosophers, the sense of 'can' clearly relevant to the free will issue applies specifically to voluntary actions. The question normally at issue is whether a man could 'of his own free will' have done other than what he did do. If this is indeed the usual question, then the weakness, or at least implausibility, of Chisholm's inference from (4) and (5) to '*S* could not have done *B* (=anything other than *A*)' is immediately apparent. In drawing his inference Chisholm must assume that the relevant sense in which a man *cannot do* otherwise may be the same as the sense in which he *cannot choose* to do otherwise. (The sameness of sense here is required by the use of the modal principle mentioned above.) Yet for most philosophers, choosing and willing are not voluntary actions. For them, it makes no more sense to speak of voluntarily willing or choosing than it does to speak of voluntarily believing and intending.[3] It may be relatively impossible to will or choose, just as it may be relatively impossible to act or move. But this kind of impossibility, it may be urged, is not the kind of impossibility that obviously limits a man's freedom.

Although the objection just made to Chisholm's inference is in my view a tenable one, it is not actually crucial to the basic strategy of his argument. Keith Lehrer, in an ingenious recent paper ('An Empirical Disproof of Determinism', loc. cit.), grants the compatibility of a man's freely doing *A* with what he calls the causal impossibility of his doing otherwise, but he

[3] The idea that willing and choosing are not voluntary actions was regarded as axiomatic by traditional writers such as F. H. Bradley and R. G. Collingwood. It has recently been defended by Wilfrid Sellars in 'Thought and Action', in Lehrer, op. cit., 105–39.

employs a variant of Chisholm's basic argument in attempting to show that the hypothetical analysis of 'could have done otherwise' so far considered must nevertheless fail. Since Lehrer's argument is simpler than Chisholm's and yet involves the same basic strategy, it will prove illuminating to examine it.

Lehrer states his argument in an even more general form than Chisholm's. His aim is to refute any analysis of '*S* can do *X*' in terms of a conditional, '*S* will do *X*, if *C* obtains', where *C* is any condition a reconciler might wish to specify. His proposed refutation is simply this. Assume that a man *S* satisfies the conditional,

(6) *S* will do *X*, if *C*.

Suppose, also, that the following are true:

(7) *S* cannot do *X*, if not-*C*.

(8) Not-*C*.

According to Lehrer, if (6) is a causal conditional (which we may grant), it is consistent with both (7) and (8). Yet these latter statements imply

(9) *S* cannot do *X*.

In view of the modal principle mentioned earlier—namely, that if *P*, *Q*, and *R* are consistent, and if *Q* and *R* entail not-*S*, then *P* is not logically equivalent to *S*—it therefore follows that the above analysis of '*S* can do *X*' must fail.

The common strategy of Chisholm's and Lehrer's argument should be obvious. The basic recipe, which can be varied to yield any number of similar arguments, is simply this: to refute a proferred equivalence of the form, *A* = If *B* then *C*, find statements *D* and *E* such that their conjunction is consistent with one of the equivalence and yet implies the negation of the other side. Lehrer's argument is simpler and less problematic than Chisholm's because he was able to find premisses *D* and *E* that imply not-*A* by the simple rule of *Modus Ponens*, while Chisholm had to rely on a far more questionable rule involving an unexplained species of modality.

The simple structure of Lehrer's argument makes it easy to locate the weakness of the basic strategy common to his and Chisholm's approach. If they are to rule out a hypothetical analysis of 'He can' or 'He could have' they must obviously prove, or give good reason for believing, that the suppositions they introduce are in fact consistent with 'He will, if' or 'He would have, if'. Obviously, they cannot simply *assume* that this consistency obtains without begging the question. If I propose an analysis of '*S* can do

X' in terms of '*S* will do *X*, if *C*', I would obviously reject the idea, on which Lehrer's argument hinges, that '*S* will do *X*, if *C*' is consistent with '*S* cannot do *X*, if not-*C*' and 'not-*C*'. For me, '*S* will do *X*, if *C*' is supposed to *mean* '*S* can do *X*'; and since the special suppositions '*S* cannot do *X*, if not-*C*' and 'not-*C*' immediately entail '*S* cannot do *X*', I would never grant that '*S* will do *X*, if *C*' is consistent with them. A similar response can be made to Chisholm's argument: his undefended claim that the suppositions (3), (4) and (5) are consistent would never be accepted by anyone offering (2) as an adequate analysis.

It is possible that someone might believe that the consistency of (3), (4), and (5)—and thus of Lehrer's (6), (7), and (8)—can be demonstrated on formal grounds. These two sets of statements, it might be thought, are instances of mutually consistent statement forms. Thus, (6), (7), and (8) could count as instances of the consistent forms, '*Q*, if *P*', '*R*, if not-*P*', and 'Not-*P*'. The assumption here is, however, completely false, and would allow one to refute any analysis that might be advanced. Suppose that one were to propose '*X* is a male sibling' as an analysis of '*X* is a brother'. If the assumption in question were sound, we could immediately refute the analysis by establishing the consistency of the forms '*P*', '*Q*', and 'Not-*R* if *Q*', and then taking '*X* is a male sibling', '*X* is an only child', and '*X* is not a brother if *X* is an only child', as the respective instance of these consistent forms. The procedure is obviously fallacious.

Another possible approach to showing the consistency of the suppositions of Chisholm and Lehrer might be to claim that they strike one 'intuitively' as consistent, or even that one is more certain that they are consistent than one is that the proposed analyses are correct. This approach is, however, useless. Obviously, if you are objecting to a proposed analysis, it will be well understood to all concerned that you find the analysis unacceptable or out of line with your intuitions, and it will be equally well understood that you would find *any* simple set of assumptions whose consistency would immediately entail the rejection of the analysis 'intuitively consistent' or 'more likely to be consistent than the analysis is likely to be correct'.

The point of the last three paragraphs is simply that if the objections of Chisholm and Lehrer are not to be regarded as absolutely worthless attempts to prove a philosophical point, an argument showing the consistency of the crucial suppositions must be provided. Chisholm does not provide such an argument in his paper, and for this reason his objection cannot be regarded as acceptable, let alone decisive. Lehrer does attempt a brief argument for the consistency of his suppositions, but it is highly questionable and far too brief for the burden it has to bear. He argues that if (6) is a causal conditional, then it is consistent with (7) and (8) because 'it is logically possible that some condition which is a sufficient condition to cause a person to do something should be a necessary condition of his being able to do it, and that the condition should fail to occur'. This argument is extremely weak because the sort of condition those defending hypothetical analyses of 'could' actually propose are states of willing, choosing, or undertaking to do something; and no basis has been established, by Lehrer or anyone else, for thinking that one may be rendered unable to do other than what one does do by the mere fact that one does not will, choose, or undertake to do other than what one is doing. As already noted, to make this latter assumption is to fall into the absurdity of thinking that if making a certain choice is ever sufficient to bring about a simple action, then even if the act performed would normally be a clear case of doing something 'of one's own free will', the fact that the choice was made rendered one unable, in the morally relevant sense of the term, to do other than what one did do.

(ii)
CANS WITHOUT IFS
KEITH LEHRER

IT is logically possible that a man could not have done what he would have done, if he willed to, chose to, tried to, or what not. So I have argued.[1] However, Bruce Aune has raised some intelligent doubts that need to be put to rest. He contends that, with some refinement, the following is true:

(E) S could have done otherwise = S would have done otherwise if he had so willed.[2]

In order to refute this thesis and any variation of it resulting from altering the 'if' clause on the right hand side of (E), it is essential to understand the philosophical use to which this thesis has been put. I shall first outline the logical status of this alleged equivalence in arguments purporting to establish the logical consistency of free action and causal determinism, and, secondly, I shall argue that, when (E) is interpreted in such a way that, if true, it would prove that consistency, then (E) is false.

From *Analysis* **29** (1 Oct. 1968), pp. 29–32. Reprinted by permission of Basil Blackwell, Publisher.

[1] *Freedom and Determinism* (New York: Random House, 1966), ed. Keith Lehrer, 19–37.

[2] Aune, Bruce, 'Hypotheticals and "Can": Another Look', *Analysis*, 191 ff. [Reprinted above, Essay III. i.]

I

Let us understand determinism as the thesis that for everything that takes place, whether it be an action or not, there was some antecedent condition causally sufficient for it. What philosophers have attempted to prove is that causal determinism as so defined is logically consistent with free action. A free action is often thought to be one such that, though it be done, the agent could have done otherwise. Therefore, the question is whether

(i) The thesis of causal determinism

is logically consistent with statements of the form

(ii) S did A and S could have done otherwise.

Those like Aune, who defend the equivalence expressed by (E) to establish the logical consistency of (i) and (ii), argue that (ii) is equivalent to

(ii′) S did A and S would have done otherwise if he had so willed

and that (ii′) is consistent with (i). This argument rests on two assumptions. The first assumption is that (E) must be understood as a *logical* equivalence. If (E) is a logical equivalence, then (ii) and (ii′) are also logically equivalent. It follows that if one of them is logically consistent with (i), then the other must be so as well. If the equivalence were not logical, then there would be no justification for concluding that (ii) is logically consistent with (i) on grounds that (ii′) is logically consistent with (i). However, to say that (E) is a logical equivalence is to make the very strong claim that it is logically impossible that one side of the equivalence should be true and the other false, and thus that it is logically impossible that S could not have done otherwise even though S would have done otherwise if he had so willed. My argument against this equivalence will only attempt to show that the latter *is* logically possible.

The second assumption concerns the interpretation of 'if' on the right hand side of (E). Austin and others have argued that the most natural way to interpret the 'if' would be as some non-causal and, indeed, non-conditional term. However, when the 'if' is so interpreted, we have no reason to accept the premiss that (ii′) is logically consistent with (i). The premiss is reasonable provided we suppose that the sentence 'S would have done otherwise if he had so willed' is a causal conditional meaning something like 'If S willed to do otherwise, causal conditions would have been altered so that S would have done otherwise'. Since the latter is logically consistent with the thesis of determinism, the former would be so as well. It is logically consistent to say both that there are sufficient conditions for what takes place and also that had something different taken place then conditions would have been sufficient for things to have turned out otherwise. Moreover, Aune grants that the 'if' statement in question should be interpreted as such a causal conditional.[3]

II

My argument depends on these two assumptions. For, I contend that it is logically possible that a person could not have done otherwise even though, had he willed to do otherwise, this would have altered conditions so that he would have done otherwise. More formally stated, it is logically possible that, S did not do A, that it is false that

(iii) S could have done A

but true that

(iv) S would have done A, if S had willed to do A

where (iv) is interpreted as a causal conditional.
My argument was that (iv) is logically consistent with the conjunction of

(v) S could have done A only if S had willed to do A

and

(vi) It is not the case that S had willed to do A

which together entail

(vii) It is not the case that S could have done A.

Since the conjunction of (iv), (v), and (vi) is consistent and entails the denial of (iii), it follows that (iv) does not entail (iii). If it did, the conjunction would be inconsistent.

Aune objects to this. Since he regards (iii) as meaning (iv), he says he would never grant that (iv) is consistent with (v) and (vi).[4] He then adds that if my argument is not to be absolutely worthless, I must offer some argument for the consistency of (iv), (v), and (vi).[5] This I now propose to do.

Earlier, in defence of the consistency claim, I contended that it is logically possible that some condition, which is a sufficient condition to cause a person to do something, should be a necessary condition of his being able to

[3] Aune says, 'According to Lehrer, if (6) is a causal conditional (which we may grant) . . .' [p. 39 above]. Statement (6) is 'S will do X if C'.

[4] Aune [p. 40 above].

[5] Aune [p. 40 above].

do it and that this condition should fail to occur.[6] Thus if the willing of S to do A is sufficient for S doing A, as (iv) states, then surely it is also logically possible that his so willing is also a necessary condition of his being able to do A, as (v) states, and, since he does not so will, he is therefore unable to do A. Against this contention Aune remarks, 'no basis has been established, by Lehrer or anyone else, for thinking that one may be rendered unable to do other than what one does do by the mere fact that one does not will, choose, or undertake to do other than what one is doing'.[7] But I do not need to show that one may be rendered unable to do otherwise by such a fact; all I need to establish is that it is logically possible to suppose that one should be so rendered. To refute this claim, it must be shown to be logically impossible that a man should be rendered unable to perform an action by not willing to perform it. And neither Aune, nor anyone else, stands a ghost of a chance of showing anything of the sort, because it is manifestly untrue.

To see this, it is only necessary to notice that, for all logic tells us, almost anything might happen as a causal consequence of my not willing to perform a certain action. It is logically possible that as a result of my not willing, not choosing, or not undertaking some action, I might lose any of my powers. If we allow ourselves to be somewhat fanciful, it is easy to imagine how this would come about. Suppose that, unknown to myself, a small object has been implanted in my brain, and that when the button is pushed by a demonic being who implanted this object, I became temporarily paralysed and unable to act. My not choosing to perform an act might cause the button to be pushed and thereby render me unable to act. However, more commonplace pathology will illustrate the same point. Suppose that I am offered a bowl of candy and in the bowl are small round red sugar balls. I do not choose to take one of the red sugar balls because I have a pathological aversion to such candy. (Perhaps they remind me of drops of blood and. . . .) It is logically consistent to suppose that if I had chosen to take the red sugar ball, I would have taken one, but, not so choosing, I am utterly unable to touch one. I can take a red candy ball only if I so choose, but my pathological aversion being what it is, I could not possibly bring myself so to choose. I could do it only if I chose to, and I do not.

Aune might reply that it is my pathological state of mind that renders me unable to perform the action, and, therefore, that my choosing to perform the act is not a necessary condition of my being able to perform it. However, such causal conditionals always contain an implicit reference to the

[6] Lehrer, 196.

[7] Aune [p. 41 above].

surrounding circumstances, and, in the circumstances under consideration, my not choosing to take the candy ball is a necessary condition of my being unable to take it. For were I to choose to take it, then I would take it, and obviously could take it. In this example, (iv), (v), and (vi) are clearly consistent. This example is logically possible, because it is logically possible that by not willing, not choosing, or not undertaking to perform an action our powers might be affected in almost any manner we can conceive, and thus render us unable to perform the action. That is why (iv), (v), and (vi) are logically consistent. And so it is logically possible that I could not do what I would have done if I had so willed. Aune says he would never grant that (iv), (v), and (vi) are logically consistent. Perhaps he could not bring himself to do that. He would if he so willed.

IV

THE INCOMPATIBILITY OF FREE WILL AND DETERMINISM*

PETER VAN INWAGEN

IN this paper I shall define a thesis I shall call 'determinism', and argue that it is incompatible with the thesis that we are able to act otherwise than we do (i.e. is incompatible with 'free will'). Other theses, some of them very different from what *I* shall call 'determinism', have at least an equal right to this name, and, therefore, I do not claim to show that *every* thesis that could be called 'determinism' without historical impropriety is incompatible with free will. I shall, however, assume without argument that what I call 'determinism' is legitimately so called.

In Part I, I shall explain what I mean by 'determinism'. In Part II, I shall make some remarks about 'can'. In Part III, I shall argue that free will and determinism are incompatible. In Part IV, I shall examine some possible objections to the argument of Part III. I shall not attempt to establish the truth or falsity of determinism, or the existence or non-existence of free will.

I

In defining 'determinism', I shall take for granted the notion of a proposition (that is, of a non-linguistic bearer of truth-value), together with

From *Philosophical Studies* **27** (1975), pp. 185–99.

*The writing of this paper was supported by a stipend from the National Endowment for the Humanities for the summer of 1973. The paper was read at a colloquium at the University of Maryland at College Park. Earlier versions were read at the University of Rochester and Syracuse University. The audiences at these colloquia are thanked for useful comments and criticism. Special thanks are due to Rolf Eberle, Keith Lehrer, Raymond Martin, and Richard Taylor. I wish to thank Carl Ginet for his acute comments on an earlier draft, and the referee [of *Philosophical Studies*] for several helpful suggestions. Of course, none of these people is responsible for any mistakes that remain.

certain allied notions such as denial, conjunction, and entailment. Nothing in this paper will depend on the special features of any particular account of propositions. The reader may think of them as functions from possible worlds to truth-values or in any other way he likes, provided they have their usual features (e.g. they are either true or false; the conjunction of a true and a false proposition is a false proposition; they obey the law of contraposition with respect to entailment).

Our definition of 'determinism' will also involve the notion of 'the state of the entire physical world' (hereinafter, 'the state of the world') at an instant. I shall leave this notion largely unexplained, since the argument of this paper is very nearly independent of its content. Provided the following two conditions are met, the reader may flesh out 'the state of the world' in any way he likes:

(i) Our concept of 'state' must be such that, given that the world is in a certain state at a certain time, nothing follows *logically* about its states at other times. For example, we must not choose a concept of 'state' that would allow as part of a description of the momentary state of the world, the clause, '. . . and, at t, the world is such that Jones's left hand will be raised 10 seconds later than t.'

(ii) If there is some observable change in the way things are (e.g. if a white cloth becomes blue, a warm liquid cold, or if a man raises his hand), this change must entail some change in the state of the world. That is, our concept of 'state' must not be so theoretical, so divorced from what is observably true, that it be possible for the world to be in the *same* state at t_1 and t_2, although (for example) Jones's hand is raised at t_1 and not at t_2.

We may now define 'determinism'. We shall apply this term to the conjunction of these two theses:

(a) For every instant of time, there is a proposition that expresses the state of the world at that instant.

(b) If A and B are any propositions that express the state of the world at some instants, then the conjunction of A with the laws of physics entails B.

By a proposition that expresses the state of the world at time t, I mean a true proposition that asserts of some state that, at t, the world is in that state. The reason for our first restriction on the content of 'state' should now be evident: if it were not for this restriction, 'the state of the world' could be defined in such a way that determinism was trivially true. We could, without this restriction, build sufficient information about the past and future into each proposition that expresses the state of the world at an instant, that, for every pair of such propositions, each *by itself* entails the other. And in that case, determinism would be a mere tautology, a thesis applicable to every conceivable state of affairs.

This amounts to saying that the 'laws of physics' clause on our definition does some work: whether determinism is true depends in the character of the laws of physics. For example, if all physical laws were vague propositions like 'In every nuclear reaction, momentum is *pretty nearly* conserved', or 'Force is *approximately* equal to mass times acceleration', then determinism would be false.

This raises the question, What is a law of physics? First, a terminological point. I do not mean the application of this term to be restricted to those laws that belong to physics in the narrowest sense of the word. I am using 'law of physics' in the way some philosophers use 'law of nature'. Thus, a law about chemical valences is a law of physics in my sense, even if chemistry is not ultimately 'reducible' to physics. I will not use the term 'law of nature', because, conceivably, *psychological* laws, including laws (if such there be) about the voluntary behaviour of rational agents, might be included under this term.[1] Rational agents are, after all, in some sense part of 'Nature'. Since I do not think that everything I shall say about laws of physics is true of such 'voluntaristic laws', I should not want to use, instead of 'laws of physics', some term like 'laws of nature' that might legitimately be applied to voluntaristic laws. Thus, for all that is said in this paper, it may be that some version of determinism based on voluntaristic laws is compatible with free will.[2] Let us, then, understand by 'law of physics' a law of nature that is not about the voluntary behaviour of rational agents.

But this does not tell us what 'laws of nature' are. There would probably be fairly general agreement that a proposition cannot be a law of nature unless it is true and contingent, and that no proposition is a law of nature if it entails the existence of some concrete individual, such as Caesar or the earth. But the proposition that there is no solid gold sphere 20 feet in diameter (probably) satisfies these conditions, though it is certainly not a law of nature.

It is also claimed sometimes that a law of nature must 'support its counter-factuals'. There is no doubt something to this. Consider, however, the proposition, 'Dogs die if exposed to virus V'. The claim that this proposition supports its counter-factuals is, I think, equivalent to the claim that 'Every

[1] For example, 'If a human being is not made to feel ashamed of lying before his twelfth birthday, then he will lie whenever he believes it to be to his advantage.'

[2] In 'The Compatibility of Free Will and Determinism', *Philosophical Review*, 1962, J. V. Canfield argues convincingly for a position that we might represent in this terminology as the thesis that a determinism based on voluntaristic laws could be compatible with free will.

dog is such that if it were exposed to virus V, it would die' is *true*. Let us suppose that this latter proposition *is* true, the quantification being understood as being over all dogs, past, present, and future. Its truth, it seems to me, is quite consistent with its being the case that dog-breeders *could* (but will not) institute a programme of selective breeding that *would* produce a sort of dog that is immune to virus V. But if dog-breeders *could* do this, then clearly 'Dogs die if exposed to virus V' is not a law of nature, since in that case the truth of the corresponding universally quantified counter-factual depends upon an accidental circumstance: if dog-breeders were to institute a certain programme of selective breeding they are quite capable of instituting, then 'Every dog is such that if it were exposed to virus V, it would die' would be false. Thus a proposition may 'support its counter-factuals' and yet not be a law of nature.

I do not think that any philosopher has succeeded in giving a (non-trivial) set of individually necessary and jointly sufficient conditions for a proposition's being a law of nature or of physics. *I* certainly do not know of any such set. Fortunately, for the purposes of this paper we need not know how to analyse the concept 'law of physics'. I shall, in Part III, argue that certain statements containing 'law of physics' are analytic. But this can be done in the absence of a satisfactory analysis of 'law of physics'. In fact, it would hardly be possible for one to *provide* an analysis of some concept if one had no pre-analytic convictions about what statements involving that concept are analytic.

For example, we do not have to have a satisfactory analysis of memory to know that 'No one can remember future events' is analytic. And if someone devised an analysis of memory according to which it was possible to remember future events, then, however attractive the analysis was in other respects, it would have to be rejected. The analyticity of 'No one can remember future events' is one of the *data* that anyone who investigates the concept of memory must take account of. Similarly, the claims I shall make on behalf of the concept of physical law seem to me to be basic and evident enough to be data that an analysis of this concept must take account of: any analysis on which these claims did not 'come out true' would be for that very reason defective.

II

It seems to be generally agreed that the concept of free will should be understood in terms of the *power* or *ability* of agents to act otherwise than they in fact do. To deny that men have free will is to assert that what a man *does* do and what he *can* do coincide. And almost all philosophers[3] agree that a necessary condition for holding an agent responsible for an act is believing that that agent *could have* refrained from performing that act.[4]

There is, however, considerably less agreement as to how 'can' (in the relevant sense) should be analysed. This is one of the most difficult questions in philosophy. It is certainly a question to which I do not know any non-trivial answer. But, as I said I should do in the case of 'law of physics', I shall make certain conceptual claims about 'can' (in the 'power' or 'ability' sense) in the absence of any analysis. Any suggested analysis of 'can' that does not support these claims will either be neutral with respect to them, in which case it will be incomplete, since it will not settle *all* conceptual questions about 'can', or it will be inconsistent with them, in which case the arguments I shall present in support of these claims will, in effect, be arguments that the analysis fails. In Part IV, I shall expand on this point as it applies to one particular analysis of 'can', the well-known 'conditional' analysis.

I shall say no more than this about the meaning of 'can'. I shall, however, introduce an idiom that will be useful in talking about ability and inability in complicated cases. Without this idiom, the statement of our argument would be rather unwieldy. We shall sometimes make claims about an agent's abilities by using sentences of the form:

S can render [could have rendered] . . . false.

where '. . .' may be replaced by names of propositions.[5] Our ordinary claims about ability can easily be translated into this idiom. For example, we translate:

He could have reached Chicago by midnight.

as

He could have rendered the proposition that he did not reach Chicago by midnight false.

and, of course, the translation from the special idiom to the ordinary idiom

[3] See, however, Harry Frankfurt, 'Alternate Possibilities and Moral Responsibility', *Journal of Philosophy*, 1969.

[4] Actually, the matter is rather more complicated than this, since we may hold a man responsible for an act we believe he could not have refrained from, provided we are prepared to hold him responsible for his being unable to refrain.

[5] In all the cases we shall consider, '. . .' will be replaced by names of *true* propositions. For the sake of logical completeness, we may stipulate that any sentence formed by replacing '. . .' with the name of a *false* proposition is trivially true. Thus, 'Kant could have rendered the proposition that $7+5=13$ false' is trivially true.

is easy enough in such simple cases. If we were interested only in everyday ascriptions of ability, the new idiom would be useless. Using it, however, we may make ascriptions of ability that it would be very difficult to make in the ordinary idiom. Consider, for example, the last true proposition asserted by Plato. (Let us assume that this description is, as logicians say, 'proper'.) One claim that we might make about Aristotle is that he could have rendered this proposition false. Now, presumably, we have no way of discovering *what* proposition the last true proposition asserted by Plato was. Still, the claim about Aristotle would seem to be either true or false. To discover its truth-value, we should have to discover under what conditions the last true proposition asserted by Plato (i.e. that proposition having as one of its accidental properties, the property of being the last true proposition asserted by Plato) would be false, and then discover whether it was within Aristotle's power to produce these conditions. For example, suppose that if Aristotle had lived in Athens from the time of Plato's death till the time of his own death, then the last true proposition asserted by Plato (whatever it was) would be false. Then, if Aristotle could have lived (i.e. if he had it within his power to live) in Athens throughout this period, he could have rendered the last true proposition asserted by Plato false. On the other hand, if the last true proposition asserted by Plato is the proposition that the planets do not move in perfect circles, then Aristotle could not have rendered the last true proposition asserted by Plato false, since it was not within his power to produce any set of conditions sufficient for the falsity of this proposition.[6]

It is obvious that the proposition expressed by 'Aristotle could have rendered the last true proposition asserted by Plato false', is a proposition that we should be hard put to express without using the idiom of rendering propositions false, or, at least, without using some very similar idiom. We shall find this new idiom very useful in discussing the relation between free will (a thesis about abilities) and determinism (a thesis about certain propositions).

III

I shall now imagine a case in which a certain man, after due deliberation, refrained from performing a certain contemplated act. I shall then argue

[6] Richard Taylor has argued (most explicitly in 'Time, Truth and Ability' by 'Diodorus Cronus', *Analysis*, 1965 that every true proposition is such that, necessarily, no one is able to render it false. On my view, this thesis is mistaken, and Taylor's arguments for it can be shown to be unsound. I shall not, however, argue for this here. I shall argue in Part III that we are unable to render *certain sorts of* true proposition false, but my arguments will depend on special features of these sorts of proposition. I shall, for example, argue that no one can render false a law of physics; but I shall not argue that this is the case because laws of physics are *true*, but because of other features that they possess.

that, if determinism is true, then that man *could not have* performed that act. Because this argument will not depend on any features peculiar to our imagined case, the incompatibility of free will and determinism *in general* will be established, since, as will be evident, a parallel argument could easily be constructed for the case of any agent and any unperformed act.

Here is the case. Let us suppose there was once a judge who had only to raise his right hand at a certain time, *T*, to prevent the execution of a sentence of death upon a certain criminal, such a hand-raising being the sign, according to the conventions of the judge's country, of a granting of special clemency. Let us further suppose that the judge—call him '*J*'—refrained from raising his hand at that time, and that this inaction resulted in the criminal's being put to death. We may also suppose that the judge was unbound, uninjured, and free from paralysis; that he decided not to raise his hand at *T* only after a period of calm, rational, and relevant deliberation; that he had not been subjected to any 'pressure' to decide one way or the other about the criminal's death; that he was not under the influence of drugs, hypnosis, or anything of that sort; and finally, that there was no element in his deliberations that would have been of any special interest to a student of abnormal psychology.

Now the argument. In this argument, which I shall refer to as the 'main argument', I shall use 'T_0' to denote some instant of time earlier than *J*'s birth, 'P_0' to denote the proposition that expresses the state of the world at T_0, '*P*' to denote the proposition that expresses the state of the world at *T*, and '*L*' to denote the conjunction into a single proposition of all laws of physics. (I shall regard *L* itself as a law of physics, on the reasonable assumption that if *A* and *B* are laws of physics, then the conjunction of *A* and *B* is a law of physics.) The argument consists of seven statements, the seventh of which follows from the first six:

(1) If determinism is true, then the conjunction of P_0 and *L* entails *P*.

(2) If *J* had raised his hand at *T*, then *P* would be false.

(3) If (2) is true, then if *J* could have raised his hand at *T*, *J* could have rendered *P* false.[7]

(4) If *J* could have rendered *P* false, and if the conjunction of P_0 and *L* entails *P*, then *J* could have rendered the conjunction of P_0 and *L* false.

[7] '*J* could have raised his hand at *T*' is ambiguous. It might mean either (roughly) '*J* possessed, at *T*, the ability to raise his hand', or '*J* possessed the ability to bring it about that his hand rose at *T*'. If *J* was unparalysed at *T* but paralysed at all earlier instants, then the latter of these would be false, though the former might be true. I mean '*J* could have raised his hand at *T*' in the latter sense.

(5) If *J* could have rendered the conjunction of P_0 and *L* false, then *J* could have rendered *L* false.

(6) *J* could not have rendered *L* false.

∴(7) If determinism is true, *J* could not have raised his hand at *T*.

That (7) follows from (1) through (6) can easily be established by truthfunctional logic. Note that all conditionals in the argument except for (2) are truth-functional. For purposes of establishing the *validity* of this argument, (2) may be regarded as a simple sentence. Let us examine the premises individually.

(1) This premiss follows from the definition of determinism.

(2) If *J* had raised his hand at *T*, then the world would have been in a different state at *T* from the state it was in fact in. (See our second condition on the content of 'the state of the world'.) And, therefore, if *J* had raised his hand at *T*, some contrary of *P* would express the state of the world at *T*. It should be emphasized that '*P*' does not *mean* 'the proposition that expresses the state of the world at *T*'. Rather, '*P*' *denotes* the proposition that expresses the state of the world at *T*. In Kripke's terminology, '*P*' is being used as a *rigid designator*, while 'the proposition that expresses the state of the world at *T*' is perforce non-rigid.[8]

(3) Since *J*'s hand being raised at *T* would have been sufficient for the falsity of *P*, there is, if *J* could have raised his hand, at least one condition sufficient for the falsity of *P* that *J* could have produced.

(4) This premiss may be defended as an instance of the following general principle:

> If *S* can render *R* false, and if *Q* entails *R*, then *S* can render *Q* false.

This principle seems to be analytic. For if *Q* entails *R*, then the denial of *R* entails the denial of *Q*. Thus, any condition sufficient for the falsity of *R* is also sufficient for the falsity of *Q*. Therefore, if there is some condition that *S* can produce that is sufficient for the falsity of *R*, there is some condition (that same condition) that *S* can produce that is sufficient for the falsity of *Q*.

(5) This premiss may be defended as an instance of the following general principle, which I take to be analytic:

> If *Q* is a true proposition that concerns only states of affairs that obtained before *S*'s birth, and if *S* can render the conjunction of *Q* and *R* false, then *S* can render *R* false.

[8] See Saul Kripke, 'Identity and Necessity', in *Identity and Individuation*, ed. Milton K. Munitz (New York, 1971).

Consider, for example, the propositions expressed by

The Spanish Armada was defeated in 1588.

and

Peter van Inwagen never visits Alaska.

The conjunction of these two propositions is quite possibly true. At any rate, let us assume it is true. Given that it is true, it seems quite clear that I can render it false if and only if I can visit Alaska. If, for some reason, it is not within my power ever to visit Alaska, then I *cannot* render it false. This is a quite trivial assertion, and the general principle (above) of which it is an instance is hardly less trivial. And it seems incontestable that premiss (5) is also an instance of this principle.

(6) I shall argue that if anyone *can* (i.e. has it within his power to) render some proposition false, then that proposition is not a law of physics. This I regard as a conceptual truth, one of the data that must be taken account of by anyone who wishes to give an analysis of 'can' or 'law'. It is this connection between these two concepts, I think, that is at the root of the incompatibility of free will and determinism.

In order to see this connection, let us suppose that both of the following are true:

(A) Nothing ever travels faster than light.

(B) Jones, a physicist, can construct a particle accelerator that would cause protons to travel at twice the speed of light.

It follows from (A) that Jones will never exercise the power that (B) ascribes to him. But whatever the reason for Jones's failure to act on his ability to render (A) false, it is clear that (A) and (B) are consistent, and that (B) entails that (A) is not a law of physics. For given that (B) is true, then Jones is able to conduct an experiment that would falsify (A); and surely it is a feature of any proposition that is a physical law that no one *can* conduct an experiment that would show it to be false.

Of course, most propositions that look initially as if they might be physical laws, but which are later decided to be non-laws, are rejected because of experiments that are actually performed. But this is not essential. In order to see this, let us elaborate the example we have been considering. Let us suppose that Jones's ability to render (A) false derives from the fact that he has discovered a mathematically rigorous proof that under certain conditions *C*, realizable in the laboratory, protons would travel faster than light. And let us suppose that this proof proceeds from premisses so obviously true that all competent physicists accept his conclusion without reservation. But suppose that conditions *C* never obtain in nature, and that actually to produce them in the laboratory would require such an expenditure of resources that Jones and his colleagues decide not to carry out the experiment. And suppose that, as a result, conditions *C* are never realized and nothing ever travels faster than light. It is evident that if all this were true, we should have to say that (A), while *true*, is not a law of physics. (Though, of course, 'Nothing ever travels faster than light except under conditions *C*' might be a law.)

The laboratories and resources that figure in this example are not essential to its point. If Jones *could* render some proposition false by performing *any* act he does not in fact perform, even such a simple act as raising his hand at a certain time, this would be sufficient to show that that proposition is not a law of physics.

This completes my defence of the premisses of the main argument. In the final part of this paper, I shall examine objections to this argument suggested by the attempts of various philosophers to establish the compatibility of free will and determinism.

IV

The most useful thing a philosopher who thinks that the main argument does not prove its point could do would be to try to show that some premiss of the argument is false or incoherent, or that the argument begs some important question, or contains a term that is used equivocally, or something of that sort. In short, he should get down to cases. Some philosophers, however, might continue to hold that free will and determinism, in the sense of Part I, are compatible, but decline to try to point out a mistake in the argument. For (such a philosopher might argue) we have, in everyday life, *criteria* for determining whether an agent could have acted otherwise than he did, and these criteria determine the *meaning* of 'could have acted otherwise'; to know the meaning of this phrase is simply to know how to apply these criteria. And since these criteria make no mention of determinism, anyone who thinks that free will and determinism are incompatible is simply confused.[9]

As regards the argument of Part III (this philosopher might continue), this argument is very complex, and this complexity must simply serve to hide some error, since its conclusion is absurd. We must treat this argument

[9] Cf. Antony Flew, 'Divine Omniscience and Human Freedom', *New Essays in Philosophical Theology*, ed. Antony Flew and Alasdair MacIntyre (London: SCM Press, 1955), 149–51 in particular.

like the infamous 'proof' that zero equals one: It may be amusing and even instructive to find the hidden error (if one has nothing better to do), but it would be a waste of time to take seriously any suggestion that it is sound.

Now I suppose we do have 'criteria', in some sense of this over-used word, for the application of 'could have done otherwise', and I will grant that knowing the criteria for the application of a term can plausibly be identified with knowing its meaning. Whether the criteria for applying 'could have done otherwise' can (as at least one philosopher has supposed[10]) be taught by simple ostension is another question. However this may be, the 'criteria' argument is simply invalid. To see this, let us examine a simpler argument that makes the same mistake.

Consider the doctrine of 'predestinarianism'. Predestinarians hold (i) that if an act is foreseen it is not free, and (ii) that all acts are foreseen by God. (I do not claim that anyone has ever held this doctrine in precisely this form.) Now suppose we were to argue that predestinarianism must be compatible with free will, since our criteria for applying 'could have done otherwise' make no reference to predestinarianism. Obviously this argument would be invalid, since predestinarianism is incompatible with free will. And the only difference I can see between this argument and the 'criteria' argument for the compatibility of free will and determinism is that predestinarianism, unlike determinism, is *obviously* incompatible with free will. But, of course, theses may be incompatible with one another even if this incompatibility is not obvious. Even if determinism cannot, like predestinarianism, be seen to be incompatible with free will on the basis of a simple formal inference, there is, nonetheless, a conceptual connection between the two theses (as we showed in our defence of premiss (6)). The argument of Part III is intended to draw out the implications of this connection. There may well be a mistake in the argument, but I do not see why anyone should think that the very idea of such an argument is misconceived.

It has also been argued that free will *entails* determinism, and, being itself a consistent thesis, is *a fortiori* compatible with determinism. The argument, put briefly, is this. To say of some person on some particular occasion that he acted freely is obviously to say at least that *he* acted on that occasion. Suppose, however, that we see someone's arm rise and it later turns out that there was *no cause whatsoever* for his arm's rising. Surely we should have to say that *he* did not really raise his arm at all. Rather, his arm's rising was a mere chance happening, that, like a muscular twitch, had nothing to do with *him*, beyond the fact that it happened to involve a part of his body. A necessary condition for this person's really having raised his hand is that *he*

[10] Flew, loc cit.

caused his hand to rise. And surely '*he* caused' means '*his* character, desires, and beliefs caused'.[11]

I think that there is a great deal of confusion in this argument, but to expose this confusion would require a lengthy discussion of many fine points in the theory of agency. I shall only point out that if this argument is supposed to refute the conclusion of Part III, it is an *ignoratio elenchi*. For I did not conclude that free will is incompatible with the thesis that every event has a cause, but rather with determinism as defined in Part I. And the denial of this thesis does not entail that there are uncaused events.

Of course, one might try to construct a similar but relevant argument for the falsity of the conclusion of Part III. But, so far as I can see, the plausibility of such an argument would depend on the plausibility of supposing that if the present movements of one's body are not completely determined by physical law and the state of the world before one's birth, then these present movements are not one's own doing, but, rather, mere random happenings. And I do not see the least shred of plausibility in this supposition.

I shall finally consider the popular 'conditional analysis' argument for the compatibility of free will and determinism. According to the advocates of this argument—let us call them 'conditionalists'—what statements of the form:

(8) *S* could have done *X*

mean is:

(9) If *S* had chosen to do *X*, *S* would have done *X*.[12]

For example, 'Smith could have saved the drowning child' means, 'If Smith had chosen to save the drowning child, Smith would have saved the drowning child.' Thus, even if determinism is true (the conditionalists argue), it is possible that Smith did not save but *could have* saved the drowning child, since the conjunction of determinism with 'Smith did not save the child' does not entail the falsity of 'If Smith had chosen to save the child, Smith would have saved the child'.

Most of the controversy about this argument centres around the question whether (9) is a correct analysis of (8). I shall not enter into the debate about

[11] Cf. R. E. Hobart, 'Free Will as Involving Determination and Inconceivable Without It', *Mind*, 1934; A. J. Ayer, 'Freedom and Necessity', in his collected *Philosophical Essays* (New York, 1954) [Essay I in this collection.]; P. H. Nowell-Smith, 'Freewill and Moral Responsibility', *Mind*, 1948; J. J. C. Smart, 'Free Will, Praise, and Blame', *Mind*, 1961.

[12] Many other verbs besides 'choose' figure in various philosophers' conditional analyses of ability: e.g. 'wish', 'want', 'will', 'try', 'set oneself'. Much of the important contemporary work on this analysis, by G. E. Moore, P. H. Nowell-Smith, J. L. Austin, Keith Lehrer, Roderick Chisholm, and others, is collected in *The Nature of Human Action*, ed. Myles Brand (Glenview Ill., 1970). See also 'Fatalism and Determinism', by Wilfrid Sellars, in *Freedom and Determinism*, ed. Keith Lehrer (New York, 1966), 141–74.

whether this analysis is correct. I shall instead question the relevance of this debate to the argument of Part III. For it is not clear that the main argument would be unsound if the conditional analysis *were* correct. Clearly the argument is *valid* whether or not (8) and (9) mean the same. But suppose the premisses of the main argument were rewritten so that every clause they contain that is of form (8) is replaced by the corresponding clause of form (9)—should we then see that any of these premisses is false? Let us try this with premiss (6), which seems, prima facie, to be the crucial premiss of the argument. We have:

(6a) It is not the case that if *J* had chosen to render *L* false, *J* would have rendered *L* false.

Now (6a) certainly seems true: If someone chooses to render false some proposition *R*, and if *R* is a law of physics, then surely he will fail. This little argument for (6a) *seems* obviously sound. But we cannot overlook the possibility that someone might discover a mistake in it and, perhaps, even construct a convincing argument that (6a) is false. Let us, therefore, assume for the sake of argument that (6a) is demonstrably false. What would this show? I submit that it would show that (6a) does not mean the same as (6), since (6) is, as I have argued, *true*.

The same dilemma confronts the conditionalist if he attempts to show, on the basis of the conditional analysis, that any of the other premisses of the argument is false. Consider the argument got by replacing every clause of form (8) in the main argument with the corresponding clause of form (9). If all the premisses of this new argument are true, the main argument is, according to the conditionalist's own theory, sound. If, on the other hand, any of the premisses of the new argument is false, then (*I* would maintain) this premiss is a counter-example to the conditional analysis. I should not be begging the question against the conditionalist in maintaining this, since I have given arguments for the truth of each of the premisses of the main argument, and nowhere in these arguments do I assume that the conditional analysis is wrong.

Of course, any or all of my arguments in defence of the premisses of the main argument may contain some mistake. But unless the conditionalist could point to some such mistake, he would not accomplish much by showing that some statement he *claimed* was equivalent to one of its premisses was false.[13]

[13] For an argument in some respects similar to what I have called the 'main argument', see Carl Ginet's admirable article, 'Might We Have No Choice?' in Lehrer, 87–104. Another argument similar to the main argument, which is (formally) much simpler than the main argument, but which is stated in language very different from that of traditional statements of the free-will problem, can be found in my 'A Formal Approach to the Problem of Free Will and Determinism', *Theoria*, 1974.

V

FREEDOM AND RESENTMENT

PETER STRAWSON

I

SOME philosophers say they do not know what the thesis of determinism is. Others say, or imply, that they do know what it is. Of these, some—the pessimists perhaps—hold that if the thesis is true, then the concepts of moral obligation and responsibility really have no application, and the practices of punishing and blaming, of expressing moral condemnation and approval, are really unjustified. Others—the optimists perhaps—hold that these concepts and practices in no way lose their *raison d'être* if the thesis of determinism is true. Some hold even that the justification of these concepts and practices requires the truth of the thesis. There is another opinion which is less frequently voiced: the opinion, it might be said, of the genuine moral sceptic. This is that the notions of moral guilt, of blame, of moral responsibility are inherently confused and that we can see this to be so if we consider the consequences either of the truth of determinism or of its falsity. The holders of this opinion agree with the pessimists that these notions lack application if determinism is true, and add simply that they also lack it if determinism is false. If I am asked which of these parties I belong to, I must say it is the first of all, the party of those who do not know what the thesis of determinism is. But this does not stop me from having some sympathy with the others, and a wish to reconcile them. Should not ignorance, rationally, inhibit such sympathies? Well, of course, though darkling, one has some inkling—some notion of what sort of thing is being talked about. This lecture is intended as a move towards reconciliation; so is likely to seem wrongheaded to everyone.

But can there be any possibility of reconciliation between such clearly

From *Proceedings of the British Academy*, vol. xlviii (1962), pp. 1–25. Reprinted by permission of the British Academy.

opposed positions as those of pessimists and optimists about determinism? Well, there might be a formal withdrawal on one side in return for a substantial concession on the other. Thus, suppose the optimist's position were put like this: (1) the facts as we know them do not show determinism to be false; (2) the facts as we know them supply an adequate basis for the concepts and practices which the pessimist feels to be imperilled by the possibility of determinism's truth. Now it might be that the optimist is right in this, but is apt to give an inadequate account of the facts as we know them, and of how they constitute an adequate basis for the problematic concepts and practices; that the reasons he gives for the adequacy of the basis are themselves inadequate and leave out something vital. It might be that the pessimist is rightly anxious to get this vital thing back and, in the grip of his anxiety, feels he has to go beyond the facts as we know them; feels that the vital thing can be secure only if, beyond the facts as we know them, there is the further fact that determinism is false. Might *he* not be brought to make a formal withdrawal in return for a vital concession?

II

Let me enlarge very briefly on this, by way of preliminary only. Some optimists about determinism point to the efficacy of the practices of punishment, and of moral condemnation and approval, in regulating behaviour in socially desirable ways.[1] In the fact of their efficacy, they suggest, is an adequate basis for these practices; and this fact certainly does not show determinism to be false. To this the pessimists reply, all in a rush, that *just* punishment and *moral* condemnation imply moral guilt and guilt implies moral responsibility and moral responsibility implies freedom and freedom implies the falsity of determinism. And to this the optimists are wont to reply in turn that it is true that these practices require freedom in a sense, and the existence of freedom in this sense is one of the facts as we know them. But what 'freedom' means here is nothing but the absence of certain conditions the presence of which would make moral condemnation or punishment inappropriate. They have in mind conditions like compulsion by another, or innate incapacity, or insanity, or other less extreme forms of psychological disorder, or the existence of circumstances in which the making of any other choice would be morally inadmissible or would be too much to expect of any man. To this list they are constrained to add other factors which, without exactly being limitations of freedom, may also make moral condemnation or punishment inappropriate or mitigate their force: as some forms of ignorance, mistake, or accident. And the general reason

[1] Cf. P. H. Nowell-Smith, 'Freewill and Moral Responsibility', *Mind*, 1948.

why moral condemnation or punishment are inappropriate when these factors or conditions are present is held to be that the practices in question will be generally efficacious means of regulating behaviour in desirable ways only in cases where these factors are *not* present. Now the pessimist admits that the facts as we know them include the existence of freedom, the occurrence of cases of free action, in the negative sense which the optimist concedes; and admits, or rather insists, that the existence of freedom in this sense is compatible with the truth of determinism. Then what does the pessimist find missing? When he tries to answer this question, his language is apt to alternate between the very familiar and the very unfamiliar.[2] Thus he may say, familiarly enough, that the man who is the subject of justified punishment, blame or moral condemnation must really *deserve* it; and then add, perhaps, that, in the case at least where he is blamed for a positive act rather than an omission, the condition of his really deserving blame is something that goes beyond the negative freedoms that the optimist concedes. It is, say, a genuinely free identification of the will with the act. And this is the condition that is incompatible with the truth of determinism.

The conventional, but conciliatory, optimist need not give up yet. He may say: Well, people often decide to do things, really intend to do what they do, know just what they're doing in doing it; the reasons they think they have for doing what they do, often really are their reasons and not their rationalizations. These facts, too, are included in the facts as we know them. If this is what you mean by freedom—by the identification of the will with the act—then freedom may again be conceded. But again the concession is compatible with the truth of the determinist thesis. For it would not follow from that thesis that nobody decides to do anything; that nobody ever does anything intentionally; that it is false that people sometimes know perfectly well what they are doing. I tried to define freedom negatively. You want to give it a more positive look. But it comes to the same thing. Nobody denies freedom in this sense, or these senses, and nobody claims that the existence of freedom in these senses shows determinism to be false.

But it is here that the lacuna in the optimistic story can be made to show. For the pessimist may be supposed to ask: But *why* does freedom in this sense justify blame, etc.? You turn towards me first the negative, and then the positive, faces of a freedom which nobody challenges. But the only reason you have given for the practices of moral condemnation and punishment in cases where this freedom is present is the efficacy of these practices in regulating behaviour in socially desirable ways. But this is not

[2] As Nowell-Smith pointed out in a later article: 'Determinists and Libertarians', *Mind*, 1954.

a sufficient basis, it is not even the right *sort* of basis, for these practices as we understand them.

Now my optimist, being the sort of man he is, is not likely to invoke an intuition of fittingness at this point. So he really has no more to say. And my pessimist, being the sort of man he is, has only one more thing to say; and that is that the admissibility of these practices, as we understand them, demands another kind of freedom, the kind that in turn demands the falsity of the thesis of determinism. But might we not induce the pessimist to give up saying this by giving the optimist something more to say?

III

I have mentioned punishing and moral condemnation and approval; and it is in connection with these practices or attitudes that the issue between optimists and pessimists—or, if one is a pessimist, the issue between determinists and libertarians—is felt to be particularly important. But it is not of these practices and attitudes that I propose, at first, to speak. These practices or attitudes permit, where they do not imply, a certain detachment from the actions or agents which are their objects. I want to speak, at least at first, of something else: of the non-detached attitudes and reactions of people directly involved in transactions with each other; of the attitudes and reactions of offended parties and beneficiaries; of such things as gratitude, resentment, forgiveness, love, and hurt feelings. Perhaps something like the issue between optimists and pessimists arises in this neighbouring field too; and since this field is less crowded with disputants, the issue might here be easier to settle; and if it is settled here, then it might become easier to settle it in the disputant-crowded field.

What I have to say consists largely of commonplaces. So my language, like that of commonplace generally, will be quite unscientific and imprecise. The central commonplace that I want to insist on is the very great importance that we attach to the attitudes and intentions towards us of other human beings, and the great extent to which our personal feelings and reactions depend upon, or involve, our beliefs about these attitudes and intentions. I can give no simple description of the field of phenomena at the centre of which stands this commonplace truth; for the field is too complex. Much imaginative literature is devoted to exploring its complexities; and we have a large vocabulary for the purpose. There are simplifying styles of handling it in a general way. Thus we may, like La Rochefoucauld, put self-love or self-esteem or vanity at the centre of the picture and point out how it may be caressed by the esteem, or wounded by the indifference or contempt, of others. We might speak, in another jargon, of the need for love, and the loss of security which results from its withdrawal; or, in another, of human self-respect and its connection with the recognition of the individual's dignity. These simplifications are of use to me only if they help to emphasize how much we actually mind, how much it matters to us, whether the actions of other people—and particularly of *some* other people—reflect attitudes towards us of goodwill, affection, or esteem on the one hand or contempt, indifference, or malevolence on the other. If someone treads on my hand accidentally, while trying to help me, the pain may be no less acute than if he treads on it in contemptuous disregard of my existence or with a malevolent wish to injure me. But I shall generally feel in the second case a kind and degree of resentment that I shall not feel in the first. If someone's actions help me to some benefit I desire, than I am benefited in any case; but if he intended them so to benefit me because of his general goodwill towards me, I shall reasonably feel a gratitude which I should not feel at all if the benefit was an incidental consequence, unintended or even regretted by him, of some plan of action with a different aim.

These examples are of actions which confer benefits or inflict injuries over and above any conferred or inflicted by the mere manifestation of attitude and intention themselves. We should consider also in how much of our behaviour the benefit or injury resides mainly or entirely in the manifestation of attitude itself. So it is with good manners, and much of what we call kindness, on the one hand; with deliberate rudeness, studied indifference, or insult on the other.

Besides resentment and gratitude, I mentioned just now forgiveness. This is a rather unfashionable subject in moral philosophy at present; but to be forgiven is something we sometimes ask, and forgiving is something we sometimes say we do. To ask to be forgiven is in part to acknowledge that the attitude displayed in our actions was such as might properly be resented and in part to repudiate that attitude for the future (or at least for the immediate future); and to forgive is to accept the repudiation and to forswear the resentment.

We should think of the many different kinds of relationship which we can have with other people—as sharers of a common interest; as members of the same family; as colleagues; as friends; as lovers; as chance parties to an enormous range of transactions and encounters. Then we should think, in each of these connections in turn, and in others, of the kind of importance we attach to the attitudes and intentions towards us of those who stand in these relationships to us, and of the kinds of *reactive* attitudes and feelings to which we ourselves are prone. In general, we demand some degree of goodwill or regard on the part of those who stand in these relationships to us, though the forms we require it to take vary widely in different connections. The range and intensity of our *reactive* attitudes towards goodwill, its absence or its opposite vary no less widely. I have mentioned, specifically, resentment and gratitude; and they are a usefully opposed pair. But, of course, there is a whole continuum of reactive attitude and feeling stretching on both sides of these and—the most comfortable area—in between them.

The object of these commonplaces is to try to keep before our minds something it is easy to forget when we are engaged in philosophy, especially in our cool, contemporary style, viz. what it is actually like to be involved in ordinary inter-personal relationships, ranging from the most intimate to the most casual.

IV

It is one thing to ask about the general causes of these reactive attitudes I have alluded to; it is another to ask about the variations to which they are subject, the particular conditions in which they do or do not seem natural or reasonable or appropriate; and it is a third thing to ask what it would be like, what it *is* like, not to suffer them. I am not much concerned with the first question; but I am with the second; and perhaps even more with the third.

Let us consider, then, occasions for resentment: situations in which one person is offended or injured by the action of another and in which—in the absence of special considerations—the offended person might naturally or normally be expected to feel resentment. Then let us consider what sorts of special considerations might be expected to modify or mollify this feeling or remove it altogether. It needs no saying now how multifarious these considerations are. But, for my purpose, I think they can be roughly divided into two kinds. To the first group belong all those which might give occasion for the employment of such expressions as 'He didn't mean to', 'He hadn't realized', 'He didn't know'; and also all those which might give occasion for the use of the phrase 'He couldn't help it', when this is supported by such phrases as 'He was pushed', 'He had to do it', 'It was the only way', 'They left him no alternative', etc. Obviously these various pleas, and the kinds of situations in which they would be appropriate, differ from each other in striking and important ways. But for my present purpose they have something still more important in common. None of them invites us to suspend towards the agent, either at the time of his action or in general, our ordinary reactive attitudes. They do not invite us to view the *agent* as one in respect of whom these attitudes are in any way inappropriate. They invite us to view the *injury* as one in respect of which a particular one of these attitudes is inappropriate. They do not invite us to see the *agent* as other than a fully responsible agent. They invite us to see the *injury* as one for which he was not fully, or at all, responsible. They do not suggest that the agent is in any way an inappropriate object of that kind of demand for goodwill or regard which is reflected in our ordinary reactive attitudes. They suggest instead that the fact of injury was not in this case incompatible with that demand's being fulfilled, that the fact of injury was quite consistent with the agent's attitude and intentions being just what we demand they should be.[3] The agent was just ignorant of the injury he was causing, or had lost his balance through being pushed or had reluctantly to cause the injury for reasons which acceptably override his reluctance. The offering of such pleas by the agent and their acceptance by the sufferer is something in no way opposed to, or outside the context of, ordinary inter-personal relationships and the manifestation of ordinary reactive attitudes. Since things go wrong and situations are complicated, it is an essential and integral element in the transactions which are the life of these relationships.

The second group of considerations is very different. I shall take them in two sub-groups of which the first is far less important than the second. In connection with the first sub-group we may think of such statements as 'He wasn't himself', 'He has been under very great strain recently', 'He was acting under post-hypnotic suggestion'; in connection with the second, we may think of 'He's only a child', 'He's a hopeless schizophrenic', 'His mind has been systematically perverted', 'That's purely compulsive behaviour on his part'. Such pleas as these do, as pleas of my first general group do not, invite us to suspend our ordinary reactive attitudes towards the agent, either at the time of his action or all the time. They do not invite us to see the agent's action in a way consistent with the full retention of ordinary inter-personal attitudes and merely inconsistent with one particular attitude. They invite us to view the agent himself in a different light from the light in which we should normally view one who has acted as he has acted. I shall not linger over the first subgroup of cases. Though they perhaps raise, in the short term, questions akin to those raised, in the long term, by the second subgroup, we may dismiss them without considering those questions by taking that admirably suggestive phrase, 'He wasn't himself', with the seriousness that—for all its being logically comic—it deserves. We shall not feel resentment against the man he is for the action done by the man he is not; or at least we shall feel less. We normally have to deal with him under normal stresses; so we shall not feel towards him, when he acts as he does

[3] Perhaps not in every case *just* what we demand they should be, but in any case *not* just what we demand they should not be. For my present purpose these differences do not matter.

under abnormal stresses, as we should have felt towards him had he acted as he did under normal stresses.

The second and more important subgroup of cases allows that the circumstances were normal, but presents the agent as psychologically abnormal—or as mòrally undeveloped. The agent was himself; but he is warped or deranged, neurotic or just a child. When we see someone in such a light as this, all our reactive attitutes tend to be profoundly modified. I must deal here in crude dichotomies and ignore the ever-interesting and ever-illuminating varieties of case. What I want to contrast is the attitude (or range of attitudes) of involvement or participation in a human relationship, on the one hand, and what might be called the objective attitude (or range of attitudes) to another human being, on the other. Even in the same situation, I must add, they are not altogether *exclusive* of each other; but they are, profoundly, *opposed* to each other. To adopt the objective attitude to another human being to see him, perhaps, as an object of social policy; as a subject for what, in a wide range of sense, might be called treatment; as something certainly to be taken account, perhaps precautionary account, of; to be managed or handled or cured or trained; perhaps simply to be avoided, though *this* gerundive is not peculiar to cases of objectivity of attitude. The objective attitude may be emotionally toned in many ways, but not in all ways: it may include repulsion or fear, it may include pity or even love, though not all kinds of love. But it cannot include the range of reactive feelings and attitudes which belong to involvement or participation with others in inter-personal human relationships; it cannot include resentment, gratitude, forgiveness, anger, or the sort of love which two adults can sometimes be said to feel reciprocally, for each other. If your attitude towards someone is wholly objective, then though you may fight him, you cannot quarrel with him, and though you may talk to him, even negotiate with him, you cannot reason with him. You can at most pretend to quarrel, or to reason, with him.

Seeing someone, then, as warped or deranged or compulsive in behaviour or peculiarly unfortunate in his formative circumstances—seeing someone so tends, at least to some extent, to set him apart from normal participant reactive attitudes on the part of one who sees him, tends to promote, at least in the civilized, objective attitudes. But there is something curious to add to this. The objective attitude is not only something we naturally tend to fall into in cases like these, where participant attitudes are partially or wholly inhibited by abnormalities or by immaturity. It is also something which is available as a resource in other cases too. We look with an objective eye on the compulsive behaviour of the neurotic or the tiresome behaviour of a very young child, thinking in terms of treatment or training. But we *can* sometimes look with something like the same eye on the behaviour of the normal and the mature. We *have* this resource and can sometimes use it: as a refuge, say, from the strains of involvement; or as an aid to policy; or simply out of intellectual curiosity. Being human, we cannot, in the normal case, do this for long, or altogether. If the strains of involvement, say, continue to be too great, then we have to do something else—like severing a relationship. But what is above all interesting is the tension there is, in us, between the participant attitude and the objective attitude. One is tempted to say: between our humanity and our intelligence. But to say this would be to distort both notions.

What I have called the participant reactive attitudes are essentially natural human reactions to the good or ill will or indifference of others towards us, as displayed in *their* attitudes and actions. The question we have to ask is: What effect would, or should, the acceptance of the truth of a general thesis of determinism have upon these reactive attitudes? More specifically, would, or should, the acceptance of the truth of the thesis lead to the decay or the repudiation of all such attitudes? Would, or should, it mean the end of gratitude, resentment, and forgiveness; of all reciprocated adult loves; of all the essentially *personal* anatgonisms?

But how can I answer, or even pose, this question without knowing *exactly* what the thesis of determinism is? Well, there is one thing we do know: that if there is a coherent thesis of determinism, then there must be a sense of 'determined' such that, if that thesis is true, then all behaviour whatever is determined in that sense. Remembering this, we can consider at least what possibilities lie formally open; and then perhaps we shall see that the question can be answered *without* knowing exactly what the thesis of determinism is. We can consider what possibilities lie open because we have already before us an account of the ways in which particular reactive attitudes, or reactive attitudes in general, may be, and, sometimes, we judge, should be, inhibited. Thus I considered earlier a group of considerations which tend to inhibit, and, we judge, should inhibit, resentment, in particular cases of an agent causing an injury, without inhibiting reactive attitudes in general towards that agent. Obviously this group of considerations cannot strictly bear upon our question; for that question concerns reactive attitudes in general. But resentment has a particular interest; so it is worth adding that it has never been claimed as a consequence of the truth of determinism that one or another of *these* considerations was operative in every case of an injury being caused by an agent; that it would follow from the truth of determinism that anyone who caused an injury *either* was quite simply ignorant of causing it *or* had acceptably overriding reasons for acquiescing reluctantly in causing it *or* . . ., etc. The prevalence of this happy state of affairs would not be a consequence of the reign of universal determinism, but of the reign of universal goodwill. We cannot, then, find here the possibility of an affirmative answer to our question, even for the particular case of resentment.

Next, I remarked that the participant attitude, and the personal reactive attitudes in general, tend to give place, and, it is judged by the civilized, should give place, to objective attitudes, just in so far as the agent is seen as excluded from ordinary adult human relationships by deep-rooted psychological abnormality—or simply by being a child. But it cannot be a consequence of any thesis which is not itself self-contradictory that abnormality is the universal condition.

Now this dismissal might seem altogether too facile; and so, in a sense, it is. But whatever is too quickly dismissed in this dismissal is allowed for in the only possible form of affirmative answer that remains. We can sometimes, and in part, I have remarked, look on the normal (those we rate as 'normal') in the objective way in which we have learned to look on certain classified cases of abnormality. And our question reduces to this: could, or should, the acceptance of the determinist thesis lead us always to look on everyone exclusively in this way? For this is the only condition worth considering under which the acceptance of determinism could lead to the decay or repudiation of participant reactive attitudes.

It does not seem to be self-contradictory to suppose that this might happen. So I suppose we must say that it is not absolutely inconceivable that it should happen. But I am strongly inclined to think that it is, for us as we are, practically inconceivable. The human commitment to participation in ordinary inter-personal relationships is, I think, too thoroughgoing and deeply rooted for us to take seriously the thought that a general theoretical conviction might so change our world that, in it, there were no longer any such things as inter-personal relationships as we normally understand them; and being involved in inter-personal relationships as we normally understand them precisely is being exposed to the range of reactive attitudes and feelings that is in question.

This, then, is a part of the reply to our question. A sustained objectivity of inter-personal attitude, and the human isolation which that would entail, does not seem to be something of which human beings would be capable, even if some general truth were a theoretical ground for it. But this is not all. There is a further point, implicit in the foregoing, which must be made explicit. Exceptionally, I have said, we can have direct dealings with human beings without any degree of personal involvement, treating them simply as creatures to be handled in our own interests, or our side's, or society's—or even theirs. In the extreme case of the mentally deranged, it is easy to see the connection between the possibility of a wholly objective attitude and the impossibility of what we understand by ordinary inter-personal relationships. Given this latter impossibility, no other civilized attitude is available than that of viewing the deranged person simply as something to be understood and controlled in the most desirable fashion. To view him as outside the reach of personal relationships is already, for the civilized, to view him in this way. For reasons of policy or self-protection we may have occasion, perhaps temporary, to adopt a fundamentally similar attitude to a 'normal' human being; to concentrate, that is, on understanding 'how he works', with a view to determining our policy accordingly or to finding in that very understanding a relief from the strains of involvement. Now it is certainly true that in the case of the abnormal, though not in the case of the normal, our adoption of the objective attitude is a consequence of our viewing the agent as *incapacitated* in some or all respects for ordinary inter-personal relationships. He is thus incapacitated, perhaps, by the fact that his picture of reality is pure fantasy, that he does not, in a sense, live in the real world at all; or by the fact that his behaviour is, in part, an unrealistic acting out of unconscious purposes; or by the fact that he is an idiot, or a moral idiot. But there is something else which, *because* this is true, is equally certainly *not* true. And that is that there is a sense of 'determined' such that (1) if determinism is true, all behaviour is determined in this sense, and (2) determinism might be true, i.e. it is not inconsistent with the facts as we know them to suppose that all behaviour might be determined in this sense, and (3) our adoption of the objective attitude towards the abnormal is the result of prior embracing of the belief that the behaviour, or the relevant stretch of behaviour, of the human being in question *is* determined in this sense. Neither in the case of the normal, then, nor in the case of the abnormal is it true that, when we adopt an objective attitude, we do so *because* we hold such a belief. So my answer has two parts. The first is that we cannot, as we are, seriously envisage ourselves adopting a thoroughgoing objectivity of attitude to others as a result of theoretical conviction of the truth of determinism; and the second is that when we do in fact adopt such an attitude in a particular case, our doing so is not the consequence of a theoretical conviction which might be expressed as 'Determinism in this case', but is a consequence of our abandoning, for different reasons in different cases, the ordinary inter-personal attitudes.

It might be said that all this leaves the real question unanswered, and that we cannot hope to answer it without knowing exactly what the thesis of determinism is. For the real question is not a question about what we actually do, or why we do it. It is not even a question about what we would *in fact* do if a certain theoretical conviction gained general acceptance. It is a question about what it would be *rational* to do if determinism were true, a question about the rational justification of ordinary inter-personal attitudes in general. To this I shall reply, first, that such a question could seem real only to one who had utterly failed to grasp the purport of the preceding answer, the fact of our natural human commitment to ordinary inter-personal attitudes. This commitment is part of the general framework of human life, not something that can come up for review as particular cases can come up for review within this general framework. And I shall reply, second, that if we could imagine what we cannot have, viz. a choice in this matter, then we could choose rationally only in the light of an assessment of the gains and losses to human life, its enrichment or impoverishment; and the truth or falsity of a general thesis of determinism would not bear on the rationality of *this* choice.[4]

V

The point of this discussion of the reactive attitudes in their relation—or lack of it—to the thesis of determinism was to bring us, if possible, nearer to a position of compromise in a more usual area of debate. We are not now to discuss reactive attitudes which are essentially those of offended parties or beneficiaries. We are to discuss reactive attitudes which are essentially not those, or only incidentally are those, of offended parties or beneficiaries, but are nevertheless, I shall claim, kindred attitudes to those I have discussed. I put resentment in the centre of the previous discussion. I shall put moral indignation—or, more weakly, moral disapprobation—in the centre of this one.

The reactive attitudes I have so far discussed are essentially reactions to the quality of others' wills towards us, as manifested in their behaviour: to their good or ill will or indifference or lack of concern. Thus resentment, or what I have called resentment, is a reaction to injury or indifference. The reactive attitudes I have now to discuss might be described as the sympathetic or vicarious or impersonal or disinterested or generalized analogues of the reactive attitudes I have already discussed. They are reactions to the qualities of others' wills, not towards ourselves, but towards others. Because of this impersonal or vicarious character, we give them

[4] The question, then, of the connection between rationality and the adoption of the objective attitude to others is misposed when it is made to seem dependent on the issue of determinism. But there is another question which should be raised, if only to distinguish it from the misposed question. Quite apart from the issue of determinism might it not be said that we should be nearer to being purely rational creatures in proportion as our relation to others was in fact dominated by the objective attitude? I think this might be said; only it would have to be added, once more, that if such a choice were possible, it would not necessarily be rational to choose to be more purely rational than we are.

different names. Thus one who experiences the vicarious analogue of resentment is said to be indignant or disapproving, or morally indignant or disapproving. What we have here is, as it were, resentment on behalf of another, where one's own interest and dignity are not involved; and it is this impersonal or vicarious character of the attitude, added to its others, which entitle it to the qualification 'moral'. Both my description of, and my name for, these attitudes are, in one important respect, a little misleading. It is not that these attitudes are essentially vicarious—one can feel indignation on one's own account—but that they are essentially capable of being vicarious. But I shall retain the name for the sake of its suggestiveness; and I hope that what is misleading about it will be corrected in what follows.

The personal reactive attitudes rest on, and reflect, an expectation of, and demand for, the manifestation of a certain degree of goodwill or regard on the part of other human beings towards ourselves; or at least on the expectation of, and demand for, an absence of the manifestation of active ill will or indifferent disregard. (What will, in particular cases, *count* as manifestations of good or ill will or disregard will vary in accordance with the particular relationship in which we stand to another human being.) The generalized or vicarious analogues of the personal reactive attitudes rest on, and reflect, exactly the same expectation or demand in a generalized form; they rest on, or reflect, that is, the demand for the manifestation of a reasonable degree of goodwill or regard, on the part of others, not simply towards oneself, but towards all those on whose behalf moral indignation may be felt, i.e. as we now think, towards all men. The generalized and non-generalized forms of demand, and the vicarious and personal reactive attitudes which rest upon, and reflect, them are connected not merely logically. They are connected humanly; and not merely with each other. They are connected also with yet another set of attitudes which I must mention now in order to complete the picture. I have considered from two points of view the demands we make on others and our reactions to their possibly injurious actions. These were the points of view of one whose interest was directly involved (who suffers, say, the injury) and of others whose interest was not directly involved (who do not themselves suffer the injury). Thus I have spoken of personal reactive attitudes in the first connection and of their vicarious analogues in the second. But the picture is not complete unless we consider also the correlates of these attitudes on the part of those on whom the demands are made, on the part of the agents. Just as there are personal and vicarious reactive attitudes associated with demands on others for oneself and demands on others for others, so there are self-reactive attitudes associated with demands on oneself for others. And here we have to mention such phenomena as feeling bound or obliged (the 'sense of obligation'); feeling compunction; feeling guilty or remorseful or at least responsible; and the more complicated phenomenon of shame.

All these three types of attitude are humanly connected. One who manifested the personal reactive attitudes in a high degree but showed no inclination at all to their vicarious analogues would appear as an abnormal case of moral egocentricity, as a kind of moral solipsist. Let him be supposed fully to acknowledge the claims to regard that others had on him, to be susceptible of the whole range of self-reactive attitudes. He would then see himself as unique both as one (*the* one) who had a general claim on human regard and as one (*the* one) on whom human beings in general had such a claim. This would be a kind of moral solipsism. But it is barely more than a conceptual possibility; if it is that. In general, though within varying limits, we demand of others for others, as well as of ourselves for others, something of the regard which we demand of others for ourselves. Can we imagine, besides that of the moral solipsist, any other case of one or two of these three types of attitude being fully developed, but quite unaccompanied by any trace, however slight, of the remaining two or one? If we can, then we imagine something far below or far above the level of our common humanity—a moral idiot or a saint. For all these types of attitude alike have common roots in our human nature and our membership of human communities.

Now, as of the personal reactive attitudes, so of their vicarious analogues, we must ask in what ways, and by what considerations, they tend to be inhibited. Both types of attitude involve, or express, a certain sort of demand for inter-personal regard. The fact of injury constitutes a prima-facie appearance of this demand's being flouted or unfulfilled. We saw, in the case of resentment, how one class of considerations may show this appearance to be mere appearance, and hence inhibit resentment, *without* inhibiting, or displacing, the sort of demand of which resentment can be an expression, without in any way tending to make us suspend our ordinary inter-personal attitudes to the agent. Considerations of this class operate in just the same way, for just the same reasons, in connection with moral disapprobation or indignation; they inhibit indignation without in any way inhibiting the sort of demand on the agent of which indignation can be an expression, the range of attitudes towards him to which it belongs. But in this connection we may express the facts with a new emphasis. We may say, stressing the moral, the generalized aspect of the demand, considerations of this group have no tendency to make us see the agent as other than a morally responsible agent; they simply make us see the injury as one for which he was not morally responsible. The offering and acceptance of such exculpatory pleas as are here in question in no way detracts in our eyes from the agent's status as a term of moral relationships. On the contrary, since things go wrong and situations are complicated, it is an essential part of the life of such relationships.

But suppose we see the agent in a different light: as one whose picture of the world is an insane delusion; or as one whose behaviour, or a part of whose behaviour, is unintelligible to us, perhaps even to him, in terms of conscious purposes, and intelligible only in tems of unconscious purposes; or even, perhaps, as one wholly impervious to the self-reactive attitudes I spoke of, wholly lacking, as we say, in moral sense. Seeing an agent in such a light as this tends, I said, to inhibit resentment in a wholly different way. It tends to inhibit resentment because it tends to inhibit ordinary inter-personal attitudes in general, and the kind of demand and expectation which those attitudes involve; and tends to promote instead the purely objective view of the agent as one posing problems simply of intellectual understanding, management, treatment, and control. Again the parallel holds for those generalized or moral attitudes towards the agent which we are now concerned with. The same abnormal light which shows the agent to us as one in respect of whom the personal attitudes, the personal demand, are to be suspended, shows him to us also as one in respect of whom the impersonal attitudes, the generalized demand, are to be suspended. Only, abstracting now from direct personal interest, we may express the facts with a new emphasis. We may say: to the extent to which the agent is seen in this light, he is not seen as one on whom demands and expectations lie in that particular way in which we think of them as lying when we speak of moral obligation; he is not, to that extent, seen as a morally responsible agent, as a term of moral relationships, as a member of the moral community.

I remarked also that the suspension of ordinary inter-personal attitudes and the cultivation of a purely objective view is sometimes possible even when we have no such reasons for it as I have just mentioned. Is this possible also in the case of the moral reactive attitudes? I think so; and perhaps it is easier. But the motives for a total suspension of moral reactive attitudes are fewer, and perhaps weaker: fewer, because only where there is antecedent personal involvement can there be the motive of seeking refuge from the strains of such involvement; perhaps weaker, because the tension between objectivity of view and the moral reactive attitudes is perhaps less than the tension between objectivity of view and the personal reactive attitudes, so that we can in the case of the moral reactive attitudes more easily secure the speculative or political gains of objectivity of view by a kind of setting on one side, rather than a total suspension, of those attitudes.

These last remarks are uncertain; but also, for the present purpose, unimportant. What concerns us now is to inquire, as previously in connection with the personal reactive attitudes, what relevance any general thesis of determinism might have to their vicarious analogues. The answers once more are parallel; though I shall take them in a slightly different order. First, we must note, as before, that when the suspension of such an attitude or such attitudes occurs in a particular case, it is *never* the consequence of the belief that the piece of behaviour in question was determined in a sense such that all behaviour *might be*, and, if determinism is true, all behaviour *is*, determined in that sense. For it is not a consequence of any general thesis of determinism which might be true that nobody knows what he's doing or that everybody's behaviour is unintelligible in terms of conscious purposes or that everybody lives in a world of delusion or that nobody has a moral sense, i.e. is susceptible of self-reactive attitudes, etc. In fact no such sense of 'determined' as would be required for a general thesis of determinism is ever relevant to our actual suspensions of moral reactive attitudes. Second, suppose it granted, as I have already argued, that we cannot take seriously the thought that theoretical conviction of such a general thesis would lead to the total decay of the personal reactive attitudes. Can we then take seriously the thought that such a conviction—a conviction, after all, that many have held or said they held—would nevertheless lead to the total decay or repudiation of the vicarious analogues of these attitudes? I think that the change in our social world which would leave us exposed to the personal reactive attitudes but not all to their vicarious analogues, the generalization of abnormal egocentricity which this would entail, is perhaps even harder for us to envisage as a real possibility than the decay of both kinds of attitude together. Though there are some necessary and some contingent differences between the ways and cases in which these two kinds of attitudes operate or are inhibited in their operation, yet, as general human capacities or pronenesses, they stand or lapse together. Finally, to the further question whether it would not be *rational*, given a general theoretical conviction of the truth of determinism, so to change our world that in it all these attitudes were wholly suspended, I must answer, as before, that one who presses this question has wholly failed to grasp the import of the preceding answer, the nature of the human commitment that is here involved: it is *useless* to ask whether it would not be rational for us to do what it is not in our nature to (be able to) do. To this I must add, as before, that if there were, say, for a moment open to us the possibility of such a godlike choice, the rationality of making or refusing it would be determined by quite other considerations than the truth or falsity of the general theoretical doctrine in question. The latter would be simply irrelevant; and this becomes ironically clear when we remember that for those convinced that the truth of determinism nevertheless really would make the one choice rational, there has always been the insuperable difficulty of explaining in intelligible terms how its falsity would make the opposite choice rational.

I am aware that in presenting the argument as I have done, neglecting the ever-interesting varieties of case, I have presented nothing more than a schema, using sometimes a crude opposition of phrase where we have a great intricacy of phenomena. In particular the simple opposition of objective attitudes on the one hand and the various contrasted attitudes which I have opposed to them must seem as grossly crude as it is central. Let me pause to mitigate this crudity a little, and also to strengthen one of my central contentions, by mentioning some things which straddle these contrasted kinds of attitude. Thus parents and others concerned with the care and upbringing of young children cannot have to their charges either kind of attitude in a pure or unqualified form. They are dealing with creatures who are potentially and increasingly capable both of holding, and being objects of, the full range of human and moral attitudes, but are not yet truly capable of either. The treatment of such creatures must therefore represent a kind of compromise, constantly shifting in one direction, between objectivity of attitude and developed human attitudes. Rehearsals insensibly modulate towards true performances. The punishment of a child is both like and unlike the punishment of an adult. Suppose we try to relate this progressive emergence of the child as a responsible being, as an object of non-objective attitudes, to that sense of 'determined' in which, if determinism is a possibly true thesis, all behaviour *may* be determined, and in which, if it is a true thesis, all behaviour *is* determined. What bearing *could* such a sense of 'determined' have upon the progressive modification of attitudes towards the child? Would it not be grotesque to think of the development of the child as a progressive or patchy emergence from an area in which its behaviour is in this sense determined into an area in which it isn't? Whatever sense of 'determined' is required for stating the thesis of determinism, it can scarcely be such as to allow of compromise, borderline-style answers to the question, 'Is this bit of behaviour determined or isn't it?' But in this matter of young children, it is essentially a borderline, penumbral area that we move in. Again, consider—a very different matter—the strain in the attitude of a psychoanalyst to his patient. *His* objectivity of attitude, *his* suspension of ordinary moral reactive attitudes, is profoundly modified by the fact that the aim of the enterprise is to make such suspension unnecessary or less necessary. Here we may and do naturally speak of restoring the agent's freedom. But here the restoring of freedom means bringing it about that the agent's behaviour shall be intelligible in terms of conscious purposes rather than in terms only of unconscious purposes. *This* is the object of the enterprise; and it is in so far as *this* object is attained that the suspension, or half-suspension, of ordinary moral attitudes is deemed no longer necessary or appropriate. And in this we see once again the *irrelevance* of that concept of 'being determined' which must be the central concept of determinism. For we cannot both agree that this object is attainable and that its attainment has this consequence and yet hold (1) that neurotic behaviour is determined in a sense in which, it may be, all behaviour is determined, and (2) that it is because neurotic behaviour is determined in this sense that objective attitudes are deemed appropriate to neurotic behaviour. Not, at least, without accusing ourselves of incoherence in our attitude to psychoanalytic treatment.

VI

And now we can try to fill in the lacuna which the pessimist finds in the optimist's account of the concept of moral responsibility, and of the bases of moral condemnation and punishment; and to fill it in from the facts as we know them. For, as I have already remarked, when the pessimist himself seeks to fill it in, he rushes beyond the facts as we know them and proclaims that it cannot be filled in at all unless determinism is false.

Yet a partial sense of the facts as we know them is certainly present to the pessimist's mind. When his opponent, the optimist, undertakes to show that the truth of determinism would not shake the foundations of the concept of moral responsibility and of the practices of moral condemnation and punishment, he typically refers, in a more or less elaborated way, to the efficacy of these practices in regulating behaviour in socially desirable ways. These practices are represented solely as instruments of policy, as methods of individual treatment and social control. The pessimist recoils from this picture; and in his recoil there is, typically, an element of emotional shock. He is apt to say, among much else, that the humanity of the offender himself is offended by *this* picture of his condemnation and punishment.

The reasons for this recoil—the explanation of the sense of an emotional, as well as a conceptual, shock—we have already before us. The picture painted by the optimists is painted in a style appropriate to a situation envisaged as wholly dominated by objectivity of attitude. The only operative notions invoked in this picture are such as those of policy, treatment, control. But a thoroughgoing objectivity of attitude, excluding as it does the moral reactive attitudes, excludes at the same time essential elements in the concepts of *moral* condemnation and *moral* responsibility. This is the reason for the conceptual shock. The deeper emotional shock is a reaction, not simply to an inadequate conceptual analysis, but to the suggestion of a change in our world. I have remarked that it is possible to cultivate an exclusive objectivity of attitude in some cases, and for some reasons, where the object of the attitude is not set aside from developed inter-personal and moral attitudes by immaturity or abnormality. And the suggestion which seems to be contained in the optimist's account is that such an attitude should be universally adopted to all offenders. This is shocking enough in the pessimist's eyes. But, sharpened by shock, his eyes see further. It would be hard to make *this* division in our natures. If to all offenders, then to all mankind. Moreover, to whom could this recommendation be, in any real sense, addressed? Only to the powerful, the authorities. So abysses seem to open.[5]

But we will confine our attention to the case of the offenders. The concepts we are concerned with are those of responsibility and guilt, qualified as 'moral', on the one hand—together with that of membership of a moral community; of demand, indignation, disapprobation and condemnation, qualified as 'moral', on the other hand—together with that of punishment. Indignation, disapprobation, like resentment, tend to inhibit or at least to limit our goodwill towards the object of these attitudes, tend to promote an at least partial and temporary withdrawal of goodwill; they do so in proportion as they are strong; and their strength is in general proportioned to what is felt to be the magnitude of the injury and to the degree to which the agent's will is identified with, or indifferent to, it. (These, of course, are not contingent connections.) But these attitudes of disapprobation and indignation are precisely the correlates of the moral demand in the case where the demand is felt to be disregarded. The making of the demand *is* the proneness to such attitudes. The holding of them does not, as the holding of objective attitudes does, involve as a part of itself viewing their object other than as a member of the moral community. The partial withdrawal of goodwill which *these* attitudes entail, the modification *they* entail of the general demand that another should, if possible, be spared suffering, is, rather, the consequence of *continuing* to view him as a member of the moral community; only as one who has offended against its demands. So the preparedness to acquiesce in that infliction of suffering on the offender which is an essential part of punishment is all of a piece with this whole range of attitudes of which I have been speaking. It is not only moral reactive attitudes towards the offender which are in question here. We must mention also the self-reactive attitudes of offenders themselves. Just as the other-reactive attitudes are associated with a readiness to acquiesce in the infliction of suffering on an offender, within the 'institution' of punishment, so the self-reactive attitudes are associated with a readiness on the part of

[5]See J. D. Mabbott's 'Freewill and Punishment', in *Contemporary British Philosophy*, 3rd ser. (London: Allen & Unwin, 1956).

the offender to acquiesce in such infliction *without* developing the reactions (e.g. of resentment) which he would normally develop to the infliction of injury upon him; i.e. with a readiness, as we say, to accept punishment[6] as 'his due' or as 'just'.

I am not in the least suggesting that these readinesses to acquiesce, either on the part of the offender himself or on the part of others, are always or commonly accompanied or preceded by indignant boilings or remorseful pangs; only that we have here a continuum of attitudes and feelings to which these readinesses to acquiesce themselves belong. Nor am I in the least suggesting that it belongs to this continuum of attitudes that we should be ready to acquiesce in the infliction of injury on offenders in a fashion which we saw to be quite indiscriminate or in accordance with procedures which we knew to be wholly useless. On the contrary, savage or civilized, we have some belief in the utility of practices of condemnation and punishment. But the social utility of these practices, on which the optimist lays such exclusive stress, is not what is now in question. What is in question is the pessimist's justified sense that to speak in terms of social utility alone is to leave out something vital in our conception of these practices. The vital thing can be restored by attending to that complicated web of attitudes and feelings which form an essential part of the moral life as we know it, and which are quite opposed to objectivity of attitude. Only by attending to this range of attitudes can we recover from the facts as we know them a sense of what we mean, i.e. of *all* we mean, when, speaking the language of morals, we speak of desert, responsibility, guilt, condemnation, and justice. But we *do* recover it from the facts as we know them. We do not have to go beyond them. Because the optimist neglects or misconstrues these attitudes, the pessimist rightly claims to find a lacuna in his account. We can fill the lacuna for him. But in return we must demand of the pessimist a surrender of his metaphysics.

Optimist and pessimist misconstrue the facts in very different styles. But in a profound sense there is something in common to their misunderstandings. Both seek, in different ways, to overintellectualize the facts. Inside the general structure or web of human attitudes and feelings of which I have been speaking, there is endless room for modification, redirection, criticism, and justification. But questions of justification are internal to the structure or relate to modifications internal to it. The existence of the general framework of attitudes itself is something we are given with the fact of human society. As a whole, it neither calls for, nor permits, an external 'rational' justification. Pessimist and optimist alike show themselves, in

[6] Of course not *any* punishment for *anything* deemed an offence.

different ways, unable to accept this.[7] The optimist's style of over-intellectualizing the facts is that of a characteristically incomplete empiricism, a one-eyed utilitarianism. He seeks to find an adequate basis for certain social practices in calculated consequences, and loses sight (perhaps wishes to lose sight) of the human attitudes of which these practices are, in part, the expression. The pessimist does not lose sight of these attitudes, but is unable to accept the fact that it is just these attitudes themselves which fill the gap in the optimist's account. Because of this, he thinks the gap can be filled only if some general metaphysical proposition is repeatedly verified, verified in all cases where it is appropriate to attribute moral responsibility. This proposition he finds it as difficult to state coherently and with intelligible relevance as its determinist contradictory. Even when a formula has been found ('contra-causal freedom' or something of the kind) there still seems to remain a gap between its applicability in particular cases and its supposed moral consequences. Sometimes he plugs this gap with an intuition of fittingness—a pitiful intellectualist trinket for a philosopher to wear as a charm against the recognition of his own humanity.

Even the moral sceptic is not immune from his own form of the wish to over-intellectualize such notions as those of moral responsibility, guilt, and blame. He sees that the optimist's account is inadequate and the pessimist's libertarian alternative inane; and finds no resource except to declare that the notions in question are inherently confused, that 'blame is metaphysical'. But the metaphysics was in the eye of the metaphysician. It is a pity that talk of the moral sentiments has fallen out of favour. The phrase would be quite a good name for that network of human attitudes in acknowledging the character and place of which we find, I suggest, the only possibility of reconciling these disputants to each other and the facts.

There are, at present, factors which add, in a slightly paradoxical way, to the difficulty of making this acknowledgement. These human attitudes themselves, in their development and in the variety of their manifestations, have to an increasing extent become objects of study in the social and psychological sciences; and this growth of human self-consciousness, which we might expect to reduce the difficulty of acceptance, in fact increases it in several ways. One factor of comparatively minor importance is an increased historical and anthropological awareness of the great variety of forms which these human attitudes may take at different times and in different cultures.

[7] Compare the question of the justification of induction. The human commitment to inductive belief-formation is original, natural, non-rational (not *ir*rational), in no way something we choose or could give up. Yet rational criticism and reflection can refine standards and their application, supply 'rules for judging of cause and effect'. Ever since the facts were made clear by Hume, people have been resisting acceptance of them.

This makes one rightly chary of claiming as essential features of the concept of morality in general, forms of these attitudes which may have a local and temporary prominence. No doubt to some extent my own descriptions of human attitudes have reflected local and temporary features of our own culture. But an awareness of variety of forms should not prevent us from acknowledging also that in the absence of *any* forms of these attitudes it is doubtful whether we should have anything that *we* could find intelligible as a system of human relationships, as human society. A quite different factor of greater importance is that psychological studies have made us rightly mistrustful of many particular manifestations of the attitudes I have spoken of. They are a prime realm of self-deception, of the ambiguous and the shady, of guilt-transference, unconscious sadism and the rest. But it is an exaggerated horror, itself suspect, which would make us unable to acknowledge the facts because of the seamy side of the facts. Finally, perhaps the most important factor of all is the prestige of these theoretical studies themselves. That prestige is great, and is apt to make us forget that in philosophy, though it also is a theoretical study, we have to take account of the facts in *all* their bearings; we are not to suppose that we are required, or permitted, as philosophers, to regard ourselves, as human beings, as detached from the attitudes which, as scientists, we study with detachment. This is in no way to deny the possibility and desirability of redirection and modification of our human attitudes in the light of these studies. But we may reasonably think it unlikely that our progressively greater understanding of certain aspects of ourselves will lead to the total disappearance of those aspects. Perhaps it is not inconceivable that it should; and perhaps, then, the dreams of some philosophers will be realized.

If we sufficiently, that is *radically*, modify the view of the optimist, his view is the right one. It is far from wrong to emphasize the efficacy of all those practices which express or manifest our moral attitudes, in regulating behaviour in ways considered desirable; or to add that when certain of our beliefs about the efficacy of some of these practices turns out to be false, then we may have good reason for dropping or modifying those practices. What *is* wrong is to forget that these practices, and their reception, the reactions to them, really *are* expressions of our moral attitudes and not merely devices we calculatingly employ for regulative purposes. Our practices do not merely exploit our natures, they express them. Indeed the very understanding of the kind of efficacy these expressions of our attitudes have turns on our remembering this. When we do remember this, and modify the optimist's position accordingly, we simultaneously correct its conceptual deficiencies and ward off the dangers it seems to entail, without recourse to the obscure and panicky metaphysics of libertarianism.

VI

FREEDOM OF THE WILL AND THE CONCEPT OF A PERSON

HARRY G. FRANKFURT

WHAT philosophers have lately come to accept as analysis of the concept of a person is not actually analysis of *that* concept at all. Strawson, whose usage represents the current standard, identifies the concept of a person as 'the concept of a type of entity such that *both* predicates ascribing states of consciousness *and* predicates ascribing corporeal characteristics . . . are equally applicable to a single individual of that single type'.[1] But there are many entities besides persons that have both mental and physical properties. As it happens—though it seems extraordinary that this should be so—there is no common English word for the type of entity Strawson has in mind, a type that includes not only human beings but animals of various lesser species as well. Still, this hardly justifies the misappropriation of a valuable philosophical term.

Whether the members of some animal species are persons is surely not to be settled merely by determining whether it is correct to apply to them, in addition to predicates ascribing corporeal characteristics, predicates that ascribe states of consciousness. It does violence to our language to endorse the application of the term 'person' to those numerous creatures which do have both psychological and material properties but which are manifestly not persons in any normal sense of the word. This misuse of language is

From *Journal of Philosophy*, vol. lxviii, No. 1 (Jan. 1971), pp. 5–20. Reprinted by permission of the author and the *Journal of Philosophy*.

[1] P. F. Strawson, *Individuals* (London: Methuen, 1959), 101–2. Ayer's usage of 'person' is similar: 'it is characteristic of persons in this sense that besides having various physical properties . . . they are also credited with various forms of consciousness' (A. J. Ayer, *The Concept of a Person* (New York: St. Martin's, 1963), 82). What concerns Strawson and Ayer is the problem of understanding the relation between mind and body, rather than the quite different problem of understanding what it is to be a creature that not only has a mind and a body but is also a person.

doubtless innocent of any theoretical error. But although the offence is 'merely verbal', it does significant harm. For it gratuitously diminishes our philosophical vocabulary, and it increases the likelihood that we will overlook the important area of inquiry with which the term 'person' is most naturally associated. It might have been expected that no problem would be of more central and persistent concern to philosophers than that of understanding what we ourselves essentially are. Yet this problem is so generally neglected that it has been possible to make off with its very name almost without being noticed and, evidently, without evoking any widespread feeling of loss.

There is a sense in which the word 'person' is merely the singular form of 'people' and in which both terms connote no more than membership in a certain biological species. In those senses of the word which are of greater philosophical interest, however, the criteria for being a person do not serve primarily to distinguish the members of our own species from the members of other species. Rather, they are designed to capture those attributes which are the subject of our most humane concern with ourselves and the source of what we regard as most important and most problematical in our lives. Now these attributes would be of equal significance to us even if they were not in fact peculiar and common to the members of our own species. What interests us most in the human condition would not interest us less if it were also a feature of the condition of other creatures as well.

Our concept of ourselves as persons is not to be understood, therefore, as a concept of attributes that are necessarily species-specific. It is conceptually possible that members of novel or even of familiar non-human species should be persons; and it is also conceptually possible that some members of the human species are not persons. We do in fact assume, on the other hand, that no member of another species is a person. Accordingly, there is a presumption that what is essential to persons is a set of characteristics that we generally suppose—whether rightly or wrongly—to be uniquely human.

It is my view that one essential difference between persons and other creatures is to be found in the structure of a person's will. Human beings are not alone in having desires and motives, or in making choices. They share these things with the members of certain other species, some of whom even appear to engage in deliberation and to make decisions based upon prior thought. It seems to be peculiarly characteristic of humans, however, that they are able to form what I shall call 'second-order desires' or 'desires of the second order'.

Besides wanting and choosing and being moved *to do* this or that, men may also want to have (or not to have) certain desires and motives. They are capable of wanting to be different, in their preferences and purposes, from what they are. Many animals appear to have the capacity for what I shall call 'first-order desires' or 'desires of the first order', which are simply desires to do or not to do one thing or another. No animal other than man, however, appears to have the capacity for reflective self-evaluation that is manifested in the formation of second-order desires.[2]

I

The concept designated by the verb 'to want' is extraordinarily elusive. A statement of the form '*A* wants to *X*'—taken by itself, apart from a context that serves to amplify or to specify its meaning—conveys remarkably little information. Such a statement may be consistent, for example, with each of the following statements: (a) the prospect of doing *X* elicits no sensation or introspectible emotional response in *A*; (b) *A* is unaware that he wants to *X*; (c) *A* believes that he does not want to *X*; (d) *A* wants to refrain from *X*-ing; (e) *A* wants to *Y* and believes that it is impossible for him both to *Y* and to *X*; (f) *A* does not 'really' want to *X*; (g) *A would rather die than X*; and so on. It is therefore hardly sufficient to formulate the distinction between first-order and second-order desires, as I have done, by suggesting merely that someone has a first-order desire when he wants to do or not to do such-and-such, and that he has a second-order desire when he wants to have or not to have a certain desire of the first order.

As I shall understand them, statements of the form '*A* wants to *X*' cover a rather broad range of possibilities.[3] They may be true even when statements like (a) through (g) are true: when *A* is unaware of any feelings concerning *X*-ing, when he is unaware that he wants to *X*, when he deceives himself about what he wants and believes falsely that he does not want to *X*, when he also has other desires that conflict with his desire to *X*, or when he is ambivalent. The desires in question may be conscious or unconscious, they need not be univocal, and *A* may be mistaken about them. There is a further source of uncertainty with regard to statements that identify

[2] For the sake of simplicity, I shall deal only with what someone wants or desires, neglecting related phenomena such as choices and decisions. I propose to use the verbs 'to want' and 'to desire' interchangeably, although they are by no means perfect synonyms. My motive in forsaking the established nuances of these words arises from the fact that the verb 'to want', which suits my purposes better so far as its meaning is concerned, does not lend itself so readily to the formation of nouns as does the verb 'to desire'. It is perhaps acceptable, albeit graceless, to speak in the plural of someone's 'wants'. But to speak in the singular of someone's 'want' would be an abomination.

[3] What I say in this paragraph applies not only to cases in which 'to *X*' refers to a possible action or inaction. It also applies to cases in which 'to *X*' refers to a first-order desire and in which the statement that '*A* wants to *X*' is therefore a shortened version of a statement—'*A* wants to want *X*'—that identifies a desire of the second order.

someone's desires, however, and here it is important for my purposes to be less permissive.

Consider first those statements of the form '*A* wants to *X*' which identify first-order desires—that is, statements in which the term 'to *X*' refers to an action. A statement of this kind does not, by itself, indicate the relative strength of *A*'s desire to *X*. It does not make it clear whether this desire is at all likely to play a decisive role in what *A* actually does or tries to do. For it may correctly be said that *A* wants to *X* even when his desire to *X* is only one among his desires and when it is far from being paramount among them. Thus, it may be true that *A* wants to *X* when he strongly prefers to do something else instead; and it may be true that he wants to *X* despite the fact that, when he acts, it is not the desire to *X* that motivates him to do what he does. On the other hand, someone who states that *A* wants to *X* may mean to convey that it is this desire that is motivating or moving *A* to do what he is actually doing or that *A* will in fact be moved by this desire (unless he changes his mind) when he acts.

It is only when it is used in the second of these ways that, given the special usage of 'will' that I propose to adopt, the statement identifies *A*'s will. To identify an agent's will is either to identify the desire (or desires) by which he is motivated in some action he performs or to identify the desire (or desires) by which he will or would be motivated when or if he acts. An agent's will, then, is identical with one or more of his first-order desires. But the notion of the will, as I am employing it, is not coextensive with the notion of first-order desires. It is not the notion of something that merely inclines an agent in some degree to act in a certain way. Rather, it is the notion of an *effective* desire—one that moves (or will or would move) a person all the way to action. Thus the notion of the will is not coextensive with the notion of what an agent intends to do. For even though someone may have a settled intention to do *X*, he may none the less do something else instead of doing *X* because, despite his intention, his desire to do *X* proves to be weaker or less effective than some conflicting desire.

Now consider those statements of the form '*A* wants to *x*' which identify second-order desires—that is, statements in which the term 'to *X*' refers to a desire of the first order. There are also two kinds of situation in which it may be true that *A* wants to want to *X*. In the first place, it might be true of *A* that he wants to have a desire to *X* despite the fact that he has a univocal desire, altogether free of conflict and ambivalence, to refrain from *x*-ing. Someone might want to have a certain desire, in other words, but univocally want that desire to be unsatisfied.

Suppose that a physician engaged in psychotherapy with narcotics addicts believes that his ability to help his patients would be enhanced if he understood better what it is like for them to desire the drug to which they are addicted. Suppose that he is led in this way to want to have a desire for the drug. If it is a genuine desire that he wants, then what he wants is not merely to feel the sensations that addicts characteristically feel when they are gripped by their desires for the drug. What the physician wants, in so far as he wants to have a desire, is to be inclined or moved to some extent to take the drug.

It is entirely possible, however, that, although he wants to be moved by a desire to take the drug, he does not want this desire to be effective. He may not want it to move him all the way to action. He need not be interested in finding out what it is like to take the drug. And in so far as he now wants only to *want* to take it, and not to *take* it, there is nothing in what he now wants that would be satisfied by the drug itself. He may now have, in fact, an altogether univocal desire *not* to take the drug; and he may prudently arrange to make it impossible for him to satisfy the desire he would have if his desire to want the drug should in time be satisfied.

It would thus be incorrect to infer, from the fact that the physician now wants to desire to take the drug, that he already does desire to take it. His second-order desire to be moved to take the drug does not entail that he has a first-order desire to take it. If the drug were now to be administered to him, this might satisfy no desire that is implicit in his desire to want to take it. While he wants to want to take the drug, he may have *no* desire to take it; it may be that *all* he wants is to taste the desire for it. That is, his desire to have a certain desire that he does not have may not be a desire that his will should be at all different than it is.

Someone who wants only in this truncated way to want to *X* stands at the margin of preciosity, and the fact that he wants to want to *X* is not pertinent to the identification of his will. There is, however, a second kind of situation that may be described by '*A* wants to *X*'; and when the statement is used to describe a situation of this second kind, then it does pertain to what *A* wants his will to be. In such cases the statement means that *A* wants the desire to *X* to be the desire that moves him effectively to act. It is not merely that he wants the desire to *X* to be among the desires by which, to one degree or another, he is moved or inclined to act. He wants this desire to be effective—that is, to provide the motive in what he actually does. Now when the statement that *A* wants to want to *X* is used in this way, it does entail that *A* already has a desire to *X*. It could not be true both that *A* wants the desire to *X* to move him into action and that he does not want to *X*. It is only if he does want to *X* that he can coherently want the desire to *X* not merely to be one of his desires but, more decisively, to be his will.[4]

[4] It is not so clear that the entailment relation described here holds in certain kinds of cases,

Suppose a man wants to be motivated in what he does by the desire to concentrate on his work. It is necessarily true, if this supposition is correct, that he already wants to concentrate on his work. This desire is now among his desires. But the question of whether or not his second-order desire is fulfilled does not turn merely on whether the desire he wants is one of his desires. It turns on whether this desire is, as he wants it to be, his effective desire or will. If, when the chips are down, it is his desire to concentrate on his work that moves him to do what he does, then what he wants at that time is indeed (in the relevant sense) what he wants to want. If it is some other desire that actually moves him when he acts, on the other hand, then what he wants at that time is not (in the relevant sense) what he wants to want. This will be so despite the fact that the desire to concentrate on his work continues to be among his desires.

II

Someone has a desire of the second order either when he wants simply to have a certain desire or when he wants a certain desire to be his will. In situations of the latter kind, I shall call his second-order desires 'second-order volitions' or 'volitions of the second order'. Now it is having second-order volitions, and not having second-order desires generally, that I regard as essential to being a person. It is logically possible, however unlikely, that there should be an agent with second-order desires but with no volitions of the second order. Such a creature, in my view, would not be a person. I shall use the term 'wanton' to refer to agents who have first-order desires but who are not persons because, whether or not they have desires of the second order, they have no second-order volitions.[5]

The essential characteristic of a wanton is that he does not care about his will. His desires move him to do certain things, without its being true of him either that he wants to be moved by those desires or that he prefers to be

which I think may fairly be regarded as non-standard, where the essential difference between the standard and the non-standard cases lies in the kind of description by which the first-order desire in question is identified. Thus, suppose that *A* admires *B* so fulsomely that, even though he does not know what *B* wants to do, he wants to be effectively moved by whatever desire effectively moves *B*; without knowing what *B*'s will is, in other words, *A* wants his own will to be the same. It certainly does not follow that *A* already has, among his desires, a desire like the one that constitutes *B*'s will. I shall not pursue here the questions of whether there are genuine counter-examples to the claim made in the text or of how, if there are, that claim should be altered.

[5] Creatures with second-order desires but no second-order volitions differ significantly from brute animals, and, for some purposes, it would be desirable to regard them as persons. My usage, which withholds the designation 'person' from them, is thus somewhat arbitrary. I adopt it largely because it facilitates the formulation of some of the points I wish to make. Hereafter, whenever I consider statements of the form '*A* wants to want to *X*', I shall have in mind statements identifying second-order volitions and not statements identifying second-order desires that are not second-order volitions.

moved by other desires. The class of wantons includes all non-human animals that have desires and all very young children. Perhaps it also includes some adult human beings as well. In any case, adult humans may be more or less wanton; they may act wantonly, in response to first-order desires concerning which they have no volitions of the second order, more or less frequently.

The fact that a wanton has no second-order volitions does not mean that each of his first-order desires is translated heedlessly and at once into action. He may have no opportunity to act in accordance with some of his desires. Moreover, the translation of his desires into action may be delayed or precluded either by conflicting desires of the first order or by the intervention of deliberation. For a wanton may possess and employ rational faculties of a high order. Nothing in the concept of a wanton implies that he cannot reason or that he cannot deliberate concerning how to do what he wants to do. What distinguishes the rational wanton from other rational agents is that he is not concerned with the desirability of his desires themselves. He ignores the question of what his will is to be. Not only does he pursue whatever course of action he is most strongly inclined to pursue, but he does not care which of his inclinations is the strongest.

Thus a rational creature, who reflects upon the suitability to his desires of one course of action or another, may none the less be a wanton. In maintaining that the essence of being a person lies not in reason but in will, I am far from suggesting that a creature without reason may be a person. For it is only in virtue of his rational capacities that a person is capable of becoming critically aware of his own will and of forming volitions of the second order. The structure of a person's will presupposes, accordingly, that he is a rational being.

The distinction between a person and a wanton may be illustrated by the difference between two narcotics addicts. Let us suppose that the physiological condition accounting for the addiction is the same in both men, and that both succumb inevitably to their periodic desires for the drug to which they are addicted. One of the addicts hates his addiction and always struggles desperately, although to no avail, against its thrust. He tries everything that he thinks might enable him to overcome his desires for the drug. But these desires are too powerful for him to withstand, and invariably, in the end, they conquer him. He is an unwilling addict, helplessly violated by his own desires.

The unwilling addict has conflicting first-order desires: he wants to take the drug, and he also wants to refrain from taking it. In addition to these first-order desires, however, he has a volition of the second order. He is not a neutral with regard to the conflict between his desire to take the drug and his desire to refrain from taking it. It is the latter desire, and not the former, that he wants to constitute his will; it is the latter desire, rather than the former, that he wants to be effective and to provide the purpose that he will seek to realize in what he actually does.

The other addict is a wanton. His actions reflect the economy of his first-order desires, without his being concerned whether the desires that move him to act are desires by which he wants to be moved to act. If he encounters problems in obtaining the drug or in administering it to himself, his reponses to his urges to take it may involve deliberation. But it never occurs to him to consider whether he wants the relation among his desires to result in his having the will he has. The wanton addict may be an animal, and thus incapable of being concerned about his will. In any event he is, in respect of his wanton lack of concern, no different from an animal.

The second of these addicts may suffer a first-order conflict similar to the first-order conflict suffered by the first. Whether he is human or not, the wanton may (perhaps due to conditioning) both want to take the drug and want to refrain from taking it. Unlike the unwilling addict, however, he does not prefer that one of his conflicting desires should be paramount over the other; he does not prefer that one first-order desire rather than the other should constitute his will. It would be misleading to say that he is neutral as to the conflict between his desires, since this would suggest that he regards them as equally acceptable. Since he has no identity apart from his first-order desires, it is true neither that he prefers one to the other nor that he prefers not to take sides.

It makes a difference to the unwilling addict, who is a person, which of his conflicting first-order desires wins out. Both desires are his, to be sure; and whether he finally takes the drug or finally succeeds in refraining from taking it, he acts to satisfy what is in a literal sense his own desire. In either case he does something he himself wants to do, and he does it not because of some external influence whose aim happens to coincide with his own but because of his desire to do it. The unwilling addict identifies himself, however, through the formation of a second-order volition, with one rather than with the other of his conflicting first-order desires. He makes one of them more truly his own and, in so doing, he withdraws himself from the other. It is in virtue of this identification and withdrawal, accomplished through the formation of a second-order volition, that the unwilling addict may meaningfully make the analytically puzzling statements that the force moving him to take the drug is a force other than his own, and that it is not of his own free will but rather against his will that this force moves him to take it.

The wanton addict cannot or does not care which of his conflicting first-order desires wins out. His lack of concern is not due to his inability to find a convincing basis for preference. It is due either to his lack of the capacity for reflection or to his mindless indifference to the enterprise of evaluating his own desires and motives.[6] There is only one issue in the struggle to which his first-order conflict may lead: whether the one or the other of his conflicting desires is the stronger. Since he is moved by both desires, he will not be altogether satisfied by what he does no matter which of them is effective. But it makes no difference *to him* whether his craving or his aversion gets the upper hand. He has no stake in the conflict between them and so, unlike the unwilling addict, he can neither win nor lose the struggle in which he is engaged. When a *person* acts, the desire by which he is moved is either the will he wants or a will he wants to be without. When a *wanton* acts, it is neither.

III

There is a very close relationship between the capacity for forming second-order volitions and another capacity that is essential to persons—one that has often been considered a distinguishing mark of the human condition. It is only because a person has volitions of the second order that he is capable both of enjoying and of lacking freedom of the will. The concept of a person is not only, then, the concept of a type of entity that has both first-order desires and volitions of the second order. It can also be construed as the concept of a type of entity for whom the freedom of its will may be a problem. This concept excludes all wantons, both infrahuman and human, since they fail to satisfy an essential condition for the enjoyment of freedom of the will. And it excludes those suprahuman beings, if any, whose wills are necessarily free.

Just what kind of freedom is the freedom of the will? This question calls for an identification of the special area of human experience to which the concept of freedom of the will, as distinct from the concepts of other sorts of freedom, is particularly germane. In dealing with it, my aim will be primarily to locate the problem with which a person is most immediately concerned when he is concerned with the freedom of his will.

According to one familiar philosophical tradition, being free is fundamentally a matter of doing what one wants to do. Now the notion of an

[6] In speaking of the evaluation of his own desires and motives as being characteristic of a person, I do not mean to suggest that a person's second-order volitions necessarily manifest a *moral* stance on his part toward his first-order desires. It may not be from the point of view of morality that the person evaluates his first-order desires. Moreover, a person may be capricious and irresponsible in forming his second-order volitions and give no serious consideration to what is at stake. Second-order volitions express evaluations only in the sense that they are preferences. There is no essential restrictions on the kind of basis, if any, upon which they are formed.

agent who does what he wants to do is by no means an altogether clear one: both the doing and the wanting, and the appropriate relation between them as well, require elucidation. But although its focus needs to be sharpened and its formulation refined, I believe that this notion does capture at least part of what is implicit in the idea of an agent who *acts* freely. It misses entirely, however, the peculiar content of the quite different idea of an agent whose *will* is free.

We do not suppose that animals enjoy freedom of the will, although we recognize that an animal may be free to run in whatever direction it wants. Thus, having the freedom to do what one wants to do is not a sufficient condition of having a free will. It is not a necessary condition either. For to deprive someone of his freedom of action is not necessarily to undermine the freedom of his will. When an agent is aware that there are certain things he is not free to do, this doubtless affects his desires and limits the range of choices he can make. But suppose that someone, without being aware of it, has in fact lost or been deprived of his freedom of action. Even though he is no longer free to do what he wants to do, his will may remain as free as it was before. Despite the fact that he is not free to translate his desires into actions or to act according to the determinations of his will, he may still form those desires and make those determinations as freely as if his freedom of action had not been impaired.

When we ask whether a person's will is free we are not asking whether he is in a position to translate his first-order desires into actions. That is the question of whether he is free to do as he pleases. The question of the freedom of his will does not concern the relation between what he does and what he wants to do. Rather, it concerns his desires themselves. But what question about them is it?

It seems to me both natural and useful to construe the question of whether a person's will is free in close analogy to the question of whether an agent enjoys freedom of action. Now freedom of action is (roughly, at least) the freedom to do what one wants to do. Analogously, then, the statement that a person enjoys freedom of the will means (also roughly) that he is free to want what he wants to want. More precisely, it means that he is free to will what he wants to will, or to have the will he wants. Just as the question about the freedom of an agent's action has to do with whether it is the action he wants to perform, so the question about the freedom of his will has to do with whether it is the will he wants to have.

It is in securing the conformity of his will to his second-order volitions, then, that a person exercises freedom of the will. And it is in the discrepancy between his will and his second-order volitions, or in his awareness that their coincidence is not his own doing but only a happy chance, that a person who does not have this freedom feels its lack. The unwilling addict's will is not free. This is shown by the fact that it is not the will he wants. It is also true, though in a different way, that the will of the wanton addict is not free. The wanton addict neither has the will he wants nor has a will that differs from the will he wants. Since he has no volitions of the second order, the freedom of his will cannot be a problem for him. He lacks it, so to speak, by default.

People are generally far more complicated than my sketchy account of the structure of a person's will may suggest. There is as much opportunity for ambivalence, conflict, and self-deception with regard to desires of the second order, for example, as there is with regard to first-order desires. If there is an unresolved conflict among someone's second-order desires, then he is in danger of having no second-order volition; for unless this conflict is resolved, he has no preference concerning which of his first-order desires is to be his will. This condition, if it is so severe that it prevents him from identifying himself in a sufficiently decisive way with *any* of his conflicting first-order desires, destroys him as a person. For it either tends to paralyse his will and to keep him from acting at all, or it tends to remove him from his will so that his will operates without his participation. In both cases he becomes, like the unwilling addict though in a different way, a helpless bystander to the forces that move him.

Another complexity is that a person may have, especially if his second-order desires are in conflict, desires and volitions of a higher order than the second. There is no theoretical limit to the length of the series of desires of higher and higher orders; nothing except common sense and, perhaps, a saving fatigue prevents an individual from obsessively refusing to identify himself with any of his desires until he forms a desire of the next higher order. The tendency to generate such a series of acts of forming desires, which would be a case of humanization run wild, also leads toward the destruction of a person.

It is possible, however, to terminate such a series of acts without cutting it off arbitrarily. When a person identifies himself *decisively* with one of his first-order desires, this commitment 'resounds' throughout the potentially endless array of higher orders. Consider a person who, without reservation or conflict, wants to be motivated by the desire to concentrate on his work. The fact that his second-order volition to be moved by this desire is a decisive one means that there is no room for questions concerning the pertinence of desires or volitions of higher orders. Suppose the person is asked whether he wants to want to concentrate on his work. He can properly insist that this question concerning a third-order desire does not arise. It would be a mistake to claim that, because he has not considered whether he wants the second-order volition he has formed, he is indifferent to the question of whether it is with this volition or with some other that he wants his will to accord. The decisiveness of the commitment he has made means that he has decided that no further question about his second-order volition, at any higher order, remains to be asked. It is relatively unimportant whether we explain this by saying that this commitment implicitly generates an endless series of confirming desires of higher orders, or by saying that the commitment is tantamount to a dissolution of the pointedness of all questions concerning higher orders of desire.

Examples such as the one concerning the unwilling addict may suggest that volitions of the second order, or of higher orders, must be formed deliberately and that a person characteristically struggles to ensure that they are satisfied. But the conformity of a person's will to his higher-order volitions may be far more thoughtless and spontaneous than this. Some people are naturally moved by kindness when they want to be kind, and by nastiness when they want to be nasty, without any explicit forethought and without any need for energetic self-control. Others are moved by nastiness when they want to be kind and by kindness when they intend to be nasty, equally without forethought and without active resistance to these violations of their higher-order desires. The enjoyment of freedom comes easily to some. Others must struggle to achieve it.

IV

My theory concerning the freedom of the will accounts easily for our disinclination to allow that this freedom is enjoyed by the members of any species inferior to our own. It also satisfies another condition that must be met by any such theory, by making it apparent why the freedom of the will should be regarded as desirable. The enjoyment of a free will means the satisfaction of certain desires—desires of the second or of higher orders—whereas its absence means their frustration. The satisfactions at stake are those which accrue to a person of whom it may be said that his will is his own. The corresponding frustrations are those suffered by a person of whom it may be said that he is estranged from himself, or that he finds himself a helpless or a passive bystander to the forces that move him.

A person who is free to do what he wants to do may yet not be in a position to have the will he wants. Suppose, however, that he enjoys both freedom of action and freedom of the will. Then he is not only free to do what he wants to do; he is also free to want what he wants to want. It seems to me that he has, in that case, all the freedom it is possible to desire or to conceive. There are other good things in life, and he may not possess some of them. But there is nothing in the way of freedom that he lacks.

It is far from clear that certain other theories of the freedom of the will meet these elementary but essential conditions: that it be understandable why we desire this freedom and why we refuse to ascribe it to animals. Consider, for example, Roderick Chisholm's quaint version of the doctrine that human freedom entails an absence of causal determination.[7] Whenever a person performs a free action, according to Chisholm, it's a miracle. The motion of a person's hand, when the person moves it, is the outcome of a series of physical causes; but some event in this series, 'and presumably one of those that took place within the brain, was caused by the agent and not by any other events' (18). A free agent has, therefore, 'a prerogative which some would attribute only to God: each of us, when we act, is a prime mover unmoved' (23).

This account fails to provide any basis for doubting that animals of subhuman species enjoy the freedom it defines. Chisholm says nothing that makes it seem less likely that a rabbit performs a miracle when it moves its leg than that a man does so when he moves his hand. But why, in any case, should anyone *care* whether he can interrupt the natural order of causes in the way Chisholm describes? Chisholm offers no reason for believing that there is a discernible difference between the experience of a man who miraculously initiates a series of causes when he moves his hand and a man who moves his hand without any such breach of the normal causal sequence. There appears to be no concrete basis for preferring to be involved in the one state of affairs rather than in the other.[8]

It is generally supposed that, in addition to satisfying the two conditions I have mentioned, a satisfactory theory of the freedom of the will necessarily provides an analysis of one of the conditions of moral responsibility. The most common recent approach to the problem of understanding the freedom of the will has been, indeed, to inquire what is entailed by the assumption that someone is morally responsible for what he has done. In my view, however, the relation between moral responsibility and the freedom of the will has been very widely misunderstood. It is not true that a person is morally responsible for what he has done only if his will was free when he did it. He may be morally responsible for having done it even though his will was not free at all.

[7] 'Freedom and Action', in *Freedom and Determinism*, ed. Keith Lehrer, (New York: Random House, 1966), 11–44. Essay II, in this collection.

[8] I am not suggesting that the alleged difference between these two states of affairs is unverifiable. On the contrary, physiologists might well be able to show that Chisholm's conditions for a free action are not satisfied, by establishing that there is no relevant brain event for which a sufficient physical cause cannot be found.

ill is free only if he is free to have the will he wants. This h regard to any of his first-order desires, he is free either to his will or to make some other first-order desire his will ver his will, then, the will of the person whose will is free could have been otherwise; he could have done otherwise than to constitute his will as he did. It is a vexed question just how 'he could have done otherwise' is to be understood in contexts such as this one. But although this question is important to the theory of freedom, it has no bearing on the theory of moral responsibility. For the assumption that a person is morally responsible for what he has done does not entail that the person was in a position to have whatever will he wanted.

This assumption *does* entail that the person did what he did freely, or that he did it of his own free will. It is a mistake, however, to believe that someone acts freely only when he is free to do whatever he wants or that he acts of his own free will only if his will is free. Suppose that a person has done what he wanted to do, that he did it because he wanted to do it, and that the will by which he was moved when he did it was his will because it was the will he wanted. Then he did it freely and of his own free will. Even supposing that he could have done otherwise, he would not have done otherwise; and even supposing that he could have had a different will, he would not have wanted his will to differ from what it was. Moreover, since the will that moved him when he acted was his will because he wanted it to be, he cannot claim that his will was forced upon him or that he was a passive bystander to its constitution. Under these conditions, it is quite irrelevant to the evaluation of his moral responsibility to inquire whether the alternatives that he opted against were actually available to him.[9]

In illustration, consider a third kind of addict. Suppose that his addiction has the same physiological basis and the same irresistible thrust as the addictions of the unwilling and wanton addicts, but that he is altogether delighted with his condition. He is a willing addict, who would not have things any other way. If the grip of his addiction should somehow weaken, he would do whatever he could to reinstate it; if his desire for the drug should begin to fade, he would take steps to renew its intensity.

The willing addict's will is not free, for his desire to take the drug will be effective regardless of whether or not he wants this desire to constitute his will. But when he takes the drug, he takes it freely and of his own free will. I am inclined to understand his situation as involving the overdetermination of his first-order desire to take the drug. This desire is his effective desire

[9] For another discussion of the considerations that cast doubt on the principle that a person is morally responsible for what he has done only if he could have done otherwise, see my 'Alternate Possibilities and Moral Responsibility', *Journal of Philosophy*, 1969, 829–39.

because he is physiologically addicted. But it is his effective desire also because he wants it to be. His will is outside his control, but, by his second-order desire that his desire for the drug should be effective, he has made this will his own. Given that it is therefore not only because of his addiction that his desire for the drug is effective, he may be morally responsible for taking the drug.

My conception of the freedom of the will appears to be neutral with regard to the problem of determinism. It seems conceivable that it should be causally determined that a person is free to want what he wants to want. If this is conceivable, then it might be causally determined that a person enjoys a free will. There is no more than an innocuous appearance of paradox in the proposition that it is determined, ineluctably and by forces beyond their control, that certain people have free wills and that others do not. There is no incoherence in the proposition that some agency other than a person's own is responsible (even *morally* responsible) for the fact that he enjoys or fails to enjoy freedom of the will. It is possible that a person should be morally responsible for what he does of his own free will and that some other person should also be morally responsible for his having done it.[10]

On the other hand, it seems conceivable that it should come about by chance that a person is free to have the will he wants. If this is conceivable, then it might be a matter of chance that certain people enjoy freedom of the will and that certain others do not. Perhaps it is also conceivable, as a number of philosophers believe, for states of affairs to come about in a way other than by chance or as the outcome of a sequence of natural causes. If it is indeed conceivable for the relevant states of affairs to come about in some third way, then it is also possible that a person should in that third way come to enjoy the freedom of the will.

[10] There is a difference between being *fully* responsible and being *solely* responsible. Suppose that the willing addict has been made an addict by the deliberate and calculated work of another. Then it may be that both the addict and this other person are fully responsible for the addict's taking the drug, while neither of them is solely responsible for it. That there is a distinction between full moral responsibility and sole moral responsibility is apparent in the following example. A certain light can be turned on or off by flicking either of two switches, and each of these switches is simultaneously flicked to the 'on' position by a different person, neither of whom is aware of the other. Neither person is solely responsible for the light's going on, nor do they share the responsibility in the sense that each is partially responsible; rather, each of them is fully responsible.

VII
FREE AGENCY*
GARY WATSON

IN this essay I discuss a distinction that is crucial to a correct account of free action and to an adequate conception of human motivation and responsibility.

I

According to one familiar conception of freedom, a person is free to the extent that he is able to do or get what he wants. To circumscribe a person's freedom is to contract the range of things he is able to do. I think that, suitably qualified, this account is correct, and that the chief and most interesting uses of the word 'free' can be explicated in its terms. But this general line has been resisted on a number of different grounds. One of the most important objections—and the one upon which I shall concentrate in this paper—is that this familiar view is too impoverished to handle talk of free actions and free will.

Frequently enough, we say, or are inclined to say, that a person is not in control of his own actions, that he is not a 'free agent' with respect to them, even though his behaviour is intentional. Possible examples of this sort of action include those which are explained by addictions, manias, and phobias of various sorts. But the concept of free action would seem to be pleonastic on the analysis of freedom in terms of the ability to get what one wants. For if a person does something intentionally, then surely he was able at that time to do it. Hence, on this analysis, he was free to do it. The familiar account would not seem to allow for any further questions, as far as

From *Journal of Philosophy*, vol. lxxii, No. 8 (Apr. 1975), pp. 205–20. Reprinted by permission of the author and the *Journal of Philosophy*.

*I have profited from discussions with numerous friends, students, colleagues, and other audiences, on the material of this essay; I would like to thank them collectively. However, special thanks are due to Joel Feinberg, Harry Frankfurt, and Thomas Nagel.

freedom is concerned, about the action. Accordingly, this account would seem to embody a conflation of free action and intentional action.

Philosophers who have defended some form of compatibilism have usually given this analysis of freedom, with the aim of showing that freedom and responsibility are not really incompatible with determinism. Some critics have rejected compatibilism precisely because of its association with this familiar account of freedom. For instance, Isaiah Berlin asks: if determinism is true,

> . . . what reasons can you, in principle, adduce for attributing responsibility or applying moral rules to [people] which you would not think it reasonable to apply in the case of compulsive choosers—kleptomaniacs, dipsomaniacs, and the like?[1]

The idea is that the sense in which actions would be free in a deterministic world allows the actions of 'compulsive choosers' to be free. To avoid this consequence, it is often suggested, we must adopt some sort of 'contracausal' view of freedom.

Now, though compatibilists from Hobbes to J. J. C. Smart have given the relevant moral and psychological concepts an exceedingly crude treatment, this crudity is not inherent in compatibilism, nor does it result from the adoption of the conception of freedom in terms of the ability to get what one wants. For the difference between free and unfree actions—as we normally discern it—has nothing at all to do with the truth or falsity of determinism.

In the subsequent pages, I want to develop a distinction between wanting and valuing which will enable the familiar view of freedom to make sense of the notion of an unfree action. The contention will be that, in the case of actions that are unfree, the agent is unable to get what he most wants, *or values*, and this inability is due to his own 'motivational system'. In this case the obstruction to the action that he most wants to do is his own will. It is in this respect that the action is unfree: the agent is obstructed in and by the very performance of the action.

I do not conceive my remarks to be a defence of compatibilism. This point of view may be unacceptable for various reasons, some of which call into question the coherence of the concept of responsibility. But these reasons do not include the fact that compatibilism relies upon the conception of freedom in terms of the ability to get what one wants, nor must it conflate free action and intentional action. If compatibilism is to be shown to be wrong, its critics must go deeper.

II

What must be true of people if there is to be a significant notion of free action? Our talk of free action arises from the apparent fact that what a

[1] *Four Essays on Liberty* (Oxford University Press, 1969), xx–xxi.

person most wants may not be what he is finally moved to get. It follows from this apparent fact that the extent to which one wants something is not determined solely by the *strength* of one's desires (or 'motives') as measured by their effectiveness in action. One (perhaps trivial) measure of the strength of the desire or want is that the agent acts upon that desire or want (trivial, since it will be non-explanatory to say that an agent acted upon that desire because it was the strongest). But, if what one most wants may not be what one most strongly wants, by this measure, then in what sense can it be true that one wants it?[2]

To answer this question, one might begin by contrasting, at least in a crude way, a Humean with a Platonic conception of practical reasoning. The ancients distinguished between the rational and the irrational parts of the soul, between Reason and Appetite. Hume employed a superficially similar distinction. It is important to understand, however, that (for Plato at least) the rational part of the soul is not to be identified with what Hume called 'Reason' and contradistinguished from the 'Passions'. On Hume's account, Reason is not a source of motivation, but a faculty of determining what is true and what is false, a faculty concerned solely with 'matters of fact' and 'relations among ideas'. It is completely dumb on the question of what to do. Perhaps Hume could allow Reason this much practical voice: given an initial set of wants and beliefs about what is or is likely to be the case, particular desires are generated in the process. In other words, a Humean might allow Reason a crucial role in deliberation. But its essential role would not be to supply motivation—Reason is not that kind of thing—but rather to calculate, within a context of desires and ends, how to fulfil those desires and serve those ends. For Plato, however, the rational part of the soul is not some kind of inference mechanism. It is itself a source of motivation. In general form, the desires of Reason are desires for 'the Good'.

Perhaps the contrast can be illustrated by some elementary notions from decision theory. On the Bayesian model of deliberation, a preference scale is imposed upon various states of affairs contingent upon courses of action open to the agent. Each state of affairs can be assigned a numerical value (initial value) according to its place on the scale; given this assignment, and the probabilities that those states of affairs will obtain if the actions are performed, a final numerical value (expected desirability) can be assigned

[2] I am going to use 'want' and 'desire' in the very inclusive sense now familiar in philosophy, whereby virtually any motivational factor that may figure in the explanation of intentional action is a want; 'desire' will be used mainly in connection with the appetites and passions.

to the actions themselves. The rational agent performs the action with the highest expected desirability.

In these terms, on the Humean picture, Reason is the faculty that computes probabilities and expected desirabilities. Reason is in this sense neutral with respect to actions, for it can operate equally on any given assignment of initial values and probabilities—it has nothing whatsoever to say about the assignment of initial values. On the Platonic picture, however, the rational part of the soul itself determines what has *value* and how much, and thus is responsible for the original ranking of alternative states of affairs.

It may appear that the difference between these conceptions is merely a difference as to what is to be called 'Reason' or 'rational', and hence is not a substantive difference. In speaking of Reason, Hume has in mind a sharp contrast between what is wanted and what is thought to be the case. What contrast is implicit in the Platonic view that the ranking of alternative states of affairs is the task of the rational part of the soul?

The contrast here is not trivial; the difference in classificatory schemes reflects different views of human psychology. For one thing, in saying this (or what is tantamount to this) Plato was calling attention to the fact that it is one thing to think a state of affairs good, worth while, or worthy of promotion, and another simply to desire or want that state of affairs to obtain. Since the notion of value is tied to (cannot be understood independently of) those of the good and worthy, it is one thing to value (think good) a state of affairs and another to desire that it obtain. However, to think a thing good is at the same time to desire it (or its promotion). Reason is thus an original spring of action. It is because valuing is essentially related to thinking or *judging* good that it is appropriate to speak of the wants that are (or perhaps arise from) evaluations as belonging to, or originating in, the rational (that is, *judging*) part of the soul; values provide *reasons* for action. The contrast is with desires, whose objects may not be thought good and which are thus, in a natural sense, blind or irrational. Desires are mute on the question of what is good.[3]

[3] To quote just one of many suggestive passages: 'We must . . . observe that within each one of us there are two sorts of ruling or guiding principle that we follow. One is an innate desire for pleasure, the other an acquired judgement that aims at what is best. Sometimes these internal guides are in accord, sometimes at variance; now one gains the mastery, now the other. And when judgement guides us rationally toward what is best, and has the mastery, that mastery is called temperance, but when desire drags us irrationally toward pleasure, and has come to rule within us, the name given to that rule is wantonness' (*Phaedrus*, 237e–238e; Hackforth trans.).

For a fascinating discussion of Plato's parts-of-the-soul doctrine, see Terry Penner's 'Thought and Desire in Plato', in Gregory Vlastos, ed., *Plato: A Collection of Critical Essays*, vol. ii (New York: Anchor, 1971). As I see it (and here I have been influenced by Penner's article), the distinction I have attributed to Plato was meant by him to be a solution to the socratic problem of *akrasia*.

Now it seems to me that—given the view of freedom as the ability to get what one wants—there can be a problem of free action only if the Platonic conception of the soul is (roughly) correct. The doctrine I shall defend is Platonic in the sense that it involves a distinction between valuing and desiring which depends upon there being independent sources of motivation. No doubt Plato meant considerably more than this by his parts-of-the-soul doctrine; but he meant at least this. The Platonic conception provides an answer to the question I posed earlier: in what sense can what one most wants differ from that which is the object of the strongest desire? The answer is that the phrase 'what one most wants' may mean either 'the object of the strongest desire' or 'what one most *values*'. This phrase can be interpreted in terms of strength or in terms of ranking order or preference. The problem of free action arises because what one desires may not be what one values, and what one most values may not be what one is finally moved to get.[4]

The tacit identification of desiring or wanting with valuing is so common[5] that it is necessary to cite some examples of this distinction in order to illustrate how evaluation and desire may diverge. There seem to be two ways in which, in principle, a discrepancy may arise. First, it is possible that what one desires is not *to any degree* valued, held to be worth while, or thought good; one assigns *no* value whatever to the object of one's desire. Second, although one may indeed value what is desired, the strength of one's desire may not properly reflect the degree to which one values its object; that is, although the object of a desire is valuable, it may not be deemed the most valuable in the situation and yet one's desire for it may be stronger than the want for what is most valued.

The cases in which one in no way values what one desires are perhaps rare, but surely they exist. Consider the case of a woman who has a sudden

---

I would argue that this distinction, though necessary, is insufficient for the task, because it does not mark the difference between ('mere') incontinence or weakness of will and psychological compulsion. This difference requires a careful examination of the various things that might be meant in speaking of the strength of a desire.

[4] Here I shall not press the rational/non-rational contrast any further than this, though Plato would have wished to press it further. However, one important and anti-Humean implication of the minimal distinction is this: it is not the case that, if a person desires to do *X*, he therefore has (or even regards himself as having) a reason to do *X*.

[5] For example, I take my remarks to be incompatible with the characterization of value R. B. Perry gives in *General Theory of Value* (Harvard University Press, 1950). In ch. 5, Perry writes: 'This, then, we take to be the original source and constant feature of all value. That which is an object of interest is *eo ipso* invested with value.' And 'interest' is characterized in the following way: '. . . liking and disliking, desire and aversion, will and refusal, or seeking and avoiding. It is to this all-pervasive characteristic of the motor-affective life, this *state, act, attitude* or *disposition of favour* or disfavor, to which we propose to give the name of "interest".'

urge to drown her bawling child in the bath; or the case of a squash player who, while suffering an ignominious defeat, desires to smash his opponent in the face with the racquet. It is just false that the mother values her child's being drowned or that the player values the injury and suffering of his opponent. But they desire these things none the less. They desire them in spite of themselves. It is not that they assign to these actions an initial value which is then outweighed by other considerations. These activities are not even represented by a positive entry, however small, on the initial 'desirability matrix'.

It may seem from these examples that this first and radical sort of divergence between desiring and valuing occurs only in the case of momentary and inexplicable urges or impulses. Yet I see no conclusive reason why a person could not be similarly estranged from a rather persistent and pervasive desire, and one that is explicable enough. Imagine a man who thinks his sexual inclinations are the work of the devil, that the very fact that he has sexual inclinations bespeaks his corrupt nature. This example is to be contrasted with that of the celibate who decides that the most fulfilling life for him will be one of abstinence. In this latter case, *one* of the things that receive consideration in the process of reaching his all-things-considered judgement is the value of sexual activity. There is something, from his point of view, to be said for sex, but there is more to be said in favour of celibacy. In contrast, the man who is estranged from his sexual inclinations does not acknowledge even a prima-facie reason for sexual activity; that he is sexually inclined toward certain activities is not even *a* consideration. Another way of illustrating the difference is to say that, for the one man, foregoing sexual relationships constitutes a *loss*, even if negligible compared with the gains of celibacy; whereas from the standpoint of the other person, no loss is sustained at all.

Now, it must be admitted, any desire may provide the basis for a reason in so far as non-satisfaction of the desire causes suffering and hinders the pursuit of ends of the agent. But it is important to notice that the reason generated in this way by a desire is a reason for *getting rid* of the desire, and one may get rid of a desire either by satisfying it or by eliminating it in some other manner (by tranquillizers, or cold showers). Hence this kind of reason differs importantly from the reasons based upon the evaluation of the activities or states of affairs in question. For, in the former case, attaining the object of desire is simply a means of eliminating discomfort or agitation, whereas in the latter case that attainment is the end itself. Normally, in the pursuit of the objects of our wants we are not attempting chiefly to relieve ourselves. We aim to satisfy, not just eliminate, desire.

Nevertheless, aside from transitory impulses, it may be that cases wherein nothing at all can be said in favour of the object of one's desire are rare. For it would seem that even the person who conceives his sexual desires to be essentially evil would have to admit that indulgence would be pleasurable, and surely that is something. (Perhaps not even this should be admitted. For indulgence may not yield pleasure at all in a context of anxiety. Furthermore, it is not obvious that pleasure is intrinsically good, independently of the worth of the pleasurable object.) In any case, the second sort of divergence between evaluation and desire remains: it is possible that, in a particular context, what one wants most strongly is not what one most values.

The distinction between valuing and desiring is not, it is crucial to see, a distinction among desires or wants according to their content. That is to say, there is nothing in the specification of the objects of an agent's desires that singles out some wants as based upon that agent's values. The distinction in question has rather to do with the *source* of the want or with its role in the total 'system' of the agent's desires and ends. It has to do with why the agent wants what he does.

Obviously, to identify a desire or want simply in terms of its content is not to identify its source(s). It does not follow from my wanting to eat that I am hungry. I may want to eat because I want to be well-nourished; or because I am hungry; or because eating is a pleasant activity. This single desire may have three independent sources. (These sources may not be altogether independent. It may be that eating is pleasurable only because I have appetites for food.) Some specifications of wants or desires—for instance, as cravings—pick out (at least roughly) the source of the motivation.

It is an essential feature of the appetites and the passions that they engender (or consist in) desires whose existence and persistence are independent of the person's judgement of the good. The appetite of hunger involves a desire to eat which has a source in physical needs and physiological states of the hungry organism. And emotions such as anger and fear partly consist in spontaneous inclinations to do various things—to attack or to flee the object of one's emotion, for example. It is intrinsic to the appetites and passions that appetitive and passionate beings can be motivated in spite of themselves. It is because desires such as these arise independently of the person's judgement and values that the ancients located the emotions and passions in the irrational part of the soul;[6] and it is because of this sort of independence that a conflict between valuing and desiring is possible.[7]

[6] Notice that most emotions differ from passions like lust in that they involve beliefs and some sort of valuation (cf. resentment). This may be the basis for Plato's positing a third part of the soul which is in a way partly rational—namely, *Thumos*.

[7] To be sure, one may attempt to cultivate or eliminate certain appetites and passions, so that the desires that result may be in this way dependent upon one's evaluations. Even so, the resulting

These points may suggest an inordinately dualistic view according to which persons are split into inevitably alien, if not always antagonistic, halves. But this view does not follow from what has been said. As central as it is to human life, it is not often noted that some activities are valued only to the extent that they are objects of the appetites. This means that such activities would never be regarded as valuable constituents of one's life were it not for one's susceptibility to 'blind' motivation—motivation independent of one's values. Sexual activity and eating are again examples. We may value the activity of eating to the degree that it provides nourishment. But we may also value it because it is an enjoyable activity, even though its having this status depends upon our appetites for food, our hunger. In the case of sex, in fact, if we were not erotic creatures, certain activities would not only lose their value to us, they might not even be physiologically possible.

These examples indicate, not that there is no distinction between desiring and valuing, but that the value placed upon certain activities depends upon their being the fulfilment of desires that arise and persist independently of what we value. So it is not that, when we value the activity of eating, we think there are reasons to eat no matter what other desires we have; rather, we value eating when food appeals to us; and, likewise, we value sexual relationships when we are aroused. Here an essential part of the *content* of our evaluation is that the activity in question be motivated by certain appetites. These activities may have value for us only in so far as they are appetitively motivated, even though to have these appetites is not *ipso facto* to value their objects.

Part of what it means to value some activities in this way is this: we judge that to cease to have such appetites is to lose something of worth. The judgement here is not merely that, if someone has these appetites, it is worth while (*ceteris paribus*) for him to indulge them. The judgement is rather that it is of value to have and (having them) to indulge these appetites. The former judgement does not account for the eunuch's loss or sorrow, whereas the latter does. And the latter judgement lies at the bottom of the discomfort one may feel when one envisages a situation in which, say, hunger is consistently eliminated and nourishment provided by insipid capsules.

It would be impossible for a non-erotic being or a person who lacked the appetite for food and drink fully to understand the value most of us attach to sex and to dining. Sexual activity must strike the non-erotic being as perfectly grotesque. Or consider an appetite that is in fact 'unnatural' (i.e. acquired): the craving for tobacco. To a person who has never known the

desires will be such that they can persist independently of one's values. It is rather like jumping from an airplane.

enticement of Lady Nicotine, what could be more incomprehensible than the filthy practice of consummating a fine meal by drawing into one's lungs the noxious fumes of a burning weed?

Thus, the relationship between evaluation and motivation is intricate. With respect to many of our activities, evaluation depends upon the possibility of our being moved to act independently of our judgement. So the distinction I have been pressing—that between desiring and valuing—does not commit one to an inevitable split between Reason and Appetite, Appetitively motivated activities may well constitute for a person the most worth-while aspects of his life.[8] But the distinction does commit us to the possibility of such a split. If there are sources of motivation independent of the agent's values, then it is possible that sometimes he is motivated to do things he does not deem worth doing. This possibility is the basis for the principal problem of free action: a person may be obstructed by his own will.

A related possibility that presents considerable problems for the understanding of free agency is this: some desires, when they arise, may 'colour' or influence what appear to be the agent's evaluations, but only temporarily. That is, when and only when he has the desire, is he inclined to think or say that what is desired or wanted is worth while or good. This possibility is to be distinguished from another, according to which one thinks it worth while to eat when one is hungry or to engage in sexual activity when one is so inclined. For one may think this even on the occasions when the appetites are silent. The possibility I have in mind is rather that what one is disposed to say or judge is temporarily affected by the presence of the desire in such a way that, both before and after the 'onslaught' of the desire, one judges that the desire's object is worth pursuing (in the circumstances) whether or not one has the desire. In this case one is likely, in a cool moment, to think it a matter for regret that one had been so influenced and to think that one should guard against desires that have this property. In other cases it may not be the desire itself that affects one's judgement, but the set of conditions in which those desires arise—e.g. the conditions induced by drugs or alcohol. (It is noteworthy that we say: 'under the influence of alcohol'.) Perhaps judgements made in such circumstances are often in some sense self-deceptive. In any event, this phenomenon raises problems about the identification of a person's values.

Despite our examples, it would be mistaken to conclude that the only desires that exhibit an independence of evaluation are appetitive or passionate desires. In Freudian terms, one may be as dissociated from the

[8] It is reported that H. G. Wells regarded the most important themes of his life to have been (1) the attainment of a World Society, and (2) sex.

demands of the super-ego as from those of the id. One may be disinclined to move away from one's family, the thought of doing so being accompanied by compunction; and yet this disinclination may rest solely upon acculturation rather than upon a current judgement of what one is to do, reflecting perhaps an assessment of one's 'duties' and interests. Or, taking another example, one may have been habituated to think that divorce is to be avoided in all cases, so that the aversion to divorce persists even though one sees no justification for maintaining one's marriage. In both of these cases, the attitude has its basis solely in acculturation and exists independently of the agent's judgement. For this reason, acculturated desires are irrational (better: non-rational) in the same sense as appetitive and passionate desires. In fact, despite the inhibitions acquired in the course of a puritan up-bringing, a person may deem the pursuit of sexual pleasure to be worth while, his judgement siding with the id rather than the super-ego. Acculturated attitudes may seem more akin to evaluation than to appetite in that they are often expressed in evaluative language ('divorce is wicked') and result in feelings of guilt when one's actions are not in conformity with them. But, since conflict is possible here, to want something as a result of acculturation is not thereby to value it, in the sense of 'to value' that we want to capture.

It is not easy to give a non-trivial account of the sense of 'to value' in question. In part, to value something is, in the appropriate circumstances, to want it, and to attribute a want for something to someone is to say that he is disposed to try to get it. So it will not be easy to draw this distinction in behavioural terms. Apparently the difference will have to do with the agent's attitude towards the various things he is disposed to try to get. We might say that an agent's values consist in those principles and ends which he—in a cool and non-self-deceptive moment—articulates as definitive of the good, fulfilling, and defensible life. That most people have articulate 'conceptions of the good', coherent life-plans, *systems* of ends, and so on, is of course something of a fiction. Yet we all have more or less long-term aims and normative principles that we are willing to defend. It is such things as these that are to be identified with our values.

The valuation system of an agent is that set of considerations which, when combined with his factual beliefs (and probability estimates), yields judgements of the form: the thing for me to do in these circumstances, all things considered, is *a*. To ascribe free agency to a being presupposes it to be a being that makes judgements of this sort. To be this sort of being, one must assign values to alternative states of affairs, that is, rank them in terms of worth.

The motivational system of an agent is that set of considerations which move him to action. We identify his motivational system by identifying what motivates him. The possibility of unfree action consists in the fact that an agent's valuational system and motivational system may not completely coincide. Those systems harmonize to the extent that what determines the agent's all-things-considered judgements also determines his actions.

Now, to be sure, since to value is also to want, one's valuational and motivational systems must to a large extent overlap. If, in appropriate circumstances, one were never inclined to action by some alleged evaluation, the claim that that was indeed one's evaluation would be disconfirmed. Thus one's valuational system must have some (considerable) grip upon one's motivational system. The problem is that there are motivational factors other than valuational ones. The free agent has the capacity to translate his values into action; his actions flow from his evaluational system.

One's evaluational system may be said to constitute one's standpoint, the point of view from which one judges the world. The important feature of one's evaluational system is that one cannot coherently dissociate oneself from it *in its entirety*. For to dissociate oneself from the ends and principles that constitute one's evaluational system is to disclaim or repudiate them, and any ends and principles so disclaimed (self-deception aside) cease to be constitutive of one's valuational system. One can dissociate oneself from one set of ends and principles only from the standpoint of another such set that one does not disclaim. In short, one cannot dissociate oneself from all normative judgements without forfeiting all standpoints and therewith one's identity as an agent.

Of course, it does not follow from the fact that one must assume some standpoint that one must have only one, nor that one's standpoint is completely determinate. There may be ultimate conflicts, irresolvable tensions, and things about which one simply does not know what to do or say. Some of these possibilities point to problems about the unity of the person. Here the extreme case is pathological. I am inclined to think that when the split is severe enough, to have more than one standpoint is to have none.

This distinction between wanting and valuing requires far fuller explication than it has received so far. Perhaps the foregoing remarks have at least shown *that* the distinction exists and is important, and have hinted at its nature. This distinction is important to the adherent of the familiar view—that talk about free action and free agency can be understood in terms of the idea of being able to get what one wants—because it gives sense to the claim that in unfree actions the agents do not get what they really or most want. This distinction gives sense to the contrast between free action and intentional action. Admittedly, further argument is required to show that such unfree agents are *unable* to get what they want; but the initial step toward this end has been taken.

At this point, it will be profitable to consider briefly a doctrine that is in many respects like that which I have been developing. The contrast will, I think, clarify the claims that have been advanced in the preceding pages.

III

In an important and provocative article,[9] Harry Frankfurt has offered a description of what he takes to be the essential feature of 'the concept of a person', a feature which, he alleges, is also basic to an understanding of 'freedom of the will'. This feature is the possession of higher-order volitions as well as first-order desires. Frankfurt construes the notion of a person's will as 'the notion of an *effective* desire—one that moves (or will or would move) a person all the way to action' [84, above]. Someone has a second-order volition, then, when he wants 'a certain desire to be his will'. (Frankfurt also considers the case of a second-order desire that is not a second-order volition, where one's desire is simply to have a certain desire and not to act upon it. For example, a man may be curious to know what it is like to be addicted to drugs; he thus desires to desire heroin, but he may not desire his desire for heroin to be effective, to be his will. In fact, Frankfurt's actual example is somewhat more special, for here the man's desire is not simply to have a desire for heroin: he wants to have a desire for heroin which has a certain source, i.e. is addictive. He wants to know what it is like to *crave* heroin.) Someone is a *wanton* if he has no second-order volitions. Finally, 'it is only because a person has volitions of the second order that he is capable both of enjoying and of lacking freedom of the will' [89, above].

Frankfurt's thesis resembles the Platonic view we have been unfolding in so far as it focuses upon 'the structure of a person's will' [82, above]. I want to make a simple point about Frankfurt's paper: namely that the 'structural' feature to which Frankfurt appeals is not the fundamental feature for either free agency or personhood; it is simply insufficient to the task he wants it to perform.

One job that Frankfurt wishes to do with the distinction between lower and higher orders of desire is to give an account of the sense in which some wants may be said to be more truly the agent's own than others (though in an obvious sense all are wants of the agent), the sense in which the agent

[9] 'Freedom of the Will and the Concept of a Person', *Journal of Philosophy*, 1971, 5–20. [Essay VI in this collection.]

'identifies' with one desire rather than another and the sense in which an agent may be unfree with respect to his own 'will'. This enterprise is similar to our own. But we can see that the notion of 'higher-order volition' is not really the fundamental notion for these purposes, by raising the question: Can't one be a wanton, so to speak, with respect to one's second-order desires and volitions?

In a case of conflict, Frankfurt would have us believe that what it is to identify with some desire rather than another is to have a volition concerning the former which is of higher order than any concerning the latter. That the first desire is given a special status over the second is due to its having an *n*-order volition concerning it, whereas the second desire has at most an (*n*−1)-order volition concerning it. But why does one necessarily care about one's higher-order volitions? Since second-order volitions are themselves simply desires, to add them to the context of conflict is just to increase the number of contenders; it is not to give a special place to any of those in contention. The agent may not care which of the second-order desires win out. The same possibility arises at each higher order.

Quite aware of this difficulty, Frankfurt writes:

> There is no theoretical limit to the length of the series of desires of higher and higher orders; nothing except common sense and, perhaps, a saving fatigue prevents an individual from obsessively refusing to identify himself with any of his desires until he forms a desire of the next higher order. [91, above.]

But he insists that

> It is possible . . . to terminate such a series of acts [i.e. the formation of ever higher-order volitions] without cutting it off arbitrarily. When a person identifies himself decisively with one of his first-order desires, this commitment 'resounds' throughout the potentially endless array of higher orders . . . The fact that his second-order volition to be moved by this desire is a decisive one means that there is no room for questions concerning the pertinence of volitions of higher orders . . . The decisiveness of the commitment he has made means that he has decided that no further question about his second-order volition, at any higher order, remains to be asked. [Ibid.]

But either this reply is lame or it reveals that the notion of a higher-order volition is not the fundamental one. We wanted to know what prevents wantonness with regard to one's higher-order volitions. What gives these volitions any special relation to 'oneself'? It is unhelpful to answer that one makes a 'decisive commitment', where this just means that an interminable ascent to higher orders is not going to be permitted. This *is* arbitrary.

What this difficulty shows is that the notion of orders of desires or volitions does not do the work that Frankfurt wants it to do. It does not tell us why or how a particular want can have, among all of a person's 'desires', the special property of being peculiarly his 'own'. There may be something to the notions of acts of identification and of decisive commitment, but these are in any case different notions from that of a second- (or *n*-) order desire. And if these are the crucial notions, it is unclear why these acts of identification cannot be themselves of the first order—that is, identification with or commitment to courses of action (rather than with or to desires)—in which case, no ascent is necessary, and the notion of higher-order volitions becomes superfluous or at least secondary.

In fact, I think that such acts of 'identification and commitment' (if one finds this way of speaking helpful) are generally to courses of action, that is, are first-order. Frankfurt's picture of practical judgement seems to be that of an agent with a given set of (first-order) desires concerning which he then forms second-order volitions. But this picture seems to be distorted. As I see it, agents frequently formulate values concerning alternatives they had not hitherto desired. Initially, they do not (or need not usually) ask themselves which of their desires they want to be effective in action; they ask themselves which course of action is most worth pursuing. The initial practical question is about courses of action and not about themselves.

Indeed, practical judgements are connected with 'second-order volitions'. For the same considerations that constitute one's on-balance reasons for doing some action, *a*, are reasons for wanting the 'desire' to do *a* to be effective in action, and for wanting contrary desires to be ineffective. But in general, evaluations are prior and of the first order. The first-order desires that result from practical judgements generate second-order volitions because they have this special status; they do not have the special status that Frankfurt wants them to have because there is a higher-order desire concerning them.

Therefore, Frankfurt's position resembles the platonic conception in its focus upon the structure of the 'soul'.[10] But the two views draw their divisions differently; whereas Frankfurt divides the soul into higher and lower orders of desire, the distinction for Plato—and for my thesis—is among independent sources of motivation.[11]

IV

In conclusion, it can now be seen that one worry that blocks the acceptance of the traditional view of freedom—and in turn, of compatibil-

[10] Frankfurt's idea of a wanton, suitably construed, can be put to further illuminating uses in moral psychology. It proves valuable, I think, in discussing the problematic phenomenon of psychopathy or sociopathy.

[11] Some very recent articles employ distinctions, for similar purposes, very like Frankfurt's and my own. See, for example, Richard C. Jeffrey, 'Preferences among Preferences', *Journal of Philosophy*, 1974, 377–91. In 'Freedom and Desire', *Philosophical Review*, 1974, 32–54, Wright Neely appeals to higher-order desires, apparently unaware of Frankfurt's development of this concept.

ism—is unfounded. To return to Berlin's question above, it is false that determinism entails that all our actions and choices have the same status as those of 'compulsive choosers' such as 'kleptomaniacs, dipsomaniacs, and the like'. What is distinctive about such compulsive behaviour, I would argue, is that the desires and emotions in question are more or less radically independent of the evaluational systems of these agents. The compulsive character of a kleptomaniac's thievery has nothing at all to do with determinism. (His desires to steal may arise quite randomly.) Rather, it is because his desires express themselves independently of his evaluational judgements that we tend to think of his actions as unfree.

The truth, of course, is that God (traditionally conceived) is the only free agent without qualification. In the case of God, who is omnipotent and omniscient, there can be no disparity between valuational and motivational systems. The dependence of motivation upon evaluation is total, for there is but a single source of motivation: his presumably benign judgement.[12] In the case of the Brutes, as well, motivation has a single source: appetite and (perhaps) passion. The Brutes (or so we normally think) have no evaluational systems. But human beings are only more or less free agents, typically less. They are free agents only in some respects. With regard to the appetites and passions, it is plain that in some situations the motivational systems of human beings exhibit an independence from their values which is inconsistent with free agency; that is to say, people are sometimes moved by their appetites and passions in conflict with their practical judgements.[13]

As Nietzsche said (probably with a rather different point in mind): 'Man's belly is the reason why man does not easily take himself for a god.'[14]

[12] God could not act *akratically*. In this respect, Socrates thought people were distinguishable from such a being only by ignorance and limited power.

[13] This possibility is a definitive feature of appetitive and passionate wants.

[14] *Beyond Good and Evil*, s. 141.

VIII

RESPONSIBILITY FOR SELF

CHARLES TAYLOR

WHAT is the notion of responsibility which is bound up with our conception of a person or self? Is there a sense in which the human agent is responsible for himself which is part of our very conception of the self?

This is certainly a commonly held idea, among 'ordinary men' as well as among philosophers. Just to mention two contemporary specimens of the latter breed: H. Frankfurt has made the point that a person is more than just a subject of desires, of choices, even of deliberation; that we attribute to persons the ability to form 'second-order desires': to want to be moved by certain desires, or 'second-order volitions': to want certain first-order desires to be the ones which move them to action.[1]

If we think of what we are as defined by our goals, by what we desire to encompass or maintain, then a person on this view is one who can raise the question: Do I really want to be what I now am? (i.e. have the desires and goals I now have?) In other words, beyond the *de facto* characterization of the subject by his goals, desires, and purposes, a person is a subject who can pose the *de jure* question: is this the kind of being I ought to be, or really want to be? There is as Frankfurt puts it a 'capacity for reflective self-evaluation . . . manifested in the formation of second-order desires' [83, above].

Or again, we can invoke Heidegger's famous formula, taken up by Sartre: 'das Seiende, dem es in seinem Sein um dieses selbst geht' (*Sein Und Zeit*, 42). The idea here, at a first approximation, is that the human subject is such that the question arises inescapably, which kind of being he is going to

From *The Identities of Persons,* ed. Amelie Oksenberg Rorty, pp. 281–99.

[1] 'Freedom of the Will and The Concept of a Person', *Journal of Philosophy*, 1971, 5–20. [Reprinted above, Essay VI in this collection.]

realize. He is not just *de facto* a certain kind of being, with certain given desires, but it is somehow 'up to' him what kind of being he is going to be.

In both these views we have the notion that human subjects are capable of evaluating what they are, and to the extent that they can shape themselves on this evaluation, are responsible for what they are in a way that other subjects of action and desire (the higher animals for instance) cannot be said to be. It is this kind of evaluation/responsibility which many believe to be essential to our notion of the self.

I

1. What is involved here? Let's look first at evaluation. Of course, in a sense the capacity to evaluate can be ascribed to any subject of desire. My dog 'evaluates' that beefsteak positively. But the kind of evaluation implicit in the above formulations is a reflective kind where we evaluate our desires themselves. It is this plainly which we are tempted to think of as essential to our notion of a self.

But the evaluation of desires or desired consummations can itself be understood in both a weak and a strong sense. To take the weaker sense, an agent could weigh desired actions simply to determine convenience, or how to make different desires compossible—he might resolve to put off eating although hungry, because later he could both eat and swim—or how to get the most overall satisfaction. But there would not yet be any evaluation in a strong sense where I class desires as being bad or unworthy, or lower; where, in other words, desires are classified in such categories as higher or lower, virtuous or vicious, more or less fulfilling, more or less refined, profound or superficial, noble or base; where they are judged as belonging to qualitatively different modes of life, fragmented or integrated, alienated or free, saintly or merely human, courageous or pusillanimous, and so on.

The difference between a reflection which is couched in qualitative distinctions and one which is not has nothing necessarily to do with calculation. The difference is rather (1) that in the latter reflection, for something to be judged good it is sufficient that it be desired, whereas in qualitative reflection there is also a use of 'good' or some other evaluative term for which being desired is not sufficient; indeed some desires or desired consummations can be judged as bad, base, ignoble, trivial, superficial, unworthy, and so on.

It follows from this (2) that when in non-qualitative reflection one desired alternative is set aside, it is only on grounds of its contingent incompatibility with a more desired alternative. But with qualitative reflection this is not necessarily the case. Some desired consummation may be eschewed not because it is incompatible with another, or if because of incompatibility, this will not be contingent. Thus I refrain from committing some cowardly act, although very tempted to do so, but this is not because this act at this moment would make any other desired act impossible, but rather because it is base.

But, of course, there is also a way in which we could characterize this alternative which would bring out incompatibility. If we examine my evaluative vision more closely, we shall see that I value courageous action as part of a mode of life; I aspire to be a certain kind of person. This would be compromised by my giving into this craven impulse. Here there is incompatibility. But this incompatibility is no longer contingent. It is not just a matter of circumstances which makes it impossible to give in to the impulse to flee and still cleave to a courageous, upright mode of life. Such a mode of life *consists* among other things in withstanding such craven impulses.

That there should be incompatibility of a non-contingent kind here is not adventitious, for qualitative reflection deploys a language of evaluative distinctions, in which different desires are described as noble or base, integrating or fragmenting, courageous or cowardly, clairvoyant or blind, and so on. But this means that they are characterized contrastively. Each concept of one of the above pairs can only be understood in relation to the other. No one can have an idea what courage is unless he knows what cowardice is, just as no one can have a notion of 'red', say, without some other colour terms with which it contrasts. And of course with evaluative terms, as with colour terms, the contrast may not just be with one other, but with several. And indeed, refining an evaluative vocabulary by introducing new terms would alter the sense of the existing terms, even as it would with our colour vocabulary.

This means that in qualitative reflection, we can characterize the alternatives contrastively; and indeed, it can be the case that we must do so if we are to express what is really desirable in the favoured alternative. But this is not so with non-qualitative reflection. Of course, in each case we are free to express the alternatives in a number of ways, some of which are and some of which are not contrastive. But if I want to identify the alternatives in terms of their desirability, the characterization ceases to be contrastive. What is going for lunching now is that I'm hungry, and it is unpleasant to wait while one's hungry and a great pleasure to eat. What's going for eating later is that I can swim. But I can identify the pleasures of eating quite independently from those of swimming; indeed, I may have enjoyed eating long before swimming entered my life (and the reverse could conceivably be true, if I spent my childhood eating something revolting like brussel sprouts—although failure to enjoy eating, no matter what one is fed, is probably a psychological impossibility). Not being contrastively described, these two desired consummations are incompatible, where they are, only contingently and circumstantially.

Reciprocally, I can describe the issue of my qualitative reflection non-contrastively. I can say that the choice is between saving my life, or perhaps avoiding pain or embarrassment, on one hand, and upholding my honour on the other. Now certainly I can understand preserving my life, and what is desirable about it, without any acquaintance with honour, and the same goes for avoiding pain and embarrassment. But the reverse is not quite the case. No one could understand 'honour' without some reference to our desire to avoid death, pain, or embarrassment, because one preserves honour among other things by a certain stance towards these. Still saving one's honour is not simply contrastively defined with saving one's life, avoiding pain and so on; there are many cases where one can save one's life without any taint to honour, without the question even arising.

But the case we are imagining is not one of these. Rather we are imagining a situation in which I save my life or avoid pain by some cowardly act. In this situation, the non-contrastive description is a cop-out. I can indeed identify the desirability of the 'lower' alternative in a way which makes no reference to the higher, for here the desirability just is that life is preserved or pain avoided. I am certainly not going to mention that the act is cowardly, for this is not part of what recommends it to me. But things are different when we come to the 'higher' alternative. This is desirable because it is an act of courage, or integrity or honour. And it is an essential part of being courageous that one eschew such craven acts as the 'lower' alternative that here beckons. Someone who doesn't understand this doesn't understand what 'courage' means. The incompatibility here is not contingent.

So in qualitative reflection, where we deploy a language of evaluative distinctions, the rejected desire is not so rejected because of some mere contingent or circumstantial conflict with another goal. Being cowardly doesn't compete with other goods by taking up the time and energy I need to pursue them, and it may not alter my circumstances in such a way as to prevent me pursuing them. The conflict is deeper; it is not contingent.

2. The utilitarian strand in our civilization would induce us to abandon the language of qualitative contrast, and this means, of course, abandon our strong evaluative languages, for their terms are only defined in contrast. And we can be tempted to redefine issues we are reflecting on in this non-qualitative fashion. For instance, let us say that I am addicted to over-eating. Now as I struggle with this addiction, in the reflection in which I

determine that moderation or controlling my irritation is better, I can be looking at the alternatives in a language of qualitative contrast. I yearn to be free of this addiction, to be the kind of person whose mere bodily appetites respond to his higher aspirations, and don't carry on remorselessly and irresistibly dragging me to incapacity and degradation.

But then I might be induced to see my problem in a quite different light. I might be induced to see it as a question of quantity of satisfaction. Eating too much cake increases the cholesterol in my blood, makes me fat, ruins my health, prevents me from enjoying all sorts of other desired consummations; so it isn't worth it. Here I have stepped away from the contrastive language of qualitative evaluation. Avoiding high cholesterol content, obesity, ill-health, or being able to climb stairs, and so on, can all be defined quite independently from my eating habits.

This is a conflict of self-interpretations. Which one we adopt will partly shape the meanings things have for us. But the question can arise which is more valid, more faithful to reality. To be in error here is thus not just to make a misdescription, as when I describe a motor vehicle as a car when it is really a truck. We think of misidentification here as in some sense distorting the reality concerned. For the man who is trying to talk me out of seeing my problem as one of dignity versus degradation, I have made a crucial misidentification. But it is not just that I have called a fear of too high cholesterol content by the name 'degradation'; it is rather that infantile fears of punishment or loss of parental love have been irrationally transferred on to obesity, or the pleasures of eating, or something of the sort (to follow a rather vulgar Freudian line). My experience of obesity, eating, and so forth, is shaped by this. But if I can get over this 'hang-up' and see the real nature of the underlying anxiety, I will see that it is largely groundless, that is, I do not really incur the risk of punishment or loss of love; in fact there is a quite other list of things at stake here: ill health, inability to enjoy the outdoor life, early death by heart attack, and so on.

So might go a modern variant of the utilitarian thrust, trying to reduce our qualitative contrasts to some homogeneous medium. In this it would be much more plausible and sophisticated than earlier variants which talked as though it were just a matter of simple misidentification, that what people sought who pined after honour, dignity, integrity, and so on, were simply other pleasurable states to which they gave these high-sounding names.

There are of course ripostes to these attempts to reduce our evaluations to a non-qualitative form. We can entertain the counter-surmise that the rejection of qualitative distinctions is itself an illusion, powered perhaps by an inability to look at one's life in the light of some of these distinctions, a failure of moral nerve, as it were; or else by the draw of a certain objectifying stance towards the world. We might hold that the most hard-bitten utilitarians are themselves moved by qualitative distinctions which remain unadmitted, that they admire the mode of life in which one calculates consciously and clairvoyantly as something higher than the life of self-indulgent illusion, and do not simply elect it as more satisfying.

We can't resolve this issue here. The point of introducing this distinction between qualitative and non-qualitative reflection is to contrast the different kinds of self that each involves. In examining this it will, I think, become overwhelmingly plausible that we are not beings whose only authentic evaluations are non-qualitative as the utilitarian tradition suggests; that if evaluation of desires is essential to our notion of the self, it is strong and not just weak evaluation which is in question.

3. Someone who evaluates non-qualitatively, that is, makes decisions like that of eating now or later, taking a holiday in the north or in the south, might be called a simple weigher of alternatives. And the other, who deploys a language of evaluative contrasts ranging over desires we might call a strong evaluator.

Now we have seen that a simple weigher is already reflective in a minimal sense, that he evaluates courses of action, and sometimes is capable of acting out of that evaluation as against under the impress of immediate desire. And this is a necessary feature of what we call a self or a person. He has reflection, evaluation and will. But in contrast to the strong evaluator he lacks something else which we often speak of with the metaphor of 'depth'.

The strong evaluator envisages his alternatives through a richer language. The desirable is not only defined for him by what he desires, or what he desires plus a calculation of consequences; it is also defined by a qualitative characterization of desires as higher and lower, noble and base, and so on. Where it is not a calculation of consequences, reflection is not just a matter of registering the conclusion that alternative A is more attractive to me, or draws me more than B. Rather the higher desirability of A over B is something I can articulate if I am reflecting a strong evaluator. I have a vocabulary of worth.

Faced with incommensurables, which is our usual predicament, the simple weigher's experiences of the superiority of A over B are inarticulable. The role of reflection is not to make these articulate, but rather to step back from the immediate situation, to calculate consequences, to compensate for the immediate force of one desire which might not be the most advantageous to follow (as when I put off lunch to swim-with-lunch later), to get over hesitation by concentrating on the inarticulate 'feel' of the alternatives.

But the strong evaluator is not similarly inarticulate. There is the beginning of a language in which to express the superiority of one alternative, the language of higher and lower, noble and base, courageous and cowardly, integrated and fragmented, and so on. The strong evaluator can articulate superiority just because he has a language of contrastive characterization. So within an experience of reflective choice between incommensurables, strong evaluation is a condition of articulacy, and to acquire a strongly evaluative language is to become (more) articulate about one's preferences.

The simple weigher's reflection is structured by a number of *de facto* desires, whereas the strong evaluator ascribes a value to those desires. He characterizes his motivation at greater depth. To characterize one desire or inclination as worthier, or nobler, or more integrated, and so forth, than others is to speak of it in terms of the kind of quality of life which it expresses and sustains. I eschew the cowardly act above because I want to be a courageous and honourable human being. Whereas for the simple weigher what is at stake is the desirability of different consummations, those defined by his *de facto* desires, for the strong evaluator reflection also examines the different possible modes of life or modes of being of the agent. Motivations or desires don't only count in virtue of the attraction of the consummations but also in virtue of the kind of life and kind of subject that these desires properly belong to.

This is what lies behind our ordinary use of the metaphor of depth applied to people. Someone is shallow in our view when we feel that he is insensitive, unaware, or unconcerned about issues touching the quality of his life which seem to us basic or important. He lives on the surface because he seeks to fulfil desires without being touched by the 'deeper' issues, what these desires express and sustain in the way of modes of life; or his concern with such issues seems to us to touch on trivial or unimportant questions, for example, he is concerned about the glamour of his life, or how it will appear, rather than the (to us) real issues of the quality of life. The complete utilitarian would be an impossibly shallow character, and we can gauge how much self-declared utilitarians really live their ideology by what importance they attribute to depth.

II

We saw that the strong evaluator reflects in another, deeper sense than the simple weigher, and this because he evaluates in a different way. And after this discussion we can perhaps see why we are tempted to make evaluation, and indeed, strong evaluation, an essential characteristic of a person. For any being who was incapable of evaluating desires (as my dog, e.g. is incapable), or who could only evaluate as a simple weigher, would lack the depth to be a potential interlocutor, a potential partner of human communion, be it as friend, lover, confidant, or whatever. And we cannot see one who could not enter into any of these relations as a normal human subject.

I would like now to turn to examine the notion of responsibility for oneself which goes along with this notion of the agent as a strong evaluator. Naturally we think of the agent as responsible, in part, for what he does; and since he is an evaluator, we think of him as responsible in part for the degree to which he acts in line with his evaluations. But we are also inclined to think of him as responsible in some sense for these evaluations themselves.

This more radical responsibility is even suggested by the word 'evaluation', which belongs to the modern, one might almost say post-Nietzschean, vocabulary of moral life. For it relates to the verb 'evaluate', and the very term here implies that this is something we do, that our evaluations emerge from our activity of evaluation, and in this sense are our responsibility. This active sense is conveyed in Frankfurt's formulation where he speaks of persons as exhibiting 'reflective self-evaluation that is manifested in the formation of second-order desires'. And when we turn to the quote from Heidegger at the beginning of this paper, the notion of responsibility is strikingly put in the idea that *Dasein's* being is in question in his being, that the kind of being we are to realize is constantly in question.

How are we to understand this responsibility? An influential strand of thought in the modern world has wanted to understand it in terms of choice. The Nietzschean term 'value', suggested by our 'evaluation', carries this idea that our 'values' are our creations, that they ultimately repose on our espousing them. But to say that they ultimately repose on our espousing them is to say that they issue ultimately from a radical choice, that is, a choice which is not grounded in any reasons. For to the extent that a choice is grounded in reasons, these are simply taken as valid and are not themselves chosen. If our 'values' are to be thought of as chosen, then they must respose finally on a radical choice in the above sense.

This is, of course, the line taken by Sarte in *L'Être et le Néant*, in which he translates verbatim the quote above from Heidegger and gives it this sense that the fundamental project which defines us reposes on a radical choice. The choice, Sartre puts it with his characteristic flair for striking formulae, is 'absurde, en ce sens qu'il est ce par quoi toutes les raisons viennent à l'être.'[2] This idea of radical choice is also defined by an influential Anglo-Saxon school of moral philosophers.

[2] *L'Être et le Néant* (Paris, 1943), 559.

But in fact we cannot understand our responsibility for our evaluations through the notion of radical choice. Not if we are to go on seeing ourselves as strong evaluators, as agents with depth. For a radical choice *between* strong evaluations is quite conceivable, but not a radical choice *of* such evaluations. To see this we might examine a famous Sartrian example, which turns out, I believe, to illustrate the exact opposite of Sartre's thesis, the example in *L'Existentialisme est un Humanisme* of the young man who is torn between remaining with his ailing mother and going off to join the Resistance. Sartre's point is that there is no way of adjudicating between these two strong claims on his moral allegiance through reason or the reliance on some kind of considerations. He has to settle the question, whichever way he goes, by radical choice.

Sartre's portrayal of the dilemma is very powerful here. But what makes it plausible is precisely what undermines his position. We see a grievous moral dilemma because the young man is faced here with two powerful moral *claims*. On one hand his ailing mother who may well die if he leaves her, and die in the most terrible sorrow, not even sure that her son still lives; on the other side the call of his country, conquered and laid waste by the enemy, and not only his country, for his enemy is destroying the very foundation of civilized and ethical relations between men. A cruel dilemma, indeed. But it is a dilemma only because the claims themselves are not created by radical choice. If they were, the grievous nature of the predicament would dissolve, for that would mean that the young man could do away with the dilemma at any moment by simply declaring one of the rival claims as dead and inoperative. Indeed, if serious claims were created by radical choice, the young man could have a grievous dilemma about whether to go and get an ice cream cone, and then again he could decide not to.

It is no argument against the view that evaluations do not repose on radical choice that there are moral dilemmas. Why should it even be surprising that the evaluations we feel called upon to assent to may conflict, even grievously, in some situations? I would argue that the reverse is the case, that moral dilemmas become inconceivable on the theory of radical choice. Now in this hypothetical case the young man has to resolve the matter by radical choice. He just has to plump for the Resistance, or for staying at home with his mother. He has no language in which the superiority of one alternative over the other can be articulated; indeed, he has not even an inchoate sense of the superiority of one over the other, they seem quite incommensurable to him. He just throws himself one way.

This is a perfectly understandable sense of radical choice. But then imagine extending this to all cases of moral action. Let us apply it to the case that I have an ailing mother and no rival obligation, as to the Resistance. Do I stay, or do I go for a holiday on the Riviera? There is no question, I should stay. Of course, I may not stay. In this sense, there is always a 'radical choice' open: whether to do what we ought or not. But the question is whether we can construe the determination of what we ought to do here as issuing from a radical choice. What would this look like? Presumably, we would be faced with the two choices, to stay with my mother or to go south. On the level of radical choice these alternatives have as yet no contrastive characterization, that is, one is not the path of duty, while the other is that of selfish indulgence, or whatever.

This contrastive description will be created by radical choice. So what does this choice consist in? Well, I might ponder the two possibilities, and then I might just find myself doing one rather than another. But this brings us to the limit where choice fades into non-choice. Do I really choose if I just start doing one of the alternatives? And above all this kind of resolution has no place for the judgement 'I owe it to my mother to stay', which is supposed to issue from the choice. What is it to have this judgement issue from radical choice? Not that on pondering the alternatives, the sense grows more and more strongly that this judgement is *right*, for this would not be an account of radical choice, but rather of our coming to see that our obligation lay here. This account would present obligations as issuing not from radical choice but from some kind of vision of our moral predicament. This choice would be grounded. What is it then for radical choice to issue in this judgement? Is it just that I find myself assenting to the judgement, as above I found myself doing one of the two actions? But then what force has 'assenting to the judgement'? I can certainly just find myself saying 'I owe it to my mother', but this is surely not what it is to assent. I can, I suppose, find myself feeling suddenly, 'I owe this to my mother'; but then what grounds are there for thinking of this as a *choice*?

In order for us to speak of choice, we cannot just find ourselves in one of the alternatives. We have in some sense to experience the pull of each and give our assent to one. But what kind of pull do the alternatives have here? What draws me to the Côte d'Azure is perhaps unproblematic enough, but what draws me to stay with my mother cannot be the sense that I owe it to her, for that *ex hypothesi* has to issue from the choice.

The agent of radical choice has to choose, if he chooses at all, like a simple weigher. And this means that he cannot be properly speaking a strong evaluator. For all his putative strong evaluations issue from simple weighings. The application of a contrastive language which makes a preference articulate reposes on fiat, a choice made between incommensurables. But then the application of the contrastive language would be in an important sense bogus. For by hypothesis the experience on which this application reposed would be more properly characterized by a preference between incommensurables; the fundamental experience which was supposed to justify this language would in fact be that of the simple weigher, not of the strong evaluator. For again by hypothesis, what leads him to call one alternative higher or more worthy is not that in his experience it appears to be so, for then his evaluations would be judgements, not choices; but rather that he is led to plump for one rather than the other after considering the attractiveness of both alternatives.

The paradox of the theory of radical choice is that it seems to make the universal feature of moral experience what we identify as the failing of rationalization, dressing up as a moral choice what is really a *de facto* preference. In fact, however, proponents of the theory would vigorously contest what I have just said; for they see the ideal agent not as a rationalizer, but as one who is aware of his choices.

Perhaps then it is that in radical choice I don't consult preferences at all. It is not that I try to see which I prefer, and then failing to get a result, I throw myself one way or the other; but rather, this kind of choice is made quite without regard to preferences. But then with regard to what is it made? Here we border on incoherence. A choice made without regard to anything, without the agent feeling any solicitation to one alternative or the other, or in complete disregard of such solicitation, is this still choice? But if this is a choice and not just an inexplicable movement, it must have been accompanied by something like: 'damn it, why should I always choose by the book? I'll take B'; or maybe he just suddenly felt that he really wanted B. In either case his choice clearly relates to his preference, however suddenly arising and from whatever reversal of criteria. But a choice utterly unrelated to the desirability of the alternatives would not be intelligible as a choice.

The theory of radical choice in fact is deeply incoherent, for it wants to maintain both strong evaluation and radical choice. It wants to have strong evaluations and yet deny their status as judgements. In fact it maintains a semblance of plausibility by surreptitiously assuming strong evaluation beyond the reach of radical choice, and that in two ways. First, the real answer to our attempted assimilation of radical moral choice to the mere preference of a simple weigher is that the choices talked about in the theory are about basic and fundamental issues, like the choice of our young man above between his mother and the Resistance. But these issues are basic and fundamental not in virtue of radical choice; their importance is given, or revealed, in an evaluation which is constated not chosen. The real force of the theory of radical choice comes from the sense that there are different moral perspectives, that there is a plurality of moral visions, as we said in the previous section, between which it seems very hard to adjudicate. We can conclude that the only way of deciding between these is by the kind of radical choice that our young man had to take.

And this in turn leads to a second strong evaluation beyond the reach of choice. If this is the predicament of man, then it plainly is a more honest, more clairvoyant, less confused and self-deluding stance, to be aware of this and take the full responsibility for the radical choice. The stance of 'good faith' is higher, and this not in virtue of radical choice, but in virtue of our characterization of the human predicament in which radical choice has such an important place. Granted this is the moral predicament of man, it is more honest, courageous, self-clairvoyant, hence a higher mode of life, to choose in lucidity than it is to hide one's choices behind the supposed structure of things, to flee from one's responsibility at the expense of lying to oneself, of a deep self-duplicity.

When we see what makes the theory of radical choice plausible, we see how strong evaluation is something inescapable in our conception of the agent and his experience; and this because it is bound up with our notion of the self. So that it creeps back in even where it is supposed to have been excluded.

III

What then is the sense we can give to the responsibility of the agent, if we are not to understand it in terms of radical choice? There is in fact another sense in which we are radically responsible. Our evaluations are not chosen. On the contrary they are articulations of our sense of what is worthy, or higher, or more integrated, or more fulfilling, and so forth. But this sense can never be fully or satisfactorily articulated. And moreover it touches on matters where there is so much room for self-deception, for distortion, for blindness and insensitivity, that the question can always arise whether one is sure, and the injunction is always in place to look again.

We touch here on a crucial feature of our evaluations—one which has given some of its plausibility to the theory of radical choice. They are not simply descriptions, if we mean by this characterizations of a fully independent object, that is, an object which is neither altered in what it is, nor in the degree or manner of its evidence to us by the description. In this way my characterization of this table as brown, or this line of mountains as jagged, is a simple description.

Our strong evaluations may be called by contrast articulations, that is, they are attempts to formulate what is initially inchoate, or confused, or badly formulated. But this kind of formulation or reformulation doesn't leave its object unchanged. To give a certain articulation is to shape our sense of what we desire or what we hold important in a certain way.

Let us take the case above of the man who is fighting obesity and who is talked into seeing it as a merely quantitative question of more satisfaction, rather than as a matter of dignity and degradation. As a result of this change, his inner struggle itself becomes transformed, it is now quite a different experience. The opposed motivations—the craving for cream cake and his dissatisfaction with himself at such indulgence—which are the 'objects' undergoing redescription here, are not independent in the sense outlined above. When he comes to accept the new interpretation of his desire to control himself, this desire itself has altered. True, it may be said on one level to have the same goal, that he stop eating cream cake, but since it is no longer understood as a seeking for dignity and self-respect it has become quite a different kind of motivation.

Of course, even here we often try to preserve the identity of the objects undergoing redescription—so deeply rooted is the ordinary descriptive model. We might think of the change, say, in terms of some immature sense of shame and degradation being detached from our desire to resist over-indulgence, which has now simply the rational goal of increasing over-all satisfaction. In this way we might maintain the impression that the elements are just rearranged while remaining the same. But on a closer look we see that on this reading, too, the sense of shame doesn't remain self-identical through the change. It dissipates altogether, or becomes something quite different.

Thus our descriptions of our motivations, and our attempts to formulate what we hold important, are not simple descriptions, in that their objects are not fully independent. And yet they are not simply arbitrary either, such that anything goes. There are more or less adequate, more or less truthful, more self-clairvoyant or self-deluding interpretations. Because of this double fact, because an articulation can be *wrong*, and yet it shapes what it is wrong about, we sometimes see erroneous articulations as involving a distortion of the reality concerned. We don't just speak of error but frequently also of illusion or delusion.

We could put the point this way. Our attempts to formulate what we hold important must, like descriptions, strive to be faithful to something. But what they strive to be faithful to is not an independent object with a fixed degree and manner of evidence, but rather a largely inarticulated sense of what is of decisive importance. An articulation of this 'object' tends to make it something different from what it was before. And by the same token a new articulation doesn't leave its 'object' evident or obscure to us in the same manner or degree as before. In the act of shaping it, it makes it accessible and/or inaccessible in new ways. Because articulations partly shape their objects in these two ways, they are intrinsically open to challenge in a way that simple descriptions are not. Evaluation is such that there is always room for re-evaluation. But our evaluations are the more open to challenge precisely in virtue of the very character of depth which we see in the self. For it is precisely the deepest evaluations which are least clear, least articulated, most easily subject to illusion and distortion. It is those which are closest to what I am as a subject, in the sense that shorn of them I would break down as a person, which are among the hardest for me to be clear about.

The question can always be posed: ought I to re-evaluate my most basic evaluations? Have I really understood what is essential to my identity? Have I truly determined what I sense to be the highest mode of life? This kind of re-evaluation will be radical, not in the sense of radical choice, however, that we choose without criteria, but rather in the sense that our looking again can be so undertaken that in principle no formulations are considered unrevisable.

What is of fundamental importance for us will already have an articulation, some notion of a certain mode of life as higher than others, or the belief that some cause is the worthiest that can be served; or the sense that belonging to this community is essential to my identity. A radical re-evaluation will call these formulations into question. But a re-evaluation of this kind, once embarked on, is of a peculiar sort. It is unlike a less than radical evaluation which is carried on within the terms of some fundamental evaluation, when I ask myself whether it would be honest to take advantage of this income-tax loophole, or smuggle something through customs. These latter can be carried on in a language which is out of dispute. In answering the questions just mentioned the term 'honest' is taken as beyond challenge. But in radical re-evaluations the most basic terms, those in which other evaluations are carried on, are precisely what is in question. It is just because all formulations are potentially under suspicion of distorting their objects that we have to see them all as revisable, that we are forced back, as it were, to the inarticulate limit from which they originate.

How then can such re-evaluations be carried on? There is certainly no metalanguage available in which I can assess rival self-interpretations. If there were, this would not be a radical re-evaluation. On the contrary the re-evaluation is carried on in the formulae available, but with a stance of attention, as it were, to what these formulae are meant to articulate and with a readiness to receive any *Gestalt* shift in our view of the situation, any quite innovative set of categories in which to see our predicament, that might come our way in inspiration.

Anyone who has struggled with a philosophical problem knows what this kind of enquiry is like. In philosophy typically we start off with a question, which we know to be badly formed at the outset. We hope that in struggling with it, we shall find that its terms are transformed, so that in the end we will answer a question which we couldn't properly conceive at the beginning. We are striving for conceptual innovation which will allow us to illuminate some matter, say an area of human experience, which would otherwise remain dark and confused. The alternative is to stick to certain fixed terms (are these propositions synthetic or analytic, is this a psychological question or a philosophical question, is this view monist or dualist?).

The same contrast can exist in our evaluations. We can attempt a radical re-evaluation, in which case we may hope that our terms will be transformed in the course of it; or we may stick to certain favoured terms, insist that all evaluations can be made in their ambit, and refuse any radical questioning. To take an extreme case, someone can adopt the utilitarian criterion and then claim to settle all further issues about action by some calculation.

The point has been made again and again by non-naturalists, existentialists and others that those who take this kind of line are ducking a major question, should I really decide on the utilitarian principle? But this doesn't mean that the alternative to this stance is a radical choice. Rather it is to look again at our most fundamental formulations, and at what they were meant to articulate, in a stance of openness, where we are ready to accept any categorical change, however radical, which might emerge. Of course we will actually start thinking of particular cases, e.g. where our present evaluations recommend things which worry us, and try to puzzle further. In doing this we will be like the philosopher with his initially ill-formed question. But we may get through to something deeper.

In fact this stance of openness is very difficult. It may take discipline and time. It is difficult because this form of evaluation is deep in a sense, and total in a sense that the other less than radical ones are not. If I am questioning whether smuggling a radio into the country is honest, or I am judging everything by the utilitarian criterion, then I have a yardstick, a definite yardstick. But if I go to the radical questioning, then it is not exactly that I have no yardstick, in the sense that anything goes, but rather that what takes the place of the yardstick is my deepest unstructured sense of what is important, which is as yet inchoate and which I am trying to bring to definition. I am trying to see reality afresh and form more adequate categories to describe it. To do this I am trying to open myself, use all of my deepest, unstructured sense of things in order to come to a new clarity.

Now this engages me at a depth that using a fixed yardstick does not. I am in a sense questioning the inchoate sense that led me to use the yardstick. And at the same time it engages my whole self in a way that judging by a yardstick does not. This is what makes it uncommonly difficult to reflect on our fundamental evaluations. It is much easier to take up the formulations that come most readily to hand, generally those which are going the rounds of our milieu or society, and live within them without too much probing. The obstacles in the way of going deeper are legion. There is not only the difficulty of such concentration, and the pain of uncertainty, but also all the distortions and repressions which make us want to turn away from this examination; and which make us resist change even when we do re-examine ourselves. Some of our evaluations may in fact become fixed and compulsive, so that we cannot help feeling guilty about X, or despising people like Y, even though we judge with the greatest degree of openness and depth at our command that X is perfectly all right, and that Y is a very admirable person. This casts light on another aspect of the term 'deep', as applied to people. We consider people deep to the extent, *inter alia*, that they are capable of this kind of radical self-reflection.

This radical evaluation is a deep reflection, and a self-reflection in a special sense: it is a reflection about the self, its most fundamental issues, and a reflection which engages the self most wholly and deeply. Because it engages the whole self without a fixed yardstick it can be called a personal reflection (the parallel to Polanyi's notion of personal knowledge is intended here); and what emerges from it is a self-resolution in a strong sense, for in this reflection the self is in question; what is at stake is the definition of those inchoate evaluations which are sensed to be essential to our identity.

Because this self-resolution is something we do, when we do it, we can be called responsible for ourselves; and because it is within limits always up to us to do it, even when we don't—indeed, the nature of our deepest evaluations constantly raises the question whether we have them right—we can be called responsible in another sense for ourselves whether we undertake this radical evaluation or not. This is perhaps Heidegger's notion in *Sein und Zeit*, quoted above, that human beings are such that their being is in question in their being, that is, their fundamental evaluations are by the very nature of this kind of subject always in question.

And it is this kind of responsibility for oneself, I would maintain, not that of radical choice, but the responsibility for radical evaluation implicit in the nature of a strong evaluator, which is essential to our notion of a person.

IX

THE CONCEIVABILITY OF MECHANISM

NORMAN MALCOLM

1. BY 'mechanism' I am going to understand a special application of physical determinism—namely, to all organisms with neurological systems, including human beings. The version of mechanism I wish to study assumes a neurophysiological theory which is adequate to explain and predict all movements of human bodies except those caused by outside forces. The human body is assumed to be as complete a causal system as is a gasoline engine. Neurological states and processes are conceived to be correlated by general laws with the mechanisms that produce movements. Chemical and electrical changes in the nervous tissue of the body are assumed to cause muscle contractions, which in turn cause movements such as blinking, breathing, and puckering of the lips, as well as movements of fingers, limbs, and head. Such movements are sometimes produced by forces (pushes and pulls) applied externally to the body. If someone forced my arm up over my head, the theory could not explain that movement of my arm. But it could explain any movement not due to an external push or pull. It could explain, and predict, the movements that occur when a person signals a taxi, plays chess, writes an essay, or walks to the store.[1]

It is assumed that the neurophysiological system of the human body is subject to various kinds of stimulation. Changes of temperature or pressure in the environment; sounds, odours; the ingestion of foods and liquids: all these will have an effect on the nerve pulses that turn on the movement-producing mechanisms of the body.

2. The neurophysiological theory we are envisaging would, as said, be rich

From *The Philosophical review*, vol. lxxvii, No. 1 (Jan. 1968), pp. 45–72. Reprinted by permission of the author and *The Philosophical Review*.

[1] If you said 'Get up!' and I got up, the theory would explain my movements in terms of neurophysiological events produced by the impact of sound waves on my auditory organs.

enough to provide systematic causal explanations of all bodily movements not due to external physical causes. These explanations should be understood as stating *sufficient* conditions of movement and not merely necessary conditions. They would employ laws that connect neurophysiological states or processes with movements. The laws would be universal propositions of the following form: whenever an organism of structure *S* is in state *q* it will emit movement *m*. Having ascertained that a given organism is of structure *S* and is in state *q*, one could deduce the occurrence of movement *m*.

It should be emphasized that this theory makes no provision for desires, aims, goals, purposes, motives, or intentions. In explaining such an occurrence as a man's walking across a room, it will be a matter of indifference to the theory whether the man's purpose, intention, or desire was to open a window, or even whether his walking across the room was intentional. This aspect of the theory can be indicated by saying that it is a 'non-purposive' system of explanation.

The viewpoint of mechanism thus assumes a theory that would provide systematic, complete, non-purposive, causal explanations of all human movements not produced by external forces. Such a theory does not at present exist. But nowadays it is ever more widely held that in the not far distant future there will be such a theory—and that it will be true. I will raise the question of whether this is conceivable. The subject belongs to an age-old controversy. It would be unrealistic for me to hope to make any noteworthy contribution to its solution. But the problem itself is one of great human interest and worthy of repeated study.

3. To appreciate the significance of mechanism, one must be aware of the extent to which a comprehensive neurophysiological theory of human behaviour would diverge from those everyday explanations of behaviour with which all of us are familiar. These explanations refer to purposes, desires, goals, intentions. 'He is running to catch the bus'. 'He is climbing the ladder in order to inspect the roof'. 'He is stopping at this store because he wants some cigars'. Our daily discourse is filled with explanations of behaviour in terms of the agent's purposes or intentions. The behaviour is claimed to occur in order that some state of affairs should be brought about or avoided—that the bus should be caught, the roof inspected, cigars purchased. Let us say that these are 'purposive' explanations.

We can note several differences between these common purposive explanations and the imagined neurophysiological explanations. First, the latter were conceived by us to be systematic—that is, to belong to a comprehensive theory—whereas the familiar purposive explanations are not organized into a theory. Second, the neurophysiological explanations do not employ the concept of purpose or intention. Third, the neurophysiological explanations embody contingent laws, but purposive explanations do not.

Let us dwell on this third point. A neurophysiological explanation of some behaviour that has occurred is assumed to have the following form:

> Whenever an organism of structure *S* is in neurophysiological state *q* it will emit movement *m*.
> Organism *O* of structure *S* was in neurophysiological state *q*.
> Therefore, *O* emitted *m*.[2]

The general form of purposive explanation is the following:

> Whenever an organism *O* has goal *G* and believes that behaviour *B* is required to bring about *G*, *O* will emit *B*.
> *O* had *G* and believed *B* was required of *G*.
> Therefore, *O* emitted *B*.

Let us compare the first premiss of a neurophysiological explanation with the first premiss of a purposive explanation. The first premiss of a neurophysiological explanation is a contingent proposition, but the first premiss of a purposive explanation is not a contingent proposition. This difference will appear more clearly if we consider how, in both cases, the first premiss would have to be qualified in order to be actually true. In both cases a *ceteris paribus* clause must be added to the first premiss, or at least be implicitly understood. (It will be more perspicuous to translate '*ceteris paribus*' as 'provided there are no countervailing factors' rather than as 'other things being equal'.)

Let us consider what '*ceteris paribus*' will mean in concrete terms. Suppose a man climbed a ladder leading to a roof. An explanation is desired. The fact is that the wind blew his hat on to the roof and he wants it back. The explanation would be spelled out in detail as follows:

> If a man wants to retrieve his hat and believes this requires him to climb a ladder, he will do so provided there are no countervailing factors.
> This man wanted to retrieve his hat and believed that this required him to climb a ladder, and there were no countervailing factors.
> Therefore, he climbed a ladder.

What sorts of things might be included under 'countervailing factors' in such a case? The unavailability of a ladder, the fear of climbing one, the belief that someone would remove the ladder while he was on the roof, and

[2] A neurophysiological *prediction* would be of the same form, with these differences: the second premiss would say that *O* is or will be in state *q* (instead of *was*), and the conclusion would say that *O will* emit *m* (instead of *emitted*).

so on. (The man's failure to climb a ladder would *not* be a countervailing factor.)

An important point emerging here is that the addition of the *ceteris paribus* clause to the first premiss turns this premiss into an a priori proposition. If there were no countervailing factors whatever (if the man knew a ladder was available, had no fear of ladders or high places, no belief that he might be marooned on the roof, and so on); if there were no hindrances or hazards, real or imagined, physical or psychological; then if the man did not climb a ladder it would not be true that he *wanted* his hat back, or *intended* to get it back.[3]

In this important recent book, *The Explanation of Behaviour*, Charles Taylor puts the point as follows:

> This is part of what we mean by 'intending *X*', that, in the absence of interfering factors, it is followed by doing *X*. I could not be said to intend *X* if, even with no obstacles or other countervailing factors, I still didn't do it.[4]

This feature of the meaning of 'intend' also holds true of 'want', 'purpose', and 'goal'.

Thus the universal premiss of a purposive explanation is an a priori principle, not a contingent law. Some philosophers have made this a basis for saying that a purposive explanation is not a causal explanation.[5] But this is a stipulation (perhaps a useful one), rather than a description of how the word 'cause' is actually used in ordinary language.

Let us consider the effect of adding a *ceteris paribus* clause to the universal premiss of a neural explanation of behaviour. Would a premiss of this form be true a priori? Certainly not. Suppose it were believed that whenever a human being is in neural state *q* his right hand will move up above his head, provided there are no countervailing factors. What could be countervailing factors? That the subject's right arm is broken or that it is tied to his side, and so on. But the exclusion of such countervailing factors would have no tendency to make the premiss true a priori. There is no connection of meaning, explicit or implicit, between the description of any neural state

[3] The correct diagnosis of such a failure will not be evident in all cases. Suppose a youth wants to be a trapeze performer in a circus, and he believes this requires daily exercise on the parallel bars. But he is lazy and frequently fails to exercise. Doesn't he really have the goal he professes to have: is it just talk? Or doesn't he really believe in the necessity of the daily exercise? Or is it that he has the goal and the belief and his laziness is a genuine countervailing factor? One might have to know him very well in order to give the right answer. In some cases there might be no definite right answer.

[4] Charles Taylor, *The Explanation of Behaviour* (London: Routledge & Kegan Paul, 1964), 33.

[5] e.g. Taylor says that the agent's intention is not a 'causal antecedent' of his behaviour, for intention and behaviour 'are not contingently connected in the normal way' ibid.).

and the description of any movement of the hand. No matter how many countervailing factors are excluded, the proposition will not lose the character of a contingent law (unless, of course, we count the failure of the hand to move as itself a countervailing factor, in which case the premiss becomes a tautology).

4. Making explicit the *ceteris paribus* conditions points up the different logical natures of the universal premisses of the two kinds of explanation. Premisses of the one sort express contingent correlations between neurological processes and behaviour. Premisses of the other sort express a priori connections between intentions (purposes, desires, goals) and behaviour.

This difference is of the utmost importance. Some students of behaviour have believed that purposive explanations of behaviour will be found to be less basic than the explanations that will arise from a future neurophysiological theory. They think that the principles of purposive explanation will turn out to be dependent on the neurophysiological laws. On this view our ordinary explanations of behaviour will often be true: but the neural explanations will also be true—and they will be *more fundamental*. Thus we could, theoretically, *by-pass* explanations of behaviour in terms of purpose, and the day might come when they simply fall into disuse.

I wish to show that neurophysiological laws could not be more basic than purposive principles. I shall understand the statement that a law L_2 is 'more basic' than a law L_1 to mean that L_1 is dependent on L_2 but L_2 is not dependent on L_1. To give an example, let us suppose there is a uniform connection between food abstinence and hunger: that is, going without food for n hours always results in hunger. This is L_1. Another law L_2 is discovered—namely, a uniform connection between a certain chemical condition of body tissue (called 'cell-starvation') and hunger. Whenever cell-starvation occurs, hunger results. It is also discovered that L_2 is more basic than L_1. This would amount to the following fact: food abstinence for n hours will not result in hunger *unless* cell-starvation occurs; and if the latter occurs, hunger will result *regardless of whether* food abstinence occurs. Thus the L_1 regularity is contingently dependent on the L_2 regularity, and the converse is not true. Our knowledge of this dependency would reveal to us the conditions under which the L_1 regularity would no longer hold.

Our comparison of the differing logical natures of purposive principles and neurophysiological laws enables us to see that the former cannot be dependent on the latter. The a priori connection between intention or purpose and behaviour cannot fail to hold. It cannot be contingently dependent on any contingent regularity. The neurophysiological explanations of behaviour could not, in the sense explained, turn out to be more basic than our everyday purposive explanations.[6]

5. There is a second important consequence of the logical difference between neurophysiological laws and purposive principles. Someone might suppose that although purposive explanations cannot be dependent on non-purposive explanations, they would be refuted by the verification of a comprehensive neurophysiological theory of behaviour. I think this view is correct: but it is necessary to understand what it *cannot* mean. It cannot mean that the principles (the universal premisses) of purposive explanations would be proved false. They cannot be proved false. It could not fail to be true that if a person wanted *X* and believed *Y* was necessary for *X*, and there were absolutely no countervailing factors, he would do *Y*.[7] This purposive principle is true a priori, not because of its form but because of its meaning—that is, because of the connection of meaning between the words. 'He wanted *X* and he realized that *Y* was necessary for *X*' and the words 'He did *Y*'. The purposive principle is not a law of nature but a conceptual truth. It cannot be confirmed or refuted by experience. Since the verification of a neurophysiological theory could never *disprove* any purposive principles, the only possible outcome of such verification, logically speaking, would be to prove that the purposive principles have no application to the world. I shall return to this point later.

6. We must come to closer grips with the exact logical relationship between neural and purposive explanations of behaviour. Can explanations of both types be true of the same bit of behaviour on one and the same occasion? Is there any rivalry between them? Some philosophers would say not. They would say that, for one thing, the two kinds of explanation explain different things. Purposive explanations explain actions. Neurophysiological explanations explain movements. Both explain behaviour: but we can say this only because we use the latter word ambiguously to cover both actions and movements. For a second point, it may be held that the two kinds of explanation belong to different 'bodies of discourse' or to different 'language games'. They employ different concepts and assumptions. One kind of explanation relates behaviour to causal laws and to concepts of biochemistry

[6] Taylor puts the point as follows:

Because explanation by intentions or purposes is like explanation by an 'antecedent' which is non-contingently linked with its consequent, i.e. because the fact that the behaviour follows from the intention other things being equal is not a contingent fact, we cannot account for this fact by more basic laws. For to explain a fact by more basic laws is to give the regularities on which this fact causally depends. But not being contingent, the dependence of behaviour on intention is not contingent on anything, and hence not on any such regularities [ibid., 44].

[7] This is true if we use 'wants *X*' to mean 'is aiming at *X*'. But sometimes we may mean no more than 'would like to have *X*', which may represent a mere wish.

and physiology, to nerve pulses and chemical reactions. The other kind of explanation relates behaviour to the desires, intentions, goals, and reasons of persons. The two forms of explanation can co-exist, because they are irrelevant to one another.[8]

It is true that the two kinds of explanation employ different concepts and, in a sense, explain different things: but are they really independent of one another? Take the example of the man climbing a ladder in order to retrieve his hat from the roof. This explanation relates his climbing to his intention. A neurophysiological explanation of his climbing would say nothing about his intention but would connect his movements on the ladder with chemical changes in body tissue or with the firing of neurons. Do the two accounts interfere with one another?

7. I believe there *would* be a collision between the two accounts if they were offered as explanations of one and the same occurrence of a man's climbing a ladder. We will recall that the envisaged neurophysiological theory was supposed to provide *sufficient* causal explanations of behaviour. Thus the movements of the man on the ladder would be *completely* accounted for in terms of electrical, chemical, and mechanical processes in his body. This would surely imply that his desire or intention to retrieve his hat had nothing to do with his movement up the ladder. It would imply that on this same occasion he would have moved up the ladder in exactly this way even if he had had no intention to retrieve his hat, or even no intention to climb the ladder. To mention his intention or purpose would be no explanation, nor even part of an explanation, of his movements on the ladder. Given the antecedent neurological states of his bodily system together with general laws correlating those states with the contractions of muscles and movements of limbs, he would have moved as he did regardless of his desire or intention. If every movement of his was completely accounted for by his antecedent neurophysiological states (his 'programming'), then it was not true that those movements occurred *because* he wanted or intended to get his hat.

8. I will briefly consider three possible objections to my claim that if mechanism were true the man would have moved up the ladder as he did

[8] The following remarks by A. I. Melden present both of these points:

Where we are concerned with causal explanations, with events of which the happenings in question are effects in accordance with some law of causality, to that extent we are not concerned with human actions at all but, at best, with bodily movements or happenings; and where we are concerned with explanations of human action, there causal factors and causal laws in the sense in which, for example, these terms are employed in the biological sciences are wholly irrelevant to the understanding we seek. The reason is simple, namely, the radically different logical characteristics of the two bodies of discourse we employ in these distinct cases—the different concepts which are applicable to these different orders of inquiry (A. I. Melden, *Free Action* (New York, 1961), 184).

even if he had not had any intention to climb the ladder. The first objection comes from a philosopher who espouses the currently popular psychophysical identity thesis. He holds that there is a neural condition that causes the man's movements up the ladder, and he further holds that the man's intention to climb the ladder (or, possibly, his having the intention) is contingently identical with the neural condition that causes the movements. Thus, if the man had not intended to climb the ladder, the cause of his movements would not have existed, and so those movements would not have occurred. My reply would be that the view that there may be a contingent identity (and not merely an extensional equivalence) between an intention (or the having of the intention) and a neural condition is not a meaningful hypothesis. One version of the identity thesis is that *A*'s intention to climb the ladder is contingently identical with some process in *A*'s brain. Verifying this identity would require the meaningless step of trying to discover whether *A*'s intention is located in his brain. One could give meaning to the notion of the location of *A*'s intention in his brain by stipulating that it has the same location as does the correlated neural process. But the identity that arose from this stipulation would not be contingent.[9] Another version of the identity thesis is that the event of Smith's having the intention *I* is identical with the event of Smith's being in neural condition *N*. This version avoids the above 'location problem': but it must take on the task (which seems hopeless) of explaining how the property 'having intention *I*' and the property 'being in neural condition *N*' could be contingently identical and not merely co-extensive.[10]

The second objection comes from an epiphenomenalist. He holds that the neurophysiological condition that contingently causes the behaviour on the ladder also contingently causes the intention to climb the ladder, but that the intention stands in no causal relation to the behaviour. If the intention had not existed, the cause of it and of the behaviour would not have existed, and so the behaviour would not have occurred. A decisive objection to epiphenomenalism is that, according to it, the relation between intention and behaviour would be purely contingent. It would be conceivable that the neurophysiological condition that always causes ladder-climbing movements should also always cause the intention to *not* climb up a ladder. Epiphenomenalism would permit it to be universally true that whenever any person intended to *not* do any action, he did it, and that whenever any

[9] This point is argued in my 'Scientific Materialism and The Identity Theory', *Dialogue*, 3 (1964); also in my forthcoming monograph, *Problems of Mind*, s. 18, to be published in the *Harper Guide to Philosophy*, ed. Arthur Danto.

[10] For an exposition of this problem see Jaegwon Kim's 'On the Psycho-Physical Identity Theory', *American Philosophical Quarterly*, 1966.

person intended to do any action, he did not do it. This is a conceptual absurdity.

The third objection springs from a philosopher who combines mechanism with logical behaviourism. He holds that some condition of the neurophysiological system causes the preparatory movements, gestures, and utterances that are expressions of the man's intention to climb the ladder; and it also causes his movements up the ladder. The component of logical behaviourism in his overall view is this: he holds that the man's having the intention to climb the ladder is simply a logical construction out of the occurrence of the expressions of intention and also the occurrence of the ladder-climbing movements. Having the intention is nothing other than the expressive behaviour plus the subsequent climbing behaviour. Having the intention is defined in terms of behaviour-events that are contingently caused by a neurophysiological condition. The supposition that the man did not have the intention to climb the ladder would be identical with the supposition that either the expressive behaviour or the climbing behaviour, or both, did not occur. If either one did not occur, then neither occurred, since by hypothesis both of them have the same cause. Thus it would be false that the man would have moved up the ladder as he did even if he had not had an intention to climb the ladder.

I think that this third position gives an unsatisfactory account of the nature of intention. Actually climbing the ladder is not a necessary condition *simpliciter* for the existence of the intention to climb the ladder. It is a necessary condition *provided* there are no countervailing factors. But there is no definite number of countervailing factors, and so they cannot be exhaustively enumerated. In addition, some of them will themselves involve the concepts of desire, belief, or purpose. For example: a man intends to climb the ladder, but also he does not want to look ridiculous; as he is just about to start climbing he is struck by the thought that he will look ridiculous; so he does not climb the ladder, although he had intended to. An adequate logical behaviourism would have to analyse away not only the initial reference to intention, but also the reference to desire, belief, purpose, and all other psychological concepts, that would occur in the listing of possible countervailing factors. There is no reason for thinking that such a programme of analysis could be carried out.

Thus a mechanist can hope to avoid the consequence that the man would have moved up the ladder as he did even if he had not had the intention of climbing the ladder, by combining his mechanist doctrine with the psychophysical identity thesis, or with epiphenomenalism, or with logical behaviourism. But these supplementary positions are so objectionable or implausible that the mechanist is not really saved from the above consequence.

9. Let us remember that the postulated neurophysiological theory is comprehensive. It is assumed to provide complete causal explanations for all bodily movements that are not produced by external physical forces. It is a closed system in the sense that it does not admit, as antecedent conditions, anything other than neurophysiological states and processes. Desires and intentions have no place in it.

If the neurophysiological theory were true, then in no cases would desires, intentions, purposes be necessary conditions of any human movements. It would never be true that a man would *not* have moved as he did if he had *not* had such and such an intention. Nor would it ever be true that a certain movement of his was due to, or brought about by, or caused by his having a certain intention or purpose. Purposive explanations of human bodily movements would *never* be true. Desires and intentions would not be even potential causes of human movements in the actual world (as contrasted with some possible world in which the neurophysiological theory did not hold true).

It might be thought that there could be two different systems of causal explanations of human movements, a purposive system and a neurophysiological system. The antecedent conditions in the one system would be the desires and intentions of human beings; in the other they would be the neurophysiological states and processes of those same human beings. Each system would provide adequate causal explanations of the same movements.

Generally speaking, it is possible for there to be a plurality of simultaneous sufficient causal conditions of an event. But if we bear in mind the comprehensive aspects of the neurophysiological theory—that is, the fact that it provides sufficient causal conditions for all movements—we shall see that desires and intentions could not be causes of movements. It has often been noted that to say *B causes C* does not mean merely that whenever *B* occurs, *C* occurs. Causation also has subjunctive and counter-factual implications: if *B were to* occur, *C would* occur; and if *B* had *not* occurred, C would *not* have occurred. But the neurophysiological theory would provide sufficient causal conditions for every human movement, and so there would be no cases at all in which a certain movement would not have occurred if the person had not had this desire or intention. Since the counter-factual would be false in all cases, desires and intentions would not be causes of human movements. They would not ever be sufficient causal conditions nor would they ever be necessary causal conditions.

10. Let us tackle this immensely important point from a different angle. Many descriptions of behaviour ascribe actions to persons: they say that someone *did* something—for example, 'He signed the cheque', 'You lifted the table', 'She broke the vase'. Two things are implied by an ascription of an 'action' to a person[11]: first, that a certain state of affairs came into existence (his signature's being present on the cheque, the table's being lifted, the vase's being broken); second, that the person intended that this state of affairs should occur. If subsequently we learn that not both conditions were satisfied, either we qualify the ascription of action or reject it entirely. If the mentioned state of affairs did not come into existence (for example, the vase was not broken), then the ascription of action ('She broke the vase') must be withdrawn. If it did come into existence but without the person's intention, then the ascription of action to the person must be diminished by some such qualification as 'unintentionally' or 'accidentally' or 'by mistake' or 'inadvertently', it being a matter of the circumstances which qualification is more appropriate. A qualified ascription of action still implies that the person played some part in bringing about the state of affairs—for example, her hand struck the vase. If she played no part at all, then it cannot rightly be said, even with qualification, that she broke the vase.

Suppose a man intends to open the door in front of him. He turns the knob and the door opens. Since turning the knob is what normally causes the door to open, we should think it right to say that *he* opened the door. Then we learn that there is an electric mechanism concealed in the door which caused the door to open at the moment he turned the knob, and furthermore that there is no causal connection between the turning of the knob and the operation of the mechanism. So his act of turning the knob had nothing to do with the opening of the door. We can no longer say that *he* opened the door: nothing he did had any causal influence on that result. We might put the matter in this way: because of the operation of the electric mechanism he had no opportunity to open the door.

The man of our example could say that at least he turned the knob. He would have to surrender this claim, however, if it came to light that still another electrical mechanism caused the knob to turn when it did, independently of the motion of his hand. The man could assert that, in any case, he moved his hand. But now the neurophysiological theory enters the scene, providing a complete causal explanation of the motion of his hand, without regard to his intention.

The problem of what to say becomes acute. Should we deny that he

[11] I am following Charles Taylor here: *The Explanation of Behaviour*, 27–32.

moved his hand? Should we admit that he moved his hand, but with some qualification? Or should we say, without qualification, that he moved his hand?

11. There is an important similarity between our three examples and an important difference. The similarity is that in all three cases a mechanism produced the intended states of affairs, and nothing the agent did had any influence on the operation of the mechanism. But there is a difference between the cases. In each of the first two, we can specify something the man did (an action) which would normally cause the intended result to occur, but which did not have that effect on this occasion. The action in the first case was turning the knob, and in the second it was gripping the knob and making a turning motion of the hand. In each of these cases there was an action, the causal efficacy of which was nullified by the operation of a mechanism. Consequently, we can rightly say that the man's action *failed* to make a contribution to the intended occurrence, and so we can deny that *he* opened the door or turned the knob.

In the third case is there something the man did which normally causes that movement of the hand? What was it? When I move my hand in the normal way is there something else *I do* that causes my hand to move? No. Various events take place in my body (for example, nerve pulses) but they cannot be said to be *actions* of mine. They are not things I do.

But in this third case the man *intended* to make a turning motion of his hand. Is this a basis for a similarity between the third case and the first two? Can we say that one's intention to move one's hand is normally a cause of the motion of one's hand, but that in our third case the causal efficacy of the intention was nullified by the operation of the neurophysiological mechanism?

On the question of whether intentions are causes of actions, Taylor says something that is both interesting and puzzling. He declares that to call something an action, in an unqualified sense 'means not just that the man who displayed this behaviour had framed the relevant intention or had this purpose, but also that *his intending it brought it about*'.[12] Now to say that *A* 'brings about' *B* is to use the language of causation. 'Brings about' is indeed a synonym for 'causes'.

12. Is there any sense at all in which a man's intention to do something can

[12] Ibid., 33 (my italics). Taylor says that an intention is *not* 'a causal antecedent' of the intended behaviour, for the reason that the intention and the behaviour are not *contingently connected*. I think he may be fairly represented as holding that an intention does *cause* the intended behaviour, although not in the sense of 'cause' in which cause and effect are contingently correlated.

be a cause of his doing it? In dealing with this point I shall use the word 'cause' in its widest sense, according to which anything that explains, or partly explains, the occurrence of some behaviour is the cause, or part of the cause, of the behaviour. To learn that a man intended to climb a ladder would not, in many cases, explain why he climbed it. It would not explain what he climbed it for, what his reason or purpose was in climbing it, whereas to say what his purpose was would, in our broad sense, give the cause or part of the cause of his climbing it.

In considering intention as a cause of behaviour *X*, it is important to distinguish between the intention to do *X* (let us call this *simple intention*) and in the intention to do something else *Y* in or by doing *X* (let us call this *further intention*). To say that a man intended to climb a ladder would not usually give a cause of his climbing it; but stating his purpose in climbing it would usually be giving the (or a) cause of the action. It is a natural use of language to ask, 'What caused you to climb the ladder?'; and it is an appropriate answer to say, 'I wanted to get my hat.' (*Question:* 'Good heavens, what caused you to vote a straight Republican ticket?' *Answer:* 'I wanted to restore the two-party system.') Our use of the language of causation is not restricted to the cases in which cause and effect are assumed to be contingently related.

13. Can the simple intention to do *X* ever be a cause of the doing of *X*? Can it ever be said that a person's intention to climb a ladder caused him to climb it, or brought about his action of climbing it? It is certainly true that whether a man does or does not intend to do *X* will make a difference in whether he will do *X*. This fact comes out strongly if we are concerned to predict whether he will do *X*; obviously, it would be important to find out whether he intends to do it. Does not this imply that his intention has 'an effect on his behaviour'?[13]

Commonly, we think of dispositions as causes of behaviour. If with the same provocation one man loses his temper and another does not, this difference in their reactions might be explained by the fact that the one man, but not the other, is of an irritable disposition. If dispositions are causes, we can hardly deny the same role to intentions. Both are useful in predicting behaviour. If I am trying to estimate the likelihood that this man is going to do so-and-so, the information that he has a disposition to do it in circumstances like these will be an affirmative consideration. I am entitled

[13] Taylor's phrase, p. 34. In my review of Taylor's book ('Explaining Behaviour', *Philosophical Review*, 1967, 97–104), I say that Taylor is wrong in holding that a simple intention *brings about* the corresponding behaviour. But now I am holding that he is partly right and partly wrong: right about previously formed simple intentions, wrong about merely concurrent simple intentions.

to give equal or possibly greater weight to the information that he intends to do it.

Not only do simple intentions have weight in predicting actions, but also they figure in the explanation of actions that have already occurred. If a man who has just been released from prison promptly climbs a flagpole, I may want an explanation of that occurrence. If I learn that he had previously made up his mind to do it, but had been prevented by his imprisonment, I have received a partial explanation of why he is climbing the flagpole, even if I do not yet know his further intention, if any, in climbing it. In general, if I am surprised at an action, it will help me to understand its occurrence if I find out that the agent had previously decided to do it but was prevented by an obstacle which has just been removed.

14. The simple intentions so far considered were formed in advance of the corresponding action. But many simple intentions are not formed in advance of the corresponding action. Driving a car, one suddenly (and intentionally) presses the brake pedal: but there was no time before this action occurred when one intended to do it. The intention existed only at the time of the action. or only *in* the action. Let us call this a merely concurrent simple intention. Can an intention of this kind be a causal factor in the corresponding action?

Here we have to remember that if the driver did not press the brake intentionally, his pressing of the brake was not unqualified action. The presence of simple intention in the action (that is, its being intentional) is an analytically necessary condition for its being unqualified action. This condition is not a cause but a defining condition of unqualified action. If this condition were not fulfilled, one would have to use some mitigating phrase—for example, that the driver pressed the brake by mistake. Thus, a simple intention that is merely concurrent cannot be a cause of the corresponding action.

15. Can we not avoid committing ourselves to the assumption that the pressing of the driver's foot on the brake was either intentional or not intentional? Can we not think of it, in a neutral way, as merely behaviour? Yes, we can. But it *was* either intentional or not intentional. If the latter, then there was no simple intention to figure as a cause of the behaviour. If the former, then the behaviour was action, and the driver's merely concurrent simple intention was a defining condition and not a cause of the behaviour. The 'neutral way' of thinking about the behaviour would be merely incomplete. It would be owing to ignorance and not to the existence of a third alternative. It is impossible, by the definition of 'action', that the

behaviour of pressing the brake should be an action and yet not be intentional. Thus it is impossible that a merely concurrent simple intention should have caused the behaviour of pressing the brake, whether the behaviour was or was not action.

To summarize this discussion of intentions as causes: we need to distinguish between simple intentions and further intentions. If an agent does *X* with the further intention *Y*, then it is proper to speak of this further intention as the (or a) cause of the doing of *X*. Simple intentions may be divided into those that are formed prior to the corresponding actions, and those that are merely concurrent with the actions. By virtue of being previously formed, a simple intention can be a cause of action. But in so far as it is merely concurrent, a simple intention cannot be a cause of the corresponding action.

16. Let us try now to appraise Taylor's view as to the causal role of intention in behaviour. He holds that it would not be true, without qualification, that one person stabbed another unless his intention to stab him 'brought about' the stabbing (ibid., 33). The example was meant to be a previously formed intention—for Taylor speaks of the agent's *deciding* to stab someone. But a majority of actions do not embody intentions formed in advance. They embody merely concurrent intentions. The latter cannot be said to cause (bring about) the corresponding actions. Possibly because he has fixed his attention too narrowly on cases of decision, Taylor errs in holding that, in general, the concept of action requires that the agent's intention should have brought about the behaviour. When the action is merely intentional (without previous intention) the agent's intention cannot be said to bring about his behaviour. In such cases his intention gives his behaviour the character of *action*, but it does this by virtue of being a defining condition of action, not by virtue of being a cause of either behaviour or action.

17. Our reflections on the relationship of intention to behaviour arose from a consideration of three examples of supposed action—opening a door, turning a knob, making a turning motion of the hand. In the first two cases we imagined mechanisms that produced the intended results independently of the agent's intervention. Consequently, we had to deny that *he* opened the door or turned the knob. Then we imagined a neurophysiological cause of the motion of his hand, and we asked whether this would imply, in turn, that *he* did not move his hand.

Is the movement of his hand independent of his 'intervention' by virtue of being independent of his intention? We saw previously (section 8) that a comprehensive neurophysiological theory would leave no room for desires and intentions as causal factors. Consequently, neither the man's previously formed simple intention to move his hand nor his further intention (to open the door) could be causes of the movement of his hand.

18. We noticed before that it is true a priori that if a man wants *Y*, or has *Y* as a goal, and believes that *X* is required for *Y*, then in the absence of countervailing factors he will do *X*. It is also true a priori that if a man forms the intention (for example, decides) to do *X*, then in the absence of countervailing factors he will do *X*. These a priori principles of action are assumed in our everyday explanations of behaviour.

We saw that mechanistic explanations could not be more basic than are explanations in terms of intentions or purposes.

We saw that the verification of mechanistic laws could not disprove the a priori principles of action.

Yet a mechanistic explanation of behaviour rules out any explanation of it in terms of the agent's intentions. If a comprehensive neurophysiological theory is true, then people's intentions never are causal factors in behaviour.

19. Thus if mechanism is true, the a priori principles of action do not apply to the world. This would have to mean one or the other of two alternatives. The first would be that people do not have intentions, purposes, or desires, or that they do not have beliefs as to what behaviour is required for the fulfilment of their desires and purposes. The second alternative would be that although they have intentions, beliefs, and so forth, there always are countervailing factors—that is, factors that interfere with the operation of intentions, desires, and decisions.

The second alternative cannot be taken seriously. If a man wants to be on the opposite bank of a river and believes that swimming it is the only thing that will get him there, he will swim it unless there are countervailing factors, such as an inability to swim or a fear of drowning or a strong dislike of getting wet. In this sense it is not true that countervailing factors are present *whenever* someone has a goal. There are not *always* obstacles to the fulfilment of any purpose or desire.

It might be objected that mechanistic causation itself is a universal countervailing factor. Now if this were so it would imply that purposes, intentions, and desires never have any effect on behaviour. But it is not a coherent position to hold that some creatures have purposes and so forth, yet that these have no effect on their behaviour. Purposes and intentions are, in concept, so closely tied to behavioural effects that the total absence of behavioural effects would mean the total absence of purposes and intentions. Thus the only position open to the exponent of mechanism is the first alternative—namely, that people do not have intentions, purposes, or beliefs.

What I have called 'a principle of action' is a conditional proposition, having an antecedent and a consequent. The whole conditional is true a priori, and therefore if the antecedent holds in a particular case, the consequent must also hold in that case. To say that the antecedent holds in a particular case means that it is true of some person (or animal). It means that the person has some desire or intention, and also has the requisite belief. If this were so, and if there were no countervailing factors, it would follow that the person would act in an appropriate manner. His intention or desire would, in our broad sense, be a cause of his action—that is, it would be a factor in the explanation of the occurrence of the action.

But this is incompatible with mechanism. A mechanist must hold, therefore, that the principles of action have no application to reality, in the sense that no one has intentions or desires or beliefs.

Some philosophers would regard this result as an adequate refutation of mechanism. But others would not. They would say that the confirmation of a comprehensive neurophysiological theory of behaviour is a logical possibility, and therefore it is logically possible that there are no desires, intentions, and so forth, and that to deny these logical possibilities is to be dogmatic and antiscientific. I will avoid adopting this 'dogmatic' and 'antiscientific' position, and will formulate a criticism of mechanism from a more 'internal' point of view.

20. I wish to make a closer approach to the question of the conceivability of mechanism. We have seen that mechanism is incompatible with purposive behaviour, but we have not yet established that it is incompatible with the existence of merely intentional behaviour. A man can do something intentionally but with no further intention: his behaviour is intentional but not purposive. One possibility is that this behaviour should embody a merely concurrent simple intention. Since such intentions are not causes of the behaviour to which they belong, their existence does not appear to conflict with mechanistic causation. Mechanism's incompatibility with purposive behaviour has not yet shown it to be incompatible with intentional behaviour as such.

But could it be true that sometimes people acted intentionally although it was never true that they acted for any purpose? Could they do things intentionally but never with any further intention?

If some intentional actions are purposeless, it does not follow that all of them could be purposeless. And I do not think this is really a possibility. I will not attempt to deal with every kind of action. But consider that subclass of actions that are activities. Any physical activity is analysable into components. If a man is painting a wall, he is grasping a brush, dipping the brush into the paint, moving his arm back and forth. He does these things in painting. They are parts of his activity of painting. If someone is rocking in a chair, he is pushing against the floor with his feet, and pressing his back against the back of the chair. These are subordinate activities in the activity of rocking. If the one who is painting is asked why he is dipping the brush into the paint, he can answer, 'I am painting this wall'. This is an explanation of what he is doing in dipping the brush, and also of what he is dipping if *for*. It is a purposive explanation. A person can put paint on a wall, or rock in a chair, or pace back and forth, without having any purpose in doing so. Still these activities could be intentional, although not for any purpose.

Whether intentional or not, these activities would be analysable into component parts. If the activity is intentional, then at least some of its components will be intentional. If none of them were, the whole to which they belong would not be intentional. A man could not be intentionally putting paint on a wall if he did not intentionally have hold of a brush. Now this is not strictly true since he might not be aware that he was holding a *brush*, rather than a roller or a cloth. But there will have to be *some* description of what he is holding according to which it is true that he is intentionally holding it and intentionally dipping it in the paint.

Thus an intentional activity must have intentional components. The components will be purposive in relation to the whole activity. If *X* is an intentional component of *Y*, one can say with equal truth that in *X*-ing one is *Y*-ing, or that one is *X*-ing in order to *Y*. In moving the pencil on the paper one is drawing a figure: but also one is moving the pencil in order to draw a figure.

I conclude that if there could be no purposive behaviour, there could be no intentional activities. Strictly speaking, this does not prove that there could be no intentional action, since many actions are not activities (for example, catching a ball or winning a race, as contrasted with playing ball or running in a race). But many of the actions that are not activities are stages in, or terminations of, activities and could not exist if the activities did not. Although I do not know how to prove the point for all cases, it seems to me highly plausible that if there could be no intentional activities there could be no intentional behaviour of any sort—so plausible that I will assume it to be so. A life that was totally devoid of activities certainly could not be a human life. My conclusion is that since mechanism is incompatible with purposive behaviour, it is incompatible with intentional activities, and consequently is incompatible with *all* intentional behaviour.

21. The long-deferred question of whether the man of our example moved his hand on the doorknob will be answered as follows. The action of moving his hand cannot be rightly ascribed to him. It should not even be ascribed to him with some qualification such as 'unintentionally' or 'accidentally', for the use of these qualifications implies that there are cases in which it is right to say of a man that he did something 'intentionally' or 'purposely'. But mechanism rules this out. On the other hand, to say 'He did not move his hand' would be misleading, not only for the reason just stated, but also for the further reason that this statement would normally carry the implication that his hand did not move—which is false. Neither the sentence 'He moved his hand' nor the sentence 'He did not move his hand' would be appropriate. We would, of course, say 'He moved his hand' if we understood this as merely equivalent to 'His hand moved'. (It is interesting that we do use these two sentences interchangeably when we are observing someone whom we know to be asleep or unconscious: we are equally ready to say either 'He moved his hand' or 'His hand moved'.) But if we came to believe in mechanism we should, in consistency, give up the ascribing of action, even in a qualified way.

22. We can now proceed directly to the question of whether mechanism is conceivable. Sometimes when philosophers ask whether a proposition is conceivable, they mean to be asking whether it is self-contradictory. Nothing in our examination has indicated that mechanism is a self-contradictory theory, and I am sure it is not. Logically speaking, the earth and the whole universe might have been inhabited solely by organisms of such a nature that all of their movements could have been completely explained in terms of the neurophysiological theory we have envisaged. We can conceive that the world might have been such that mechanism was true. In this sense mechanism is conceivable.

But there is a respect in which mechanism is not conceivable. This is a consequence of the fact that mechanism is incompatible with the existence of any intentional behaviour. The speech of human beings is, for the most part, intentional behaviour. In particular, stating, asserting, or saying that so-and-so is true requires the intentional uttering of some sentence. If mechanism is true, therefore, no one can state or assert anything. In a sense, no one can *say* anything. Specifically, no one can assert or state that mechanism is true. If anyone were to assert this, the occurrence of his intentional 'speech act' would imply that mechanism is false.

Thus there is a logical absurdity in asserting that mechanism is true. It is not that the doctrine of mechanism is self-contradictory. The absurdity lies in the human act of asserting the doctrine. The occurrence of this act of assertion is inconsistent with the content of the assertion. The mere proposition that mechanism is true is not self-contradictory. But the conjunctive proposition. 'Mechanism is true and someone asserts it to be true' *is* self-contradictory. Thus anyone's assertion that mechanism is true is necessarily false. The assertion implies its own falsity by virtue of providing a counter-example to what is asserted.

23. A proponent of mechanism might claim that since the absurdity we have been describing is a mere 'pragmatic paradox' and not a self-contradiction in the doctrine of mechanism, it does not provide a sense in which mechanism is inconceivable. He may say that the paradox is similar to the paradox of a man's asserting that he himself is unconscious. There is an inconsistency between this man's act of stating he is unconscious and what he states. His act of stating it implies that what he states is false. But this paradox does not establish that a man cannot be unconscious, or that we cannot conceive that a man should be unconscious.

Now there is some similarity between the paradox of stating that oneself is unconscious and the paradox of stating that mechanism is true. But there is an important difference. *I* cannot state, without absurdity, that *I* am unconscious. But anyone else can, without absurdity, state that I am unconscious. There is only one person (myself) whose act of stating this proposition is inconsistent with the proposition. But an assertion of mechanism by any person whomsoever is inconsistent with mechanism. That I am unconscious is not (in consistency) statable by me. The unstatability is relative to only one person. But the unstatability of mechanism is absolute.

Furthermore, no one can consistently assert that although mechanism is unstatable it may be true. For this assertion, too, would require an intentional utterance (speech act) and so would be incompatible with mechanism.

We have elucidated a sense in which mechanism can properly be said to be inconceivable. The sense is that no one can consistently assert (or state, or say) that mechanism is, or may be, true.

If someone were to insist on asserting that mechanism is or may be true, his only recourse (if he were to be consistent) would be to adopt a form of solipsism. He could claim that mechanism is true for other organisms but not for himself. In this way he would free his assertion of inconsistency, but at the cost of accepting the embarrassments and logical difficulties of solipsism. He would also be repudiating the scientific respectability of mechanism by denying the universality of the envisaged neurophysiological laws.

24. Our criticism that mechanism is not a consistently statable doctrine is, of course, purely logical in nature. It consists in deducing a consequence of mechanism. Now one may feel that this consequence cannot refute mechanism or jeopardize its status as a scientific theory. It would seem to be up to science alone to determine whether or not there is a comprehensive neurophysiological theory to explain all bodily movements in accordance with universal laws. If scientific investigation should confirm such a theory, then so be it! To confirm it would be to confirm its consequence. If confirming the theory were to prove that people do not have desires, purposes, or goals, then this result would have to be swallowed, no matter how upsetting it would be not only to our ordinary beliefs but also to our ordinary concepts.

Almost anyone will feel some persuasiveness in this viewpoint. Determinism is a painful problem because it creates a severe tension between two viewpoints, each of which is strongly attractive: one is that the concepts of purpose, intention, and desire, of our ordinary language, cannot be rendered void by scientific advance; the other is that those concepts cannot prescribe limits to what it is possible for empirical science to achieve.

Let us see what would be the effect on our thinking of a scientific confirmation of mechanism. Suppose I am playing catch with a small boy. The ball escapes his grasp and he runs after it. Any observer would agree that the boy is running after the ball. This description implies that the purpose of the boy's running is to get the ball, or that he is running because he wants to capture the ball.

Now suppose a neurological technician could explain and predict every movement of the boy's limbs without regard to the whereabouts of the ball, solely in terms of the changing states of the boy's neurophysiological system. Or, what is worse, suppose the technician could control the boy's movements by altering the states of his central nervous system at will—that is, by 'programming'. We can imagine that it should be impossible for us to tell in a given instance, by observation of the boy's outward behaviour and circumstances, whether the boy's limbs were responding to programming or whether he was running in order to retrieve the ball. And suppose that in many instances when we thought the behaviour was intentional, it was subsequently proved to us that exactly the same inner physiological processess occurred as on those occasions when the technician controlled the boy's movements. We can also suppose that the neurologist's predictions of behaviour would be both more reliable and more accurate than are the predictions based on purposive assumptions.

If such demonstrations occurred on a massive scale, we should be learning that the principles of purposive explanation have a far narrower application than we had thought. On more and more occasions we (that is, each one of us) would be forced to regard other human beings as mechanisms. The ultimate outcome of this development would be that we should cease to think of the behaviour of others as being influenced by desires and intentions.

25. Having become believers in mechanistic explanations of the behaviour of others, could each of us also come to believe that mechanistic causation is the true doctrine for his own case? Not if we realized what this would imply, for each of us would see that he could not include himself within the scope of the doctrine. Saying or doing something *for a reason* (in the sense of grounds as well as in the sense of purpose) implies that the saying or doing is intentional. Since mechanism is incompatible with the intentionality of behaviour, my acceptance of mechanism as true for myself would imply that I am incapable of saying or doing anything for a reason. There could be *a* reason (that is, a cause) but there could not be such a thing as *my* reason. There could not, for example, be such a thing as my reason for stating that mechanism is true. Thus my assertion of mechanism would involve a second paradox. Not only would the assertion be inconsistent, in the sense previously explained, but also it would imply that I am incapable of having rational grounds for asserting anything, including mechanism.

Once again we see that mechanism engenders a form of solipsism. In asserting mechanism I must deny its application to my own case: for otherwise my assertion would imply that I could not be asserting mechanism on rational grounds.

26. Some philosophers hold that if mechanism is true then a radical revision of our concepts is required. We need to junk all such terms as 'intentionally', 'unintentionally', 'purposely', 'by mistake', 'deliberately', 'accidentally', and so on. The classifying of utterances such as 'asserting', 'repeating', 'quoting', 'mimicking', 'translating', and so forth, would have to be abandoned. We should need an entirely new repertoire of descriptions of a sort that would be compatible with the viewpoint of mechanism.

I think these philosophers have not grasped the full severity of the predicament. If mechanism is true, not only should we give up speaking of 'asserting', but also of 'describing' or even of 'speaking'. It would not even be right to say that a person *meant* something by the noise that came from him. No marks or sounds would mean anything. There could not be *language*.

A proponent of mechanism should not think that at present we are using the wrong concepts and that a revision is called for. If he is right, we do not use concepts at all. There is nothing to revise—and nothing to say. The motto of a mechanist ought to be: One cannot speak, therefore one must be silent.

27. To conclude: We have uncovered two respects in which mechanism is not a conceivable doctrine. The first is that the occurrence of an act of asserting mechanism is inconsistent with mechanism's being true. The second is that the asserting of mechanism implies that the one who makes the assertion cannot be making it on rational grounds.

In order to avoid these paradoxes, one must deny that mechanism is universally true. One can hold that it is true for others but not for oneself. It is highly ironical that the affirmation of mechanism requires one to affirm its metaphysical and methodological opposite—solipsism.

The inconceivability of mechanism, in the two respects we have elucidated, does not establish that mechanism is false. It would seem, logically speaking, that a comprehensive neurophysiological theory of human behaviour ought to be confirmable by scientific investigation. Yet the assertion that this confirmation had been achieved would involve the two paradoxes we have elucidated. Mechanism thus presents a harsh, and perhaps insoluble, antimony to human thought.

Concluding unscientific postscript: I must confess that I am not entirely convinced of the correctness of the position I have taken in respect of the crux of this paper—namely, the problem of whether it is possible for there to be both a complete neurophysiological explanation and also a complete purposive explanation of one and the same sequence of movements. I do not believe I have really proved this to be impossible. On the other hand, it is true that for me (and for others, too) a sequence of sounds tends to lose the aspect of speech (language) when we conceive of those sounds as being caused neurophysiologically (especially if we imagine a technician to be controlling the production of the sounds). Likewise, a sequence of movements loses the aspect of action. Is this tendency due to some false picture or to some misleading analogy? Possibly so; but also possibly not. Perhaps the publication of the present paper will be justified if it provokes a truly convincing defence of the compatibility of the two forms of explanation.[14]

[14] A number of people have read various versions of this paper and I have profited from their criticisms. I am especially indebted to Elizabeth Anscombe, Keith Donnellan, Philippa Foot, G. H. von Wright, and Ann Wilbur. They are not responsible for the mistakes I have retained.

X

MECHANISM AND RESPONSIBILITY

DANIEL C. DENNETT

I

IN the eyes of many philosophers the old question of whether determinism (or indeterminism) is incompatible with moral responsibility has been superseded by the hypothesis that *mechanism* may well be. This is a prior and more vexing threat to the notion of responsibility, for mechanism is here to stay, unlike determinism and its denial, which go in and out of fashion. The mechanistic style of explanation, which works so well for electrons, motors, and galaxies, has already been successfully carried deep into man's body and brain, and the open question now is not whether mechanistic explanation of human motion is possible, but just whether it will ultimately have crucial gaps of randomness (like the indeterminists' mechanistic explanation of electrons) or not (like the mechanistic explanation of macroscopic systems such as motors and billiards tables). In either case the believer in responsibility has problems, for it seems that whenever a particular bit of human motion can be given an entirely mechanistic explanation—with or without the invocation of 'random' interveners—any non-mechanistic, rational purposive explanation of the same motions is otiose. For example, if we are on the verge of characterizing a particular bit of human motion as a well-aimed kick in the pants, and a doctor can show us that in fact the extensor muscles in the leg were contracted by nerve impulses triggered by a 'freak' (possibly random?) epileptic discharge in the brain, we will have to drop the search for purposive explanations of the motion, and absolve the kicker from all responsibility. Or so it seems. A more central paradigm might be as follows. Suppose a man is found who cannot, or will not, say the word 'father'. Otherwise, we may suppose, he

From *Essays on Freedom of Action,* ed. Ted Honderich (1973), pp. 159–84. Reprinted by permission of the publisher, Routledge & Kegan Paul Ltd.

seems perfectly normal, and even expresses surprise at his 'inability' to say 'that word I can't say'. A psychoanalyst might offer a plausible explanation of his behaviour in terms of unconscious hatred and desires and beliefs about his father, and a layman might say: 'Nonsense! This man is just playing a joke. I suspect he's made a bet that he can go a year without saying "father" and is doing all this deliberately.' But if a neurosurgeon were to come along and establish that a tiny lesion in the speech centre of the brain caused by an aneurysm (random or not) was causally responsible for the lacuna in the man's verbal repertory (not an entirely implausible discovery in the light of Penfield's remarkable research), both the analyst's and the layman's candidates for explanation would have the rug pulled out from under them. Since a mere mechanistic happening in the brain, random or not, was the cause of the quirk, the man cannot have had reasons, unconscious or ordinary, for it, and cannot be held responsible for it. Or so it seems.

The principle that seems to some philosophers to emerge from such examples is that *the mechanistic displaces the purposive*, and any mechanistic (or causal) explanation of human motions takes priority over, indeed renders false, any explanation in terms of desires, beliefs, intentions. Thus Hospers says, 'Let us note that the more *thoroughly* and *in detail* we know the causal factors leading a person to behave as he does, the more we tend to exempt him from responsibility.'[1] And Malcolm has recently supported the view that 'although purposive explanations cannot be dependent on non-purposive explanations, they would be refuted by the verification of a comprehensive neurophysiological theory of behaviour'.[2] I want to argue that this principle is false, and that it is made plausible only by focusing attention on the wrong features of examples like those above. The argument I will unwind strings together arguments and observations from a surprisingly diverse group of recent writers, and perhaps it is fair to say that my share of the argument is not much. I will try to put the best face on this eclecticism by claiming that my argument provides a more fundamental and unified ground for these variously expressed discoveries about the relations between responsibility and mechanism.

II

The first step in reconciling mechanism and responsibility is getting clearer about the nature of the apparently warring sorts of explanations

[1] J. Hospers, 'What Means This Freedom?' in *Determinism and Freedom in the Age of Modern Science*, ed. Sidney Hook (New York: Collier, 1958), 133.

[2] N. Malcolm, 'The Conceivability of Mechanism', *Philosophical Review*, 1968, 51. [Essay IX in this collection, 132.]

involved. Explanations that serve to ground verdicts of responsibility are couched at least partly in terms of the beliefs, intentions, desires, and reasons of the person or agent held responsible. There is a rough consensus in the literature about the domain of such explanations, but different rubrics are used: they are the 'purposive' or 'rational' or 'action' or 'Intentional' explanations of behaviour. I favour the term 'Intentional' (from the scholastics, via Brentano, Chisholm, and other revivalists), and shall capitalize it to avoid confusion with 'intend' and its forms, thereby freeing the latter terms for more restrictive duty. *Intentional explanations*, then, cite thoughts, desires, beliefs, intentions, rather than chemical reactions, explosions, electric impulses, in explaining the occurrence of human motions. There is a well-known controversy debating whether (any) Intentional explanations are ultimately only causal explanations—Melden and Davidson[3] are the initial protagonists—but I shall avoid the centre of this controversy and the related controversy about whether a desire or intention could be identical with a physical state or event, and rest with a more modest point, namely that Intentional explanations are at least not causal explanations *simpliciter*. This can be brought out by contrasting genuine Intentional explanations with a few causal hybrids.

Not all explanations containing Intentional terms are Intentional explanations. Often a belief or desire or other Intentional phenomenon (Intentional in virtue of being referred to by Intentional idioms) is cited as a cause or (rarely) effect in a perfectly Humean sense of cause and effect.

(1) His belief that the gun was loaded caused his heart attack

(2) His obsessive desire for revenge caused his ulcers

(3) The thought of his narrow escape from the rattler made him shudder.

These sentences betray their Humean neature by being subject to the usual rules of evidence for causal assertions. We do not know at this time how to go about confirming (1), but whatever techniques and scientific knowledge we might have recourse to, our tactic would be to show that no other conditions inside or outside the man were sufficient to bring on the heart attack, and that the belief (however we characterize or embody it) together with the prevailing conditions brought about the heart attack in a law-governed way. Now this sort of account may be highly suspect, and ringed with metaphysical difficulties, yet it is undeniable that this is roughly the story we assume to be completable in principle when we assert (1). It may

[3] A. I. Melden, *Free Action* (London: Routledge & Kegan Paul, 1961); D. Davidson, 'Actions, Reasons and Causes', *Journal of Philosophy*, 1963, 685–700.

seem at first that (1) is not purely causal, for the man in question can tell us, infallibly or non-inferentially, that it was his belief that caused his heart attack. But this is false. The man is in no better position than we to say what caused his heart attack. It may feel to him as if this was the cause of the attack, but he may well be wrong; his only *knowledge* is of the temporal juxtaposition of the events. Similarly, (2) would be falsified if it turned out that the man's daily consumption of a quart of gin was more than sufficient to produce his ulcers, however strong and sincere his intuitions that the vengefulness was responsible. We are apt to think we have direct, non-inferential experience of thoughts causing shudders, as asserted in (3), but in fact we have just what Hume says we have; fallible experience over the years of regular conjunction.

These explanations are not Intentional because they do not explain by *giving a rationale* for the *explicandum*. Intentional explanations explain a bit of behaviour, an action, or a stretch of inaction, by making it reasonable in the light of certain beliefs, intentions, desires ascribed to the agent. (1) to (3) are to be contrasted in this regard with

(4) He threw himself to the floor because of his belief that the gun was loaded

(5) His obsessive desire for revenge led him to follow Jones all the way to Burma

(6) He refused to pick up the snake because at that moment he thought of his narrow escape from the rattler.

The man's heart attack in (1) is not made *reasonable* in the light of his belief (though we might say we can now understand how it happened), but his perhaps otherwise inexplicable action in (4) is. Sentence (5) conspicuously has 'led' where its counterpart has 'caused', and for good reason. Doubts about (5) would not be settled by appeal to inductive evidence of past patterns of constant conjunctions, and the man's own pronouncements about his trip to Burma have an authority his self-diagnosis in (2) lacks.

The difference in what one is attempting to provide in mechanistic and Intentional explanations is especially clear in the case of 'psychosomatic' disorders. One can say—in the manner of (1) and (2)—that a desire or belief merely *caused* a symptom, say, paralysis, *or* one can say that a desire or belief led a person to *want* to be paralysed—to become paralysed *deliberately*. The latter presumes to be a purely Intentional explanation, a case of making the paralysis—as an *intended condition*—*reasonable* in the light of certain beliefs and desires, e.g. the desire to be waited on, the belief that relatives must be made to feel guilty.

III

Intentional explanations have the actions of persons as their primary domain, but there are times when we find Intentional explanations (and predictions based on them) not only useful but indispensable for accounting for the behaviour of complex machines. Consider the case of the chess-playing computer, and the different stances one can choose to adopt in trying to predict and explain its behaviour. First there is the *design stance*. If one knows exactly how the computer's program has been designed (and we will assume for simplicity that this is not a learning or evolving program but a static one), one can predict the computer's designed response to any move one makes. One's prediction will come true provided only that the computer performs as designed, that is, without breakdown. In making a prediction from the design stance, one *assumes* there will be no malfunction, and predicts, as it were, from the blueprints alone. We generally adopt this stance when making predictions about the behaviour of mechanical objects, e.g. 'As the typewriter carriage approaches the margin, a bell will ring (provided the machine is in working order)', and more simply, 'Strike the match and it will light'. We also often adopt this stance in predictions involving natural objects: 'When spring comes new buds will burst on these twigs'. The essential feature of the design stance is that we make predictions solely from knowledge of or assumptions about the system's design, often without making any examination of the innards of the particular object.

Second, there is what we may call the *physical stance*. From this stance our predictions are based on the actual state of the particular system, and are worked out by applying whatever knowledge we have of the laws of nature. It is from this stance alone that we can predict the malfunction of systems (unless, as sometimes happens these days, a system is *designed* to malfunction after a certain time, in which case malfunctioning in one sense becomes a part of its proper functioning). Instances of predictions from the physical stance are common enough: 'If you turn on that switch you'll get a nasty shock', and, 'When the snows come that branch will break right off' are cases in point. One seldom adopts the physical stance in dealing with a computer just because the number of critical variables in the physical constitution of a computer would overwhelm the most prodigious human calculator. Significantly, the physical stance is generally reserved for instances of breakdown, where the condition preventing normal operation is generalized and easily locatable, e.g. 'Nothing will happen when you type in your question, because it isn't plugged in' or, 'It won't work with all that flood water in it'. Attempting to give a physical account or prediction of the chess-playing computer would be a pointless and herculean labour, but it would work in principle. One could predict the response it would make in a chess game by tracing out the effects of the input energies all the way through the computer until once more type was pressed against paper and a response was printed.

There is a third stance one can adopt towards a system, and that is the *Intentional stance*. This tends to be most appropriate when the system one is dealing with is too complex to be dealt with effectively from the other stances. In the case of the chess-playing computer one adopts this stance when one tries to predict its response to one's move by figuring out what a good or reasonable response would be, given the information the computer has about the situation. Here one assumes not just the absence of malfunction, but the rationality of design or programming as well. Of course the stance is pointless, in view of its extra assumption, in cases where one has no reason to believe in the system's rationality. In weather predicting one is not apt to make progress by wondering what clever move the wise old West Wind will make next. Prediction from the Intentional stance assumes rationality in the system, but not necessarily perfect rationality. Rather, our pattern of inference is that we start with the supposition of what we take to be perfect rationality, and then alter our premiss in individual cases as we acquire evidence of individual foibles and weaknesses of reason. This bias in favour of rationality is particularly evident in the tactics of chess players, who set out to play a new opponent by assuming that he will make reasonable responses to their moves, and then seeking out weaknesses. The opponent who started from an assumption of irrationality would be foolhardy in the extreme. But notice, in this regard, how the designer of a chess-playing program might himself be able to adopt the design stance and capitalize from the very beginning on flaws in rationality he knew were built into the program. In the early days of chess-playing programs, this tactic was feasible, but today, with evolving programs capable of self-improvement, designers are no longer capable of maintaining the design stance in playing against their own programs, and must resort, as any outsider would, to the Intentional stance in trying to outwit their own machines.

Whenever one can successfully adopt the Intentional stance toward an object, I call that object an *Intentional system*. The success of the stance is of course a matter settled pragmatically, without reference to whether the object *really* has beliefs, intentions, and so forth, so whether or not any computer can be conscious, or have thoughts or desires, some computers undeniably *are* Intentional systems, for they are systems whose behaviour can be predicted, and most efficiently predicted, by adopting the Intentional stance toward them.[4]

This tolerant assumption of rationality is the hallmark of the Intentional stance with regard to people as well as computers. We start by assuming rationality in our transactions with other adult human beings, and adjust our predictions as we learn more about personalities. We do not *expect* new acquaintances to react irrationally to particular topics, but when they do we adjust our strategies accordingly. The presumption that we will be able to communicate with our fellow men is founded on the presumption of their rationality, and this is so strongly entrenched in our inference habits that when our predictions prove false we first cast about for external mitigating factors (he must not have heard, he must not know English, he must not have seen x, been aware that y, etc.) before questioning the rationality of the system as a whole. In extreme cases personalities may prove to be so unpredictable from the Intentional stance that we abandon it, and if we have accumulated a lot of evidence in the meanwhile about the nature of response patterns in the individual, we may find that the design stance can be effectively adopted. This is the fundamentally different attitude we occasionally adopt toward the insane. To watch an asylum attendant manipulate an obsessively counter-suggestive patient, for instance, is to watch something radically unlike normal interpersonal relations. It need hardly be added that in the area of behaviour (as opposed to the operation of internal organs, for instance) we hardly ever know enough about the physiology of individuals to adopt the physical stance effectively, except for a few dramatic areas, like the surgical care of epileptic seizures.

IV

The distinction of stance I have drawn appears closely related to MacKay's distinction between the 'personal aspect' and the 'mechanical aspect' of some systems. Of central importance in MacKay's account is his remarking that the choice of stance is 'up to us', a matter of *decision*, not discovery.[5] Having chosen to view our transactions with a system from the Intentional stance, certain characterizations of events necessarily arise, but that these arise *rightly* cannot be a matter of proof. Much the same distinction, I believe, is presented in a different context by Strawson, who

[4] For a more detailed analysis of the concept, see my 'Intentional Systems', *Journal of Philosophy*, 1971, 87–106, where in particular the notions of rationality of design and Intentionality of information-processing systems are discussed at length.

[5] D. M. MacKay, 'The Use of Behavioural Language to Refer to Mechanical Processes', *British Journal for the Philosophy of Science*, 1962, 89–103. See also H. Putnam, 'Robots: Machines or Artificially Created Life?', read at the American Philosophical Association, Eastern Division meeting, 1964, subsequently published in *Philosophy of Mind*, ed. Stuart Hampshire (New York: Harper & Row, 1966), 91.

contrasts 'participation in a human relationship' with 'the objective attitude'. 'If your attitude toward someone is wholly objective, then though you may fight him, you cannot quarrel with him, and though you may talk to him, even negotiate with him, you cannot reason with him. You can at most pretend to quarrel, or to reason, with him.'[6] Both MacKay and Strawson say a great deal that is illuminating about the conditions and effects of adopting the personal or participant attitude toward someone (or something), but in their eagerness to establish the implications for ethics of the distinction, they endow it with a premature moral dimension. That is, both seem to hold that adopting the personal attitude toward a system (human or not) involves admitting the system into the moral community. MacKay says, in discussing the effect of our adopting the attitude toward a particular animate human body,[7]

> At the personal level, Joe will have established some personal claims on us, and we on Joe. We shall not be able rightly to tamper with his brain, for example, nor feel free to dismantle his body. . . . He has become 'one of us', a member of the linguistic community—not, be it noted, by virtue of the particular *stuff* of which his brain is built . . . but by virtue of the particular kinds of mutual interaction that it can sustain with our own—interaction which at the personal level we describe as that of person-to-person.

MacKay is, I believe, conflating two choices into one. The first choice, to ascend from the mechanistic to the Intentional stance, as portrayed by our chess-playing designer, has no moral dimension. One is guilty of no monstrosities if one dismembers the computer with whom one plays chess, or even the robot with whom one has long conversations. One adopts the Intentional stance toward any system one assumes to be (roughly) rational, where the complexities of its operation preclude maintaining the design stance effectively. The second choice, to adopt a truly moral stance toward the system (thus viewing it as a person), might often turn out to be psychologically irresistible given the first choice, but it is logically distinct. Consider in this context the hunter trying to stalk a tiger by thinking what *he* would do if he were being hunted down. He has adopted the Intentional stance toward the tiger, and perhaps very effectively, but though the psychological tug is surely there to disapprove of the hunting of any creature wily enough to deserve the Intentional treatment, it would be hard to sustain a charge of either immorality or logical inconsistency against the hunter. We might, then, distinguish a fourth stance, above the Intentional stance,

[6] P. F. Strawson, 'Freedom and Resentment', *Proceedings of the British Academy*, 1962, reprinted in *Studies in the Philosophy of Thought and Action*, ed. P. F. Strawson (Oxford University Press, 1968), 79. [Essay V in this collection, 66.]

[7] MacKay, 102.

called the *personal stance*. The personal stance presupposes the Intentional stance (note that the Intentional stance presupposes neither lower stance) and seems to cursory views at least to be just the annexation of moral commitment to the Intentional. (A less obvious relative of my distinctions of stance is Sellars's distinction between the manifest and scientific images of man. Sellars himself draws attention to its kinship to Strawson: 'Roughly, the manifest image corresponds to the world as conceived by P. F. Strawson. . . . The manifest image is, in particular, a framework in which the distinctive features of persons are conceptually irreducible to features of non-persons, e.g. animals and merely material things.'[8] A question I will not attempt to answer here is whether Sellars's manifest image lines up more with the more narrow, and essentially moral, personal stance or the broader Intentional stance.)

Something like moral commitment can exist in the absence of the Intentional stance, as Strawson points out, but it is not the same; the objective attitude—my design or physical stances—'may include pity or even love, though not all kinds of love'. The solicitude of a gardener for his flowers, or for that matter, of a miser for his coins, cannot amount to moral commitment, because of the absence of the Intentional. (Parenthetical suggestion: is the central fault in utilitarianism a confusion of gardener-solicitude with person-solicitude?)

Since the second choice (of moral commitment) is like the first in being just a choice, relative to ends and desires and not provably right or wrong, it is easy to see how they can be run together. When they are, important distinctions are lost. Strawson's union of the two leads him to propose, albeit cautiously, a mistaken contrast: 'But what is above all interesting is the tension there is, in us, between the participant attitude and the objective attitude. One is tempted to say: between our humanity and our intelligence. But to say this would be to distort both notions.'[9] The distortion lies in allying the non-Intentional, mechanistic stances with the coldly rational and intelligent, and the Intentional stance with the emotional. The Intentional stance of one chess player toward another (or the hunter toward his prey) can be as coldly rational as you wish, and alternatively one can administer to one's automobile in a bath of sentiment.

Distinctions are also obscured if one makes *communicating with* a system the hallmark of Intentionality or rationality. Adopting the Intentional

[8] W. Sellars, 'Fatalism and Determinism', in *Freedom and Determinism*, ed. Keith Lehrer (New York: Random House, 1966), 145. A. Flew, 'A Rational Animal', in *Brain and Mind*, ed. J. R. Smythies (London: Routledge & Kegan Paul, 1968), 111–35, and A. Rorty, 'Slaves and Machines', *Analysis*, 1962, 118–20, develop similar distinctions.

[9] Strawson, 80 [67 above.]

stance toward the chess-playing computer is not necessarily viewing one's moves as *telling* the computer anything (I do not have to *tell* my human opponent where I moved—he can *see* where I moved); it is merely predicting its responses with the assumption that it will respond rationally to its *perceptions*. Similarly, the hunter stalking the tiger will be unlikely to try to *communicate* with the tiger (although in an extended sense even this might be possible—consider the sort of *entente* people have on occasion claimed to establish with bears encountered on narrow trails, etc.), but he will plan his strategy on his assessment of what the tiger would be reasonable to *believe* or *try*, given its perceptions. As Grice has pointed out,[10] one thing that sets communication as a mode of interaction apart from others is that in attempting a particular bit of communication with A, one intends to produce in A some response *and* one intends A to recognize that one intends to produce in him this response *and* one intends that A produce this response on the basis of this recognition. When one's assessment of the situation leads to the belief that these intentions are not apt to be fulfilled, one does not try to communicate with A, but one does not, on these grounds, necessarily abandon the Intentional stance. A may simply not understand any language one can speak, or any language at all (e.g. the tiger). One can still attempt to influence A's behaviour by relying on A's rationality. For instance, one can throw rocks at A in an effort to get A to leave, something that is apt to work with Turk or tiger, and in each case what one does is at best marginal communication.[11]

Communication, then, is not a separable and higher *stance* one may choose to adopt toward something, but a type of interaction one may attempt within the Intentional stance. It can be seen at a glance that the set of intentions described by Grice would not be fulfilled with any regularity in any community where there was no *trust* among the members, and hence communication would be impossible, and no doubt this sort of consideration contributes to the feeling that the Intentional community (or at least the smaller *communicating* community) is co-extensive with the moral community, but of course the only conclusion validly drawn from Grice's analysis here is a pragmatic one: if one wants to influence A's behaviour, and A is capable of communicating, then one will be able to establish a very *effective* means of influence by establishing one's trustworthiness in A's eyes (by

[10] H. P. Grice, 'Meaning', *Philosophical Review*, 1957; 'Utterer's Meaning and Intentions', *Philosophical Review*, 1969.

[11] J. Bennett, in *Rationality* (London: Routledge & Kegan Paul, 1964), offers an extended argument to the effect that communication and rationality are essentially linked, but his argument is vitiated, I believe, by its reliance on an artificially restrictive sense of rationality—a point it would take too long to argue here. See my 'Intentional Systems', loc. cit., for arguments for a more generous notion of rationality.

hook or by crook). It is all too easy, however, to see interpersonal, convention-dependent communication as the mark of the Intentional—perhaps just because Intentional systems process information—and thus make the crucial distinction out to be between 'poking at' a system (to use MacKay's vivid phrase) and communicating with it. Not only does this way of putting the matter wrongly confuse the system's perception of communications with its perception more generally, but it is apt to lead to a moralistic inflation of its own. The notion of communication is apt to be turned into something mystical or semi-divine—synonyms today are 'rap', 'groove', 'dig', 'empathize'. The critical sense of communication, though, is one in which the most inane colloquies between parent and teenager (or man and bear) count as communication. (MacKay himself has on occasion suggested that the personal attitude is to be recognized in Buber's famous I–Thou formula, which is surely inflation.) The ethical implication to be extracted from the distinction of stance is not that the Intentional stance is a moral stance, but that it is a precondition of any moral stance, and hence if it is jeopardized by any triumph of mechanism, the notion of moral responsibility is jeopardized in turn.

V

Reason, not regard, is what sets off the Intentional from the mechanistic; we do not just reason about what Intentional systems will do, we reason about how they will reason. And so it is that our predictions of what an Intentional system will do are formed on the basis of what would be reasonable (for anyone) to do under the circumstances, rather than on what a wealth of experience with this system or similar systems might inductively suggest the system will do. It is the absence from the mechanistic stances of this presupposition of rationality that gives rise to the widespread feeling that there is an antagonism between predictions or explanations from these different stances. The feeling ought to be dissipated at least in part by noting that the absence of a presupposition of rationality is not the same as a presupposition of non-rationality.

Suppose someone asks me whether a particular desk calculator will give 108 as the product of 18 and 6.[12] I work out the sum on a piece of paper and say, 'Yes'. He responds with, 'I know that it *should*, but will it? You see, it was designed by my wife, who is no mathematician.' He hands me her blueprints and asks for a prediction (from the design stance). In working on this prediction the assumption of rationality, or good design, is useless, so I abandon, it, not as false but as question-begging. Similarly, if in response to

[12] Cf. L. W. Beck, 'Agent, Actor, Spectator, and Critic', *Monist* (1965), 175–9.

is initial question I reply, 'It's an IBM, so yes', he may reply, 'I know it's *esigned* to give that answer, but I just dropped it, so maybe it's broken'. In etting out to make this prediction I will be unable to avail myself of the ssumption that the machine is designed to behave in a certain way, so I bandon it. My prediction does not depend on any assumptions about ationality or design, but neither does it rescind any.

One reason we are tempted to suppose that mechanistic explanations reclude Intentional explanations is no doubt that since mechanistic xplanations (in particular, physical explanations) are for the most part ttempted, or effective, only in cases of malfunction or breakdown, where he rationality of the system is obviously impaired, we associate the physical xplanation with a failure of Intentional explanation, and ignore the ossibility that a physical explanation will go through (however superfluous, umbersome, unfathomable) in cases where Intentional explanation is roceeding smoothly. But there is a more substantial source of concern than his, raised by MacIntyre.[13]

> ehaviour is rational—in this arbitrarily, defined sense—if, and only if, it can be nfluenced, or inhibited by the adducing of some logically relevant consideration. . . But this means that if a man's behaviour is rational it cannot be determined by the tate of his glands or any other antecedent causal factor. For if giving a man more or etter information or suggesting a new argument to him is a both necessary and ufficient condition for, as we say, changing his mind, then we exclude, for this ccasion at least, the possibility of other sufficient conditions. . . . Thus to show that ehaviour is rational is enough to show that it is not causally determined in the sense f being the effect of a set of sufficient conditions *operating independently of the agent's eliberation or possibility of deliberation* [my italics]. So the discoveries of the hysiologist and psychologist may indefinitely increase our knowledge of why men ehave irrationally but they could never show that rational behaviour in this sense as causally determined.

AacIntyre's argument offers no licence for the introduction of the italicized hrase above, and without it his case is damaged, as we shall see later, when he effect of prediction is discussed. More fundamental, however, is his nisleading suggestion that the existence of sufficient conditions for events n a system puts that system in a strait-jacket, as it were, and thus denies it he flexibility required of a truly rational system. There is a grain of truth in his, which should be uncovered. In elaborating the distinction between tances, I chose for an example a system of rather limited versatility; the hess-playing system is unequipped even to play checkers or bridge, and nput appropriate to these other games would reveal the system to be as non-ational and unresponsive as any stone. There is a fundamental difference etween such limited-purpose systems and systems that are supposed to be

[13] A. C. MacIntyre, 'Determinism', *Mind*, 1957, 248 f.

capable of responding appropriately to input of all sorts. For although it i possible in principle to design a system that can be guaranteed to respon appropriately (relative to some stipulated ends) to any limited number o inputs given fixed, or finitely ambiguous or variable, environmenta 'significance', there is no way to design a system that can be guaranteed t react appropriately under *all* environmental conditions. A detailed argumen for this claim would run on too long for this occasion, and I have presente the major steps of it elsewhere,[14] so I will try to establish at leas comprehension, if not conviction, for the claim by a little thought experiment about *tropistic behaviour*. Wooldridge gives a lucid account of tropism:[15]

> When the time comes for egg laying the wasp *Sphex* builds a burrow for the purpos and seeks out a cricket which she stings in such a way as to paralyse but not kill it. Sh drags the cricket into the burrow, lays her eggs alongside, closes the burrow, then flie away, never to return. In due course, the eggs hatch and the wasp grubs feed off th paralysed cricket, which has not decayed, having been kept in the wasp equivalent o deep freeze. To the human mind, such an elaborately organized and seemingl purposeful routine conveys a convincing flavour of logic and thoughtfulness—unti more details are examined. For example, the wasp's routine is to bring the paralyse cricket to the burrow, leave it on the threshold, go inside to see that all is well, emerge and then drag the cricket in. If, while the wasp is inside making her preliminar inspection the cricket is moved a few inches away, the wasp, on emerging from th burrow, will bring the cricket back to the threshold, but not inside, and will the repeat the preparatory procedure of entering the burrow to see that everything is a right. If again the cricket is removed a few inches while the wasp is inside, once agai the wasp will move the cricket up to the threshold and re-enter the burrow for a fina check. The wasp never thinks of pulling the cricket straight in. On one occasion, thi procedure was repeated forty times, always with the same result.

The experiment unmasks the behaviour as a tropism, rigid within the limit set on the significance of the input, however felicitous its operation unde normal circumstances. The wasp's response lacks that free-wheelin flexibility in response to the situation that Descartes so aptly honoured a the infinity of the rational mind. For the notion of a perfectly rational perfectly adaptable system, to which all input compatible with its inpu organs is significant and comprehensible is the notion of an unrealizabl physical system. For let us take the wasp's tropism and improve on it. Tha is, suppose we take on the role of wasp designers, and decide to enlarge th sub-routine system of the tropism to ensure a more rational fit betwee behaviour and *whatever* environment the wasp may run into. We think u one stymieing environmental condition after another, and in each cas

[14] *Content and Consciousness* (London: Routledge & Kegan Paul, 1969).

[15] D. Wooldridge, *The Machinery of the Brain* (New York: McGraw-Hill, 1963), 82.

design sub-routines to detect and surmount the difficulty. There will always be room for yet one more set of conditions in which the rigidly mechanical working-out of response will be unmasked, however long we spend improving the system. Long after the wasp's behaviour has become so perspicacious that we would not think of calling it tropistic, the fundamental nature of the system controlling it will not have changed; it will just be more complex. In this sense any behaviour controlled by a finite mechanism must be tropistic.

What conclusion should be drawn from this about human behaviour? That human beings, as finite mechanical systems, are not rational after all? Or that the demonstrable rationality of man proves that there will always be an inviolable *terra incognita*, an infinite and non-mechanical mind beyond the grasp of physiologists and psychologists? It is hard to see what evidence could be adduced in support of the latter conclusion, however appealing it may be to some people, since for every awe-inspiring stroke of genius cited in its favour (the Einstein–Shakespeare gambit), there are a thousand evidences of lapses, foibles, bumbling and bullheadedness to suggest to the contrary that man is only imperfectly rational. Perfection is hard to prove, and nothing short of perfection sustains the argument. The former alternative also lacks support, for although in the case of the wasp we can say that its behaviour has been shown to be *merely* mechanically controlled, what force would the 'merely' have if we were to entertain the notion that the control of man's more versatile behaviour is merely mechanical? The denigration might well be appropriate if in a particular case the mechanical explanation of a bit of behaviour was short and sweet (consider explanations of the knee-jerk reflex or our hypothetical man who cannot say 'father'), but we must also consider cases in which the physiologist or cybernetician hands us twenty volumes of fine print and says, 'Here is the design of this man's behavioural control system'. Here is a case where the philosopher's preference for simple examples leads him astray, for of course any *simple* mechanistic explanation of a bit of behaviour will disqualify it for plausible Intentional characterization, make it a mere happening and not an action, but we cannot generalize from simple examples to complex, for it is precisely the simplicity of the examples that grounds the crucial conclusion.

The grain of truth in MacIntyre's contention is that *any* system that can be explained mechanistically—at whatever length—must be in an extended sense tropistic, and this can enhance the illusion that mechanistic and Intentional explanations cannot coexist. But the only implication that could be drawn from the *general* thesis of man's ultimately mechanistic organization would be that man must, then, be imperfectly rational, in the sense that he cannot be so designed as to *ensure* rational responses to all contingencies, hardly an alarming or counter-intuitive finding; and from any *particular* mechanistic explanation of a bit of behaviour it would not follow that that particular bit of behaviour was or was not a rational response to the environmental conditions at the time, for the mere fact that the response *had* to follow, given its causal antecedents, casts no more doubt on its rationality than the fact that the computer *had* to answer '108' casts doubts on the arithmetic correctness of its answer.

What, then, can we say about the hegemony of mechanistic explanations over Intentional explanations? Not that it does not exist, but that it is misdescribed if we suppose that whenever the former are confirmed, they drive out the latter. It is rather that mechanistic predictions, eschewing any presuppositions of rationality, can put the lie to Intentional predictions when a system happens to fall short of rationality in its response, whether because of weakness of 'design', or physically predictable breakdown. It is the presuppositions of Intentional explanation that put prediction of *lapses* in principle beyond its scope, whereas lapses are in principle predictable from the mechanistic standpoint, provided they are not the result of truly random events.[16]

VI

It was noted earlier that the search for a watershed to divide the things we are responsible for from the things we are not comes to rest usually with a formulation roughly harmonious with the distinction drawn here between the Intentional and the mechanistic. Many writers have urged that we are responsible for just those events that are our intentional *actions* (and for their forseeable results), and a great deal has been written in an effort to distinguish action from mere happening. The performing of actions is the restricted privilege of rational beings, persons, conscious agents, and one establishes that something is an action not by examining its causal ancestory but by seeing whether certain sorts of talk about *reasons* for action are appropriate in the context. On this basis we exculpate the insane, with whom one is unable to reason, unable to communicate; we also excuse the results of physical *force majeure* against which reason cannot prevail, whether the force is external (the chains that bind) or internal (the pain that makes me cry out, revealing our position to the enemy). This fruitful distinction between reason giving and cause giving is often, however, the

[16] In practice we predict lapses at the Intentional level ('You watch! He'll forget all about your knight after you move the queen') on the basis of loose-jointed inductive hypotheses about individual or widespread human frailties. These hypotheses are expressed in Intentional terms, but if they were given rigorous support, they would in the process be recast as predictions from the design or physical stance.

source of yet another misleading intuition about the supposed antagonism between mechanism and responsibility. 'Roughly speaking,' Anscombe says, 'it establishes something as a reason if one argues against it.'[17] One is tempted to go on: a reason is the sort of thing one can argue against with some hope of success, but one cannot argue against a causal chain. There is of course a sense in which this is obvious: one cannot argue with what has no ears to hear, for instance. But if one tries to get the point into a form where it will do some work, namely: 'the presentation of an argument cannot affect a causal chain', it is simply false. Presentations of arguments have all sorts of effects on the causal milieu: they set air waves in motion, cause ear drums to vibrate, and have hard to identify but important effects deep in the brain of the audience. So although the presentation of an argument may have no detectable effect on the trajectory of a cannon-ball, or closer to home, on one's *autonomic* nervous system, one's perceptual system is designed to be sensitive to the sorts of transmissions of energy that must occur for an argument to be communicated. The perceptual system can, of course, be affected in a variety of ways; if I sneak up behind someone and yell 'flinch, please!' in his ear, the effects wrought by my utterance would not constitute an action in obedience to my request, not because they were effects of a cause, but because the intricate sort of causal path that in general would have to have existed for an Intentional explanation to be appropriate was short-circuited. An Intentional system is precisely the sort of system to be affected by the input of information, so the discovery in such a system of a causal chain culminating in a bit of behaviour does not at all license the inference: 'since the behaviour was caused we could not have argued him out of it', for a prior attempt to argue him out of it would have altered the causal ancestry of the behaviour, perhaps effectively.

The crucial point when assessing responsibility is whether or not the antecedent inputs achieve their effects as inputs of information or by short-circuit. The possibility of short-circuiting or otherwise tampering with an Intentional system gives rise to an interesting group of perplexities about the extent of responsibility in cases where there has been manipulation. We are generally absolved of responsibility in cases where we have been manipulated by others, but there is no one principle of innocence by reason of manipulation. To analyse the issue we must first separate several distinct excusing conditions that might be lumped together under the heading of manipulation.

First, one may disclaim responsibility for an act if one has been led to commit the act by deliberately false information communicated by another,

[17] G. E. M. Anscombe, *Intention* (Oxford: Blackwell, 1957), 24.

and one might put this: 'he manipulated me, by forging documents'. The principle in such cases has nothing to do with one's Intentional system being tampered with, and in fact the appeal to the deliberate malice of the other party is a red herring.[18] The principle invoked to determine guilt or innocence in such cases is simply whether the defendant had reasonably good evidence for the beliefs which led to his act (and which, if true, would have justified it presumably). The plain evidence of one's senses is normally adequate when what is at issue is the presentation of a legal document, and so normally one is absolved when one has been duped by a forgery, but not, of course, if the forgery is obvious or one has any evidence that would lead a reasonable man to be suspicious. And if the evidence that misled one into a harmful act was produced by mere chance or an 'act of God' (such as a storm carrying away a 'Stop' sign) the principle is just the same. When one is duped in this manner by another, one's Intentional system has not been tampered with, but rather exploited.

The cases of concern to us are those in which one's behaviour is altered by some non-rational, non-Intentional interference. Here, cases where a person's body is merely mechanically interposed in an ultimately harmful result do not concern us either (e.g. one's arm is bumped, spilling Jones's beer, or less obviously, one is drugged, and hence is unable to appear in court). One is excused in such cases by an uncomplicated application of the *force majeure* principle. The only difficult cases are those in which the non-rational, non-Intentional interference alters one's beliefs and desires, and subsequently, one's actions. Our paradigm here is the idea—still fortunately science fiction—of the neurosurgeon who 'rewires' me and in this way inserts a belief or desire that was not there before. The theme has an interesting variation which is not at all fictional: the mad scientist might discover enough about a man's neural *design* (or program) to figure out that certain inputs would have the effect of reprogramming the man, quite independent of any apparent sense they might have for the man to react to rationally. For instance, the mad scientist might discover that flashing the letters of the alphabet in the man's eyes at a certain speed would cause him (in virtue of his imperfectly rational design) to believe that Mao is God. We have, in fact, fortuitously hit upon such ways of 'unlocking' a person's mind in hypnotism and brain-washing, so the question of responsibility in such cases is not academic. Some forms of psychotherapy, especially those involving drugs, also apparently fall under this rubric. Again it should be noted that the introduction of an evil manipulator in the examples is superfluous. If I am led to believe that Mao is God by a brain haemorrhage

[18] Cf. D. M. MacKay, 'Comments on Flew', in Smythies, 130.

or eating tainted meat, or by being inadvertently hypnotized by the monotony of the railroad tracks, the same puzzling situation prevails.

Philosophers have recognized that something strange is going on in these cases, and have been rightly reluctant to grant that such descriptions as I have just given are fully coherent. Thus Melden says,[19]

> If by introducing an electrode into the brain of a person, I succeed in getting him to believe that he is Napoleon, that surely is not a rational belief that he has, nor is he responsible for what he does in consequence of this belief, however convinced he may be that he is fully justified in acting as he does.

Why, though, is the man not responsible? Not because of the absurdity of the belief, for if a merely negligent evidence-gatherer came to believe some absurdity, his consequent action would not be excused, and if the electrode-induced belief happened to be true but just previously unrecognized by the man, it seems we would still deny him responsibility. (I do not think this is obvious. Suppose a benevolent neurosurgeon implants the belief that honesty is the best policy in the heads of some hardened criminals; do we, on grounds of non-rational implantation, deny these people status in the society as responsible agents?) The non-rationality, it seems, is not to be ascribed to the *content* of the belief, but somehow to the manner in which it is believed or acquired. We do, of course, absolve the insane, for they are *in general* irrational, but in this case we cannot resort to this precedent for the man has, *ex hypothesi*, only one non-rational belief. Something strange indeed is afoot here, for as was mentioned before, the introduction of the evil manipulator adds nothing to the example, and if we allow that the presence of one non-rationally induced belief absolves from responsibility, and if the absurdity or plausibility of a belief is independent of whether it has been rationally acquired or not, it seems we can never be sure whether a man is responsible for his actions, for it just may be that one of the beliefs (true or false) that is operative in a situation has been produced by non-rational accident, in which case the man would be ineligible for praise or blame. Can it be that there is a tacit assumption that no such accidents have occurred in those cases where we hold men responsible? This line is unattractive, for suppose it were *proved* in a particular case that Smith was led to some deed by a long and intricate argument, impeccably formulated by him, with the exception of one joker, a solitary premiss non-rationally induced. Our tacit assumption would be shown false; would we deny him responsibility?

A bolder scepticism toward such examples has been defended by MacIntyre: 'If I am right the concept of causing people to change their

[19] Melden, 214.

beliefs or to make moral choices, by brain-washing or drugs, for example, is not a possible concept.'[20] Hampshire, while prepared to countenance causing beliefs in others, finds a conceptual difficulty in the reflexive case: 'I must regard my own beliefs as formed in response to free inquiry; I could not otherwise count them as beliefs.'[21] Flew vehemently attacks MacIntyre's proposal:[22]

> If it did hold it would presumably rule out as logically impossible all indoctrination by such non-rational techniques. The account of Pavlovian conditionings in Aldous Huxley's *Brave New World* would be not a nightmare fantasy but contradictory nonsense. Again if this consequence did hold, one of the criteria for the use of the term *belief* would have to be essentially backward-looking. Yet this is surely not the case. The actual criteria are concerned with the present and future dispositions of the putative believer; and not at all with how he may have been led, or misled, into his beliefs.

Flew's appeal to the reality of brain-washing is misplaced, however, for what is at issue is how the results of brain-washing are to be coherently described, and MacIntyre is right to insist that there is a conceptual incoherency in the suggestion that in brain-washing one causes beliefs, *tout simple*. Elsewhere[23] I have argued that there *is* an essential backward-looking criterion of belief; here I shall strike a more glancing blow at Flew's thesis. Suppose for a moment that we put ourselves in the position of a man who wakes up to discover a non-rationally induced belief in his head (he does not know it was non-rationally induced; he merely encounters this new belief in the course of reflection, let us say). What would this be like? We can tell several different stories, and to keep the stories as neutral as possible, let us suppose the belief induced is false, but not wild: the man has been induced to believe that he has an older brother in Cleveland.

In the first story, Tom is at a party and in response to the question, 'Are you an only child?' he replies, 'I have an older brother in Cleveland.' When he is asked, 'What is his name?' Tom is baffled. Perhaps he says something like this: 'Wait a minute. Why do I think I have a brother? No name or face or experiences come to mind. Isn't that strange: *for a moment* I had this feeling of conviction that I had an older brother in Cleveland, but now that I think back on my childhood, I remember perfectly well I was an only child.' If Tom has come out of his brainwashing still predominantly rational, his induced belief can last only a moment once it is uncovered. For this reason, our earlier example of the impeccable practical reasoning flawed by a lone induced belief is an impossibility.

[20] Quoted by Flew, 118.

[21] S. Hampshire, *Freedom of the Individual* (New York: Harper & Row, 1965), 87.

[22] Flew, 120.

[23] *Content and Consciousness*.

In the second story, when Tom is asked his brother's name, he answers 'Sam' and proceeds to answer a host of other obvious questions, relates incidents from his childhood, and so forth. Not *one* belief has been induced, but an indefinitely large stock of beliefs, and other beliefs have been wiped out. This is a more stable situation, for it may take a long time before Tom encounters a serious mismatch between this large and interrelated group and his other beliefs. Indeed, the joint, as it were, between this structure of beliefs and his others may be obscured by some selective and hard-to-detect amnesia, so that Tom never is brought up with any hard-edge contradictions.

In the third story, Tom can answer no questions about his brother in Cleveland, but insists that he believes in him. He refuses to acknowledge that well-attested facts in his background make the existence of such a brother a virtual impossibility. He says bizarre things like, 'I know I am an only child and have an older brother living in Cleveland.' Other variations in the story might be interesting, but I think we have touched the important points on the spectrum with these three stories. In each story the question of Tom's responsibility can be settled in an intuitively satisfactory way by the invocation of familiar principles. In the first case, while it would be *hubris* to deny that a neurosurgeon might some day be able to set up Tom in this strange fashion, if he can do it without disturbing Tom's prevailing rationality the effect of the surgery on Tom's beliefs will be evanescent. And since we impose a general and flexible obligation on any rational man to inspect his relevant beliefs before undertaking important action, we would hold Tom responsible for any rash deed he committed while under the temporary misapprehension induced in him. Now if it turned out to be physically impossible to insert a single belief without destroying a large measure of Tom's rationality, as in the third story, we would not hold Tom responsible, on the grounds of insanity—his rationality would have been so seriously impaired as to render him invulnerable to rational communication. In the second story determining responsibility must wait on answers to several questions. Has Tom's rationality been seriously impaired? If not, we must ask the further question: did he make a reasonable effort to examine the beliefs on which he acted? If the extent of his brainwashing is so great, if the fabric of falsehoods is so broad and well-knit, that a reasonable man taking normal pains could not be expected to uncover the fraud, then Tom is excused. Otherwise not.

With this in mind we can reconsider the case of the hardened criminals surgically rehabilitated. Are they responsible citizens now, or zombies? If the surgeon has worked so delicately that their rationality is not impaired (perhaps improved!), they are, or can become, responsible. In such a case the surgeon will not so much have implanted a belief as implanted a suggestion and removed barriers of prejudice so that the suggestion *will be* believed, given the right sort of evidential support. If on the other hand the patients become rigidly obsessive about honesty, while we may feel safe allowing them to run loose in the streets, we will have to admit that they are less than persons, less than responsible agents. A bias in favour of true beliefs can be detected here: since it is hard to bring an evidential challenge to bear against a true belief (for lack of challenging evidence—unless we fabricate or misrepresent), the flexibility, or more specifically rationality, of the man whose beliefs all seem to be true is hard to establish. And so, if the rationality of the hardened criminal's new belief in honesty is doubted, it can be established, if at all, only by deliberately trying to shake the belief!

The issue between Flew and MacIntyre can be resolved, then, by noting that one cannot directly and simply cause or implant a belief, for a belief is essentially something that has been *endorsed* (by commission or omission) by the agent on the basis of its conformity with the rest of his beliefs. One may well be able to produce a zombie, either surgically or by brainwashing, and one might even be able to induce a large network of false beliefs in a man, but if so, their persistence *as beliefs* will depend, not on the strength of any sutures, but on their capacity to win contests against conflicting claims in evidential showdowns. A parallel point can be made about desires and intentions. Whatever might be induced in me is either fixed and obsessive, in which case I am not responsible for where it leads me, or else, in MacIntyre's phrase, 'can be influenced or inhibited by the adducing of some logically relevant consideration', in which case I am responsible for *maintaining* it.

VII

I believe the case is now complete against those who suppose there to be an unavoidable antagonism between the Intentional and the mechanistic stance. The Intentional stance toward human beings, which is a precondition of any ascriptions of responsibility, *may* coexist with mechanistic explanations of their motions. The other side of this coin, however, is that we *can* in principle adopt a mechanistic stance toward human bodies and their motions, so there remains an important question to be answered. *Might* we abandon the Intentional stance altogether (thereby of necessity turning our backs on the conceptual field of morality, agents, and responsibility) in favour of a purely mechanistic world view, or is this an alternative that can be ruled out on logical or conceptual grounds? This question has been approached in a number of different ways in the literature, but there is near unanimity about the general shape of the answer: for Strawson the question is whether considerations (of determinism, mechanism, etc.) could lead us to look on everyone exclusively in the 'objective' way, abandoning the 'participant' attitude altogether. His decision is that this could not transpire, and he compares the commitment to the participant attitude to our commitment to induction, which is 'original, natural, non-rational (not *ir*rational), in no way something we choose or could give up'.[24] Hampshire puts the point in terms of the mutual dependence of 'two kinds of knowledge', roughly, inductive knowledge and knowledge of one's intentions. 'Knowledge of the natural order derived from observation is inconceivable without a decision to test this knowledge, even if there is only the test that constitutes a change of point of view in observation of external objects.'[25] In other words, one cannot *have* a world view of any sort without having beliefs, and one could not have beliefs without having intentions, and having intentions requires that one view *oneself*, at least, Intentionally, as a rational agent. Sellars makes much the same point in arguing that 'the scientific image cannot replace the manifest without rejecting its own foundation'.[26] Malcolm says, 'The motto of the mechanist ought to be: One cannot speak, therefore one must be silent.'[27] But here Malcolm has dropped the ball on the goal line; how is the mechanist to *follow* his 'motto', and how *endorse* the 'therefore'? The doctrine that emerges from all these writers is that you can't get there from here, that to assert that the Intentional is eliminable 'is to imply pragmatically that there is at least one person, namely the one being addressed, if only oneself, with regard to whom the objective attitude cannot be the only kind of attitude that is appropriate to adopt'.[28] Recommissioning Neurath's ship of Knowledge, we can say that the consensus is that there is at least one plank in it that cannot be replaced.

Caution is advisable whenever one claims to have proved that something cannot happen. It is important to see what does not follow from the consensus above. It does not follow, though Malcolm thinks it does,[29] that there are some things in the world, namely human beings, of which mechanism as an embracing theory cannot be true, for there is no

[24] Strawson, 94. [79n. above]

[25] This is of course an echo of Strawson's examination of the conditions of knowledge in a 'no-space world' in *Individuals* (London: Methuen, 1959).

[26] W. Sellars, *Science, Perception and Reality* (London: Routledge & Kegan Paul, 1963), 21.

[27] Malcolm, 71. [149 above.]

[28] J. E. Llewelyn, 'The Inconceivability of Pessimistic Determinism', *Analysis,* 1966, 39–44. Having cited all these authorities, I must acknowledge my own failure to see this point in *Content and Consciousness*, 190. This is correctly pointed out by R. L. Franklin in his review in the *Australasian Journal of Philosophy*, 1970.

[29] Malcolm, 71. [149 above.]

incompatibility between mechanistic and Intentional explanation. Nor does it follow that we will always characterize some things Intentionally, for we may all be turned into zombies next week, or in some other way the human race may be incapacitated for communication and rationality. All that is the case is that we, *as persons*, cannot *adopt* exclusive mechanism (by eliminating the Intentional stance altogether). A corollary to this which has been much discussed in the literature recently is that we, as persons, are curiously immune to certain sorts of predictions. If I cannot help but have a picture of myself as an Intentional system, I am bound, as MacKay has pointed out, to have an *underspecified* description of myself, 'not in the sense of leaving any parts unaccounted for, but in the sense of being compatible with more than one state of the parts'.[30] This is because no information system can carry a complete true representation of itself (whether this representation is in terms of the physical stance or any other). And so I cannot even in principle have all the data from which to predict (from any stance) my own future.[31] Another person might in principle have the data to make all such predictions, but he could not tell them all to me without of necessity falsifying the antecedents on which the prediction depends by interacting with the system whose future he is predicting, so I can never be put in the position of being obliged to believe them. As an Intentional system I have an epistemic horizon that keeps my own future as an Intentional system indeterminate. Again, a word of caution: this barrier to prediction is not one we are going to run into in our daily affairs; it is not a barrier preventing or rendering incoherent predictions I might make about my own future decisions, as Pears for one has pointed out.[32] It is just that since I must view myself as a person, a full-fledged Intentional system, there is no complete biography of my future I would be right to accept.

All this says nothing about the impossibility of dire depersonalization in the future. Wholesale abandonment of the Intentional is in any case a less pressing concern than partial erosion of the Intentional domain, an eventuality against which there are no conceptual guarantees at all. If the growing area of success in mechanistic explanation of human behaviour does not in itself rob us of responsibility, it does make it more pragmatic, more effective or efficient, for people on occasion to adopt less than the

[30] MacKay, 'On the Logical Indeterminacy of a Free Choice', *Mind*, 1960, 31–40; 'The Use of Behavioural Language to Refer to Mechanical Processes', loc cit.; 'The Bankruptcy of Determinism', unpublished, read June 1969, at University of California at Santa Barbara.

[31] Cf. K. Popper, 'Indeterminism in Quantum Physics and Classical Physics', *British Journal for the Philosophy of Science*, 1950.

[32] D. F. Pears, 'Pretending and Deciding', *Proceedings of the British Academy*, 1964, reprinted in *Studies in the Philosophy of Thought and Action*, ed. Strawson, 97–133.

Intentional stance toward others. Until fairly recently the only well-known generally effective method of getting people to do what you wanted them to was to treat them as persons. One might threaten, torture, trick, misinform, bribe them, but at least these were forms of control and coercion that appealed to or eploited man's rationality. One did not attempt to adopt the design stance or the physical stance, just because it was so unlikely that one could expect useful behavioural results. The advent of brainwashing, subliminal advertising, hypnotism and even psychotherapy (all invoking variations on the design stance), and the more direct physical tampering with drugs and surgical intervention, for the first time make the choice of stance a genuine one. In this area many of the moral issues are easily settled; what dilemmas remain can be grouped, as MacKay has observed, under the heading of treating a person as less than a person *for his own good*. What if mass hypnosis could make people stop wanting to smoke? What if it could make them give up killing? What if a lobotomy will make an anguished man content? I argued earlier that in most instances we must ask for much more precise descriptions of the changes wrought, if we are to determine whether the caused change has impaired rationality and hence destroyed responsibility. But this leaves other questions still unanswered.

XI
MORAL LUCK
THOMAS NAGEL

KANT believed that good or bad luck should influence neither our moral judgement of a person and his actions, nor his moral assessment of himself.

> The good will is not good because of what it effects or accomplishes or because of its adequacy to achieve some proposed end; it is good only because of its willing, i.e., it is good of itself. And, regarded for itself, it is to be esteemed incomparably higher than anything which could be brought about by it in favour of any inclination or even of the sum total of all inclinations. Even if it should happen that, by a particularly unfortunate fate or by the niggardly provision of a stepmotherly nature, this will should be wholly lacking in power to accomplish its purpose, and if even the greatest effort should not avail it to achieve anything of its end, and if there remained only the good will (not as a mere wish but as the summoning of all the means in our power), it would sparkle like a jewel in its own right, as something that had its full worth in itself. Usefulness or fruitlessness can neither diminish nor augment this worth.[1]

He would presumably have said the same about a bad will: whether it accomplishes its evil purposes is morally irrelevant. And a course of action that would be condemned if it had a bad outcome cannot be vindicated if by luck it turns out well. There cannot be moral risk. This view seems to be wrong, but it arises in response to a fundamental problem about moral responsibility to which we possess no satisfactory solution.

The problem develops out of the ordinary conditions of moral judgement. Prior to reflection it is intuitively plausible that people cannot be morally assessed for what is not their fault, or for what is due to factors beyond their control. Such judgement is different from the evaluation of something as a good or bad thing, or state of affairs. The latter may be present in addition

From: *Mortal Questions*, by Thomas Nagel (Cambridge University Press, 1979), pp. 24–38. Reprinted by permission of Cambridge University Press.

[1] *Foundations of the Metaphysics of Morals*, s. 1, par. 3.

to moral judgement, but when we blame someone for his actions we are not merely saying it is bad that they happened, or bad that he exists: we are judging *him*, saying he is bad, which is different from his being a bad thing. This kind of judgement takes only a certain kind of object. Without being able to explain exactly why, we feel that the appropriateness of moral assessment is easily undermined by the discovery that the act or attribute, no matter how good or bad, is not under the person's control. While other evaluations remain, this one seems to lose its footing. So a clear absence of control, produced by involuntary movement, physical force, or ignorance of the circumstances, excuses what is done from moral judgement. But what we do depends in many more ways than these on what is not under our control—what is not produced by a good or a bad will, in Kant's phrase. And external influences on this broader range are not usually thought to excuse what is done from moral judgement, positive or negative.

Let me give a few examples, beginning with the type of case Kant has in mind. Whether we succeed or fail in what we try to do nearly always depends to some extent on factors beyond our control. This is true of murder, altruism, revolution, the sacrifice of certain interests for the sake of others—almost any morally important act. What has been done, and what is morally judged, is partly determined by external factors. However jewel-like the good will may be in its own right, there is a morally significant difference between rescuing someone from a burning building and dropping him from a twelfth-storey window while trying to rescue him. Similarly, there is a morally significant difference between reckless driving and manslaughter. But whether a reckless driver hits a pedestrian depends on the presence of the pedestrian at the point where he recklessly passes a red light. What we do is also limited by the opportunities and choices with which we are faced, and these are largely determined by factors beyond our control. Someone who was an officer in a concentration camp might have led a quiet and harmless life if the Nazis had never come to power in Germany. And someone who led a quiet and harmless life in Argentina might have become an officer in a concentration camp if he had not left Germany for business reasons in 1930.

I shall say more later about these and other examples. I introduce them here to illustrate a general point. Where a significant aspect of what someone does depends on factors beyond his control, yet we continue to treat him in that respect as an object of moral judgement, it can be called moral luck. Such luck can be good or bad. And the problem posed by this phenomenon, which led Kant to deny its possibility, is that the broad range of external influences here identified seems on close examination to undermine moral assessment as surely as does the narrower range of familiar excusing conditions. If the condition of control is consistently applied, it threatens to erode most of the moral assessments we find it natural to make. The things for which people are morally judged are determined in more ways than we at first realize by what is beyond their control. And when the seemingly natural requirement of fault or responsibility is applied in light of these facts, it leaves few pre-reflective moral judgements intact. Ultimately, nothing or almost nothing about what a person does seems to be under his control.

Why not conclude, then, that the condition of control is false—that it is an initially plausible hypothesis refuted by clear counter-examples? One could in that case look instead for a more refined condition which picked out the *kinds* of lack of control that really undermine certain moral judgements, without yielding the unacceptable conclusion derived from the broader condition, that most or all ordinary moral judgements are illegitimate.

What rules out this escape is that we are dealing not with a theoretical conjecture but with a philosophical problem. The condition of control does not suggest itself merely as a generalization from certain clear cases. It seems *correct* in the further cases to which it is extended beyond the original set. When we undermine moral assessment by considering new ways in which control is absent, we are not just dicovering what *would* follow given the general hypothesis, but are actually being persuaded that in itself the absence of control is relevant in these cases too. The erosion of moral judgement emerges not as the absurd consequence of an over-simple theory, but as a natural consequence of the ordinary idea of moral assessment, when it is applied in view of a more complete and precise account of the facts. It would therefore be a mistake to argue from the unacceptability of the conclusions to the need for a different account of the conditions of moral responsibility. The view that moral luck is paradoxical is not a *mistake*, ethical or logical, but a perception of one of the ways in which the intuitively acceptable conditions of moral judgement threaten to undermine it all.

It resembles the situation in another area of philosophy, the theory of knowledge. There too conditions which seem perfectly natural, and which grow out of the ordinary procedures for challenging and defending claims to knowledge, threaten to undermine all such claims if consistently applied. Most sceptical arguments have this quality: they do not depend on the imposition of arbitrarily stringent standards of knowledge, arrived at by misunderstanding, but appear to grow inevitably from the consistent application of ordinary standards.[2] There is a substantive parallel as well, for epistemological scepticism arises from consideration of the respects in

[2] See Thompson Clark, 'The Legacy of Skepticism', *Journal of Philosophy*, 1972, 754–69.

which our beliefs and their relation to reality depends on factors beyond our control. External and internal causes produce our beliefs. We may subject these processes to scrutiny in an effort to avoid error, but our conclusions at this next level also result, in part, from influences which we do not control directly. The same will be true no matter how far we carry the investigation. Our beliefs are always, ultimately, due to factors outside our control, and the impossibility of encompassing those factors without being at the mercy of others leads us to doubt whether we know anything. It looks as though, if any of our beliefs are true, it is pure biological luck rather than knowledge.

Moral luck is like this because while there are various respects in which the natural objects of moral assessment are out of our control or influenced by what is out of our control, we cannot reflect on these facts without losing our grip on the judgements.

There are roughly four ways in which the natural objects of moral assessment are disturbingly subject to luck. One is the phenomenon of constitutive luck—the kind of person you are, where this is not just a question of what you deliberately do, but of your inclinations, capacities, and temperament. Another category is luck in one's circumstances—the kind of problems and situations one faces. The other two have to do with the causes and effects of action: luck in how one is determined by antecedent circumstances, and luck in the way one's actions and projects turn out. All of them present a common problem. They are all opposed by the idea that one cannot be more culpable or estimable for anything than one is for that fraction of it which is under one's control. It seems irrational to take or dispense credit or blame for matters over which a person has no control, or for their influence on results over which he has partial control. Such things may create the conditions for action, but action can be judged only to the extent that it goes beyond these conditions and does not just result from them.

Let us first consider luck, good and bad, in the way things turn out. Kant, in the above-quoted passage, has one example of this in mind, but the category covers a wide range. It includes the truck driver who accidentally runs over a child, the artist who abandons his wife and five children to devote himself to painting,[3] and other cases in which the possibilities of

[3] Such a case, modelled on the life of Gauguin, is discussed by Bernard Williams in 'Moral Luck' *Proceedings of the Aristotelian Society*, supplementary volume, 1976, 115–35 (to which the original version of this essay was a reply). He points out that though success or failure cannot be predicted in advance, Gauguin's most basic retrospective feelings about the decision will be determined by the development of his talent. My disagreement with Williams is that his account fails to explain why such retrospective attitudes can be called moral. If success does not permit Gauguin to justify himself to others, but still determines his most basic feelings, that shows only that his most basic feelings need not be moral. It does not show that morality is subject to luck. If the retrospective judgement were moral, it would imply the truth of a hypothetical judgement

success and failure are even greater. The driver, if he is entirely without fault, will feel terrible about his role in the event, but will not have to reproach himself. Therefore, this example of agent-regret[4] is not yet a case of *moral* bad luck. However, if the driver was guilty of even a minor degree of negligence—failing to have his brakes checked recently, for example—then if that negligence contributes to the death of the child, he will not merely feel terrible. He will blame himself for the death. And what makes this an example of moral luck is that he would have to blame himself only slightly for the negligence itself if no situation arose which required him to brake suddenly and violently to avoid hitting a child. Yet the *negligence* is the same in both cases, and the driver has no control over whether a child will run into his path.

The same is true at higher levels of negligence. If someone has had too much to drink and his car swerves on to the sidewalk, he can count himself morally lucky if there are no pedestrians in its path. If there were, he would be to blame for their deaths, and would probably be prosecuted for manslaughter. But if he hurts no one, although his recklessness is exactly the same, he is guilty of a far less serious legal offence and will certainly reproach himself and be reproached by others much less severely. To take another legal example, the penalty for attempted murder is less than that for successful murder—however similar the intentions and motives of the assailant may be in the two cases. His degree of culpability can depend, it would seem, on whether the victim happened to be wearing a bullet-proof vest, or whether a bird flew into the path of the bullet—matters beyond his control.

Finally, there are cases of decision under uncertainty—common in public and in private life. Anna Karenina goes off with Vronsky, Gauguin leaves his family, Chamberlain signs the Munich agreement, the Decembrists persuade the troops under their command to revolt against the czar, the American colonies declare their independence from Britain, you introduce two people in an attempt at match-making. It is tempting in all such cases to feel that some decision must be possible, in the light of what is known at the time, which will make reproach unsuitable no matter how things turn out. But this is not true; when someone acts in such ways he takes his life, or his moral position, into his hands, because how things turn out determines what he has done. It is possible *also* to assess the decision from the point of view of what could be known at the time, but this is not the end of the story. If the Decembrists had succeeded in overthrowing Nicholas I in 1825 and

made in advance, of the form 'If I leave my family and become a great painter, I will be justified by success; if I don't become a great painter, the act will be unforgivable.'

[4] Williams's term *ibid.*

establishing a constitutional regime, they would be heroes. As it is, not only did they fail and pay for it, but they bore some responsibility for the terrible punishments meted out to the troops who had been persuaded to follow them. If the American Revolution had been a bloody failure resulting in greater repression, then Jefferson, Franklin and Washington would still have made a noble attempt, and might not even have regretted it on their way to the scaffold, but they would also have had to blame themselves for what they had helped to bring on their compatriots. (Perhaps peaceful efforts at reform would eventually have succeeded.) If Hitler had not overrun Europe and exterminated millions, but instead had died of a heart attack after occupying the Sudetenland, Chamberlain's action at Munich would still have utterly betrayed the Czechs, but it would not be the great moral disaster that has made his name a household word.[5]

In many cases of difficult choice the outcome cannot be foreseen with certainty. One kind of assessment of the choice is possible in advance, but another kind must await the outcome, because the outcome determines what has been done. The same degree of culpability or estimability in intention, motive, or concern is compatible with a wide range of judgements, positive or negative, depending on what happened beyond the point of decision. The *mens rea* which could have existed in the absence of any consequences does not exhaust the grounds of moral judgement. Actual results influence culpability or esteem in a large class of unquestionably ethical cases ranging from negligence through political choice.

That these are genuine moral judgements rather than expressions of temporary attitude is evident from the fact that one can say *in advance* how the moral verdict will depend on the results. If one negligently leaves the bath running with the baby in it, one will realize, as one bounds up the stairs toward the bathroom, that if the baby has drowned one has done something awful, whereas if it has not one has merely been careless. Someone who launches a violent revolution against an authoritarian regime knows that if he fails he will be responsible for much suffering that is in vain, but if he succeeds he will be justified by the outcome. I do not mean that *any* action can be retroactively justified by history. Certain things are so bad in themselves, or so risky, that no results can make them all right. Nevertheless, when moral judgement does depend on the outcome, it is objective and timeless and not dependent on a change of standpoint produced by success or failure. The judgement after the fact follows from an hypothetical

[5] For a fascinating but morally repellent discussion of the topic of justification by history, see Maurice Merleau-Ponty, *Humanisme et Terreur* (Paris; Gallimard, 1947), translated as *Humanism and Terror* (Boston: Beacon Press, 1969).

judgement that can be made beforehand, and it can be made as easily by someone else as by the agent.

From the point of view which makes responsibility dependent on control, all this seems absurd. How is it possible to be more or less culpable depending on whether a child gets into the path of one's car, or a bird into the path of one's bullet? Perhaps it is true that what is done depends on more than the agent's state of mind or intention. The problem then is, why is it not irrational to base moral assessment on what people do, in this broad sense? It amounts to holding them responsible for the contributions of fate as well as for their own—provided they have made some contribution to begin with. If we look at cases of negligence or attempt, the pattern seems to be that overall culpability corresponds to the product of mental or intentional fault and the seriousness of the outcome. Cases of decision under uncertainty are less easily explained in this way, for it seems that the overall judgement can even shift from positive to negative depending on the outcome. But here too it seems rational to subtract the effects of occurrences subsequent to the choice, that were merely possible at the time, and concentrate moral assessment on the actual decision in light of the probabilities. If the object of moral judgement is the *person*, then to hold him accountable for what he has done in the broader sense is akin to strict liability, which may have its legal uses but seems irrational as a moral position.

The result of such a line of thought is to pare down each act to its morally essential core, an inner act of pure will assessed by motive and intention. Adam Smith advocates such a position in *The Theory of Moral Sentiments*, but notes that it runs contrary to our actual judgements.

> But how well soever we may seem to be persuaded of the truth of this equitable maxim, when we consider it after this manner, in abstract, yet when we come to particular cases, the actual consequences which happen to proceed from any action, have a very great effect upon our sentiments concerning its merit or demerit, and almost always either enhance or diminish our sense of both. Scarce, in any one instance, perhaps, will our sentiments be found, after examination, to be entirely regulated by this rule, which we all acknowledge ought entirely to regulate them.[6]

Joel Feinberg points out further that restricting the domain of moral responsibility to the inner world will not immunize it to luck. Factors beyond the agent's control, like a coughing fit, can interfere with his decisions as surely as they can with the path of a bullet from his gun.[7] Nevertheless the tendency to cut down the scope of moral assessment is

[6] Pt. II, s. 3, Introduction, par. 5.

[7] 'Problematic Responsibility in Law and Morals', in Joel Feinberg, *Doing and Deserving* (Princeton University Press, 1970).

pervasive, and does not limit itself to the influence of effects. It attempts to isolate the will from the other direction, so to speak, by separating out constitutive luck. Let us consider that next.

Kant was particularly insistent on the moral irrelevance of qualities of temperament and personality that are not under the control of the will. Such qualities as sympathy or coldness might provide the background against which obedience to moral requirements is more or less difficult, but they could not be objects of moral assessment themselves, and might well interfere with confident assessment of its proper object—the determination of the will by the motive of duty. This rules out moral judgement of many of the virtues and vices, which are states of character that influence choice but are certainly not exhausted by dispositions to act deliberately in certain ways. A person may be greedy, envious, cowardly, cold, ungenerous, unkind, vain, or conceited, but *behave* perfectly by a monumental effort of will. To possess these vices is to be unable to help having certain feelings under certain circumstances, and to have strong spontaneous impulses to act badly. Even if one controls the impulses, one still has the vice. An envious person hates the greater success of others. He can be morally condemned as envious even if he congratulates them cordially and does nothing to denigrate or spoil their success. Conceit, likewise, need not be displayed. It is fully present in someone who cannot help dwelling with secret satisfaction on the superiority of his own achievements, talents, beauty, intelligence, or virtue. To some extent such a quality may be the product of earlier choices; to some extent it may be amenable to change by current actions. But it is largely a matter of constitutive bad fortune. Yet people are morally condemned for such qualities, and esteemed for others equally beyond control of the will: they are assessed for what they are *like*.

To Kant this seems incoherent because virtue is enjoined on everyone and therefore must in principle be possible for everyone. It may be easier for some than for others, but it must be possible to achieve it by making the right choices, against whatever temperamental background.[8] One may want to have a generous spirit, or regret not having one, but it makes no sense to condemn oneself or anyone else for a quality which is not within the control of the will. Condemnation implies that you should not be like that, not that it is unfortunate that you are.

Nevertheless, Kant's conclusion remains intuitively unacceptable. We

[8] 'If nature has put little sympathy in the heart of a man, and if he, though an honest man, is by temperament cold and indifferent to the sufferings of others, perhaps because he is provided with special gifts of patience and fortitude and expects or even requires that others should have the same—and such a man would certainly not be the meanest product of nature—would not he find in himself a source from which to give himself a far higher worth than he could have got by having a good-natured temperament?' (*Foundation of the Metaphysics of Morals*, s. 1, par. 11.)

may be persuaded that these moral judgements are irrational, but they reappear involuntarily as soon as the argument is over. This is the pattern throughout the subject.

The third category to consider is luck in one's circumstances, and I shall mention it briefly. The things we are called upon to do, the moral tests we face, are importantly determined by factors beyond our control. It may be true of someone that in a dangerous situation he would behave in a cowardly or heroic fashion, but if the situation never arises, he will never have the chance to distinguish or disgrace himself in this way, and his moral record will be different.[9]

A conspicuous example of this is political. Ordinary citizens of Nazi Germany had an opportunity to behave heroically by opposing the regime. They also had an opportunity to behave badly, and most of them are culpable for having failed this test. But it is a test to which the citizens of other countries were not subjected, with the result that even if they, or some of them, would have behaved as badly as the Germans in like circumstances, they simply did not and therefore are not similarly culpable. Here again one is morally at the mercy of fate, and it may seem irrational upon reflection, but our ordinary moral attitudes would be unrecognizable without it. We judge people for what they actually do or fail to do, not just for what they would have done if circumstances had been different.[10]

This form of moral determination by the actual is also paradoxical, but we can begin to see how deep in the concept of responsibility the paradox is embedded. A person can be morally responsible only for what he does; but what he does results from a great deal that he does not do; therefore he is not morally responsible for what he is and is not responsible for. (This is not a contradiction, but it is a paradox.)

[9] Cf. Thomas Gray, 'Elegy Written in a Country Churchyard':

> Some mute inglorious Milton here may rest,
> Some Cromwell, guiltless of his country's blood.

An unusual example of circumstantial moral luck is provided by the kind of moral dilemma with which someone can be faced through no fault of his own, but which leaves him with nothing to do which is not wrong. See ch. 5 of *Mortal Questions*, and Bernard Williams, 'Ethical Consistency', *Proceedings of the Aristotelian Society*, supplementary volume, 1965, reprinted in *Problems of the Self* (Cambridge University Press, 1973), 166–86.

[10] Circumstantial luck can extend to aspects of the situation other than individual behaviour. For example, during the Vietnam War even U.S. citizens who had opposed their country's actions vigorously from the start often felt compromised by its crimes. Here they were not even responsible; there was probably nothing they could do to stop what was happening, so the feeling of being implicated may seem unintelligible. But it is nearly impossible to view the crimes of one's own country in the same way that one views the crimes of another country, no matter how equal one's lack of power to stop them in the two cases. One *is* a citizen of one of them, and has a connection with its actions (even if only through taxes that cannot be withheld)—that one does not have with the other's. This makes it possible to be ashamed of one's country, and to feel a victim of moral bad luck that one was an American in the 1960s.

It should be obvious that there is a connection between these problems about responsibility and control and an even more familiar problem, that of freedom of the will. That is the last type of moral luck I want to take up, though I can do no more within the scope of this essay than indicate its connection with the other types.

If one cannot be responsible for consequences of one's acts due to factors beyond one's control, or for antecedents of one's acts that are properties of temperament not subject to one's will, or for the circumstances that pose one's moral choices, then how can one be responsible even for the stripped-down acts of the will itself, if *they* are the product of antecedent circumstances outside of the will's control?

The area of genuine agency, and therefore of legitimate moral judgement, seems to shrink under this scrutiny to an extensionless point. Everything seems to result from the combined influence of factors, antecedent and posterior to action, that are not within the agent's control. Since he cannot be responsible for them, he cannot be responsible for their results—though it may remain possible to take up the aesthetic or other evaluative analogues of the moral attitudes that are thus displaced.

It is also possible, of course, to brazen it out and refuse to accept the results, which indeed seem unacceptable as soon as we stop thinking about the arguments. Admittedly, if certain surrounding circumstances had been different, then no unfortunate consequences would have followed from a wicked intention, and no seriously culpable act would have been performed; but since the circumstances were *not* different, and the agent *in fact* succeeded in perpetrating a particularly cruel murder, *that* is what he did, and that is what he is responsible for. Similarly, we may admit that if certain antecedent circumstances had been different, the agent would never have developed into the sort of person who would do such a thing; but since he *did* develop (as the inevitable result of those antecedent circumstances) into the sort of swine he is, and into the person who committed such a murder, *that* is what he is blameable for. In both cases one is responsible for what one actually does—even if what one actually does depends in important ways on what is not within one's control. This compatibilist account of our moral judgements would leave room for the ordinary conditions of responsibility—the absence of coercion, ignorance, or involuntary movement—as part of the determination of what someone has done—but it is understood not to exclude the influence of a great deal that he has not done.[11]

[11] The corresponding position in epistemology would be that knowledge consists of true beliefs formed in certain ways, and that it does not require all aspects of the process to be under the knower's control, actually or potentially. Both the correctness of these beliefs and the process by

The only thing wrong with this solution is its failure to explain how sceptical problems arise. For they arise not from the imposition of an arbitrary external requirement, but from the nature of moral judgement itself. Something in the ordinary idea of what someone does must explain how it can seem necessary to subtract from it anything that merely happens—even though the ultimate consequence of such subtraction is that nothing remains. And something in the ordinary idea of knowledge must explain why it seems to be undermined by any influences on belief not within the control of the subject—so that knowledge seems impossible without an impossible foundation in autonomous reason. But let us leave epistemology aside and concentrate on action, character, and moral assessment.

The problem arises, I believe, because the self which acts and is the object of moral judgement is threatened with dissolution by the absorption of its acts and impulses into the class of events. Moral judgement of a person is judgement not of what happens to him, but of him. It does not say merely that a certain event or state of affairs is fortunate or unfortunate or even terrible. It is not an evaluation of a state of the world, or of an individual as part of the world. We are not thinking just that it would be better if he were different, or did not exist, or had not done some of the things he has done. We are judging *him*, rather than his existence or characteristics. The effect of concentrating on the influence of what is not under his control is to make this responsible self seem to disappear, swallowed up by the order of mere events.

What, however, do we have in mind that a person must *be* to be the object of these moral attitudes? While the concept of agency is easily undermined, it is very difficult to give it a positive characterization. That is familiar from the literature on Free Will.

I believe that in a sense the problem has no solution, because something in the idea of agency is incompatible with actions being events, or people being things. But as the external determinants of what someone has done are gradually exposed, in their effect on consequences, character, and choice itself, it becomes gradually clear that actions are events and people things. Eventually nothing remains which can be ascribed to the responsible self, and we are left with nothing but a portion of the larger sequence of events, which can be deplored or celebrated, but not blamed or praised.

Though I cannot define the idea of the active self that is thus undermined, it is possible to say something about its sources. There is a close connection between our feelings about ourselves and our feelings about others. Guilt

which they are arrived at would therefore be importantly subject to luck. The Nobel Prize is not awarded to people who turn out to be wrong, no matter how brilliant their reasoning.

and indignation, shame and contempt, pride and admiration are internal and external sides of the same moral attitudes. We are unable to view ourselves simply as portions of the world, and from inside we have a rough idea of the boundary between what is us and what is not, what we do and what happens to us, what is our personality and what is an accidental handicap. We apply the same essentially internal conception of the self to others. About ourselves we feel pride, shame, guilt, remorse—and agent-regret. We do not regard our actions and our characters merely as fortunate or unfortunate episodes—though they may also be that. We cannot *simply* take an external evaluative view of ourselves—of what we most essentially are and what we do. And this remains true even when we have seen that we are not responsible for our own existence, or our nature, or the choices we have to make, or the circumstances that give our acts the consequences they have. Those acts remain ours and we remain ourselves, despite the persuasiveness of the reasons that seem to argue us out of existence.

It is this internal view that we extend to others in moral judgement—when we judge *them* rather than their desirability or utility. We extend to others the refusal to limit ourselves to external evaluation, and we accord to them selves like our own. But in both cases this comes up against the brutal inclusion of humans and everything about them in a world from which they cannot be separated and of which they are nothing but contents. The external view forces itself on us at the same time that we resist it. One way this occurs is through the gradual erosion of what we do by the subtraction of what happens.[12]

The inclusion of consequences in the conception of what we have done is an acknowledgement that we are parts of the world, but the paradoxical character of moral luck which emerges from this acknowledgement shows that we are unable to operate with such a view, for it leaves us with no one to be. The same thing is revealed in the appearance that determinism obliterates responsibility. Once we see an aspect of what we or someone else does as something that happens, we lose our grip on the idea that it has been done and that we can judge the doer and not just the happening. This explains why the absence of determinism is no more hospitable to the concept of agency than is its presence—a point that has been noticed often. Either way the act is viewed externally, as part of the course of events.

The problem of moral luck cannot be understood without an account of

[12] See P. F. Strawson's discussion of the conflict between the objective attitude and personal reactive attitudes in 'Freedom and Resentment', *Proceedings of the British Academy*, 1962, reprinted in *Studies in the Philosophy of Thought and Action*, ed. P. F. Strawson (Oxford University Press, 1968), in P. F. Strawson, *Freedom and Resentment and Other Essays* (London: Methuen, 1974), and above, Essay V in this collection.

the internal conception of agency and its special connection with the moral attitudes as opposed to other types of value. I do not have such an account. The degree to which the problem has a solution can be determined only by seeing whether in some degree the incompatibility between this conception and the various ways in which we do not control what we do is only apparent. I have nothing to offer on that topic either. But it is not enough to say merely that our basic moral attitudes toward ourselves and others are determined by what is actual; for they are also threatened by the sources of that actuality, and by the external view of action which forces itself on us when we see how everything we do belongs to a world that we have not created.

NOTES ON THE CONTRIBUTORS

SIR ALFRED AYER was Wykeham Professor of Logic at Oxford from 1959 to 1978 and is a Fellow of Wolfson College, Oxford.

RODERICK M. CHISHOLM is Andrew W. Mellon Professor of Humanities at Brown University.

BRUCE AUNE is a member of the Department of Philosophy at the University of Massachusetts at Amherst.

KEITH LEHRER is a member of the Department of Philosophy at the University of Arizona in Tucson.

PETER VAN INWAGEN is a member of the Department of Philosophy at Syracuse University.

SIR PETER STRAWSON is Waynflete Professor of Metaphysical Philosophy at Oxford and a Fellow of Magdalen College, Oxford.

HARRY G. FRANKFURT is a member of the Department of Philosophy at Yale University.

GARY WATSON is a member of the Department of Philosophy at the University of California at Irvine.

CHARLES TAYLOR is Chichele Professor of Social and Political Theory and a Fellow at All Souls College, Oxford.

NORMAN MALCOLM is Professor of Philosophy Emeritus at Cornell University.

DANIEL C. DENNETT is a member of the Department of Philosophy at Tufts University.

THOMAS NAGEL is a member of the Department of Philosophy at New York University.

SELECTED BIBLIOGRAPHY

BOOKS

AYERS, M. *The Refutation of Determinism*. London: Methuen, 1968.

BEROFSKY, B. *Determinism*. Princeton University Press, 1971.

FINGARETTE, H. *On Responsibility*. New York: Basic Books, 1967.

GLOVER, J. *Responsibility*. New York: Humanities Press, 1970.

HAMPSHIRE, STUART. *Freedom of the Individual*. New York: Harper and Row, 1965.

KENNY, A. J. P. *Will, Freedom, and Power*. Oxford: Basil Blackwell, 1976.

——. *Freewill and Responsibility*. London: Routledge & Kegan Paul, 1978.

MELDEN, A. I. *Free Action*. London: Routledge & Kegan Paul, 1961.

SORABJI, RICHARD. *Necessity, Cause and Blame: Perspectives on Aristotle's Theory*. Cornell University Press, 1980.

THORP, JOHN. *Free Will: A Defence Against Neurophysiological Determinism*. London: Routledge & Kegan Paul, 1980.

COLLECTIONS AND ANTHOLOGIES

BEROFSKY, B. *Free Will and Determinism*. New York: Harper and Row, 1966.

DWORKIN, G. *Determinism, Free Will, and Moral Responsibility*. Englewood Cliffs: Prentice-Hall, 1970.

FEINBERG, J. *Doing and Deserving*. Princeton University Press, 1970.

HONDERICH, T. *Essays on Freedom of Action*. London: Routledge & Kegan Paul, 1973.

LEHRER, K. *Freedom and Determinism*. New York: Random House, 1966.

MORGENBESSER, S. and WALSH, J. J. *Free Will*. Englewood Cliffs: Prentice-Hall, 1962.

MORRIS, H. *Freedom and Responsibility*. Stanford University Press, 1961.

PEARS, D. *Freedom and the Will*. London: MacMillan & Co., 1963.

ARTICLES

ANSCOMBE, G. E. M. 'Soft Determinism'. In *Contemporary Aspects of Philosophy*. Ed. Gilbert Ryle. Stocksfield: Oriel Press, 1976, 148–60.

ARMSTRONG, DAVID. 'The Freedom of the Will'. *The Pluralist*, August 1965, 21–5.

AUDI, ROBERT. 'Moral Responsibility, Freedom, and Compulsion'. *American Philosophical Quarterly*, 1974, 1–14.

AUNE, BRUCE. 'Free Will, "Can", and Ethics: A Reply to Lehrer'. *Analysis*, 1969–70, 77–83.

AYER, A. J. 'Free-Will and Rationality'. In *Philosophical Subjects*. Ed. Zak Van Straaten. Oxford: Clarendon Press, 1980, 1–13.

BENNETT, JONATHAN. 'Accountability'. In *Philosophical Subjects*, 14–47.

CHISHOLM, R. M. 'He Could Have Done Otherwise'. *Journal of Philosophy*, 1967, 409–17.

——. 'The Agent as Cause'. In *Action Theory*. Ed. M. Brand and D. Walton. Dordrecht, Holland: D. Reidel, 1976, 199–212.

DAVIDSON, DONALD. 'Mental Events'. In *Experience and Theory*. Ed. L. Foster and J. Swanson. University of Massachusetts Press, 1970, 79–101. Reprinted in Donald Davidson, *Essays on Actions and Events*. Oxford: Clarendon Press, 207–25.

——. 'Psychology as Philosophy'. In *Philosophy of Psychology*. Ed. S. C. Brown. London: The Macmillan Press, 1974, 41–52. Reprinted in Donald Davidson, *Essays on Actions and Events*. Oxford: Clarendon Press, 1979, 229–39.

——. 'Freedom to Act'. In *Essays on Freedom of Action*. Ed. Ted Honderich. London: Routledge & Kegan Paul, 1973, 139–56. Reprinted in Donald Davidson, *Essays on Actions and Events*. Oxford: Clarendon Press, 1979, 63–81.

DENNETT, DANIEL C. 'On Giving Libertarians What They Say They Want'. In *Brainstorms*. D. C. Dennett. Montgomery, Vt.: Bradford Books, 1978, 286–99.

DWORKIN, GERALD. 'Acting Freely'. *Nous*, 1970, 367–83.

——. 'Autonomy and Behavior Control'. *Hastings Center Report*, Hastings-on-Hudson, New York, February 1976, 23–8.

FEINBERG, JOEL. 'What Is So Special about Mental Illness?' In *Doing and Deserving*. Joel Feinberg. Princeton University Press, 1970, 272–92.

FOLEY, R. 'Compatibilism and Control over the Past'. *Analysis*, 1979, 70–4.

FOOT, PHILIPPA. 'Free Will as Involving Determinism'. *Philosophical Review*, 1957, 439–50.

FRANKFURT, HARRY. 'Alternate Possibilities and Moral Responsibility'. *Journal of Philosophy*, 1969, 829–39.

——. 'Coercion and Moral Responsibility'. In *Essays in Freedom of Action*, 63–86.

——. 'Three Concepts of Free Action'. *Proceedings of the Aristotelian Society*, supplementary volume, 1975, 113–25.

——. 'Identification and Externality'. In *The Identity of Persons*. Ed. A. O. Rorty. University of California Press, 1976, 239–51.

GALLOIS, A. 'Van Inwagen on Free Will and Determinism'. *Philosophical Studies*, 1977, 99–105.

GOLDMAN, ALVIN. 'The Compatibility of Mechanism and Purpose'. *Philosophical Review*, 1969, 468–82.

GREENSPAN, P. S. 'Behavior Control and Freedom of Action'. *Philosophical Review*, 1978, 225–40.

HONDERICH, TED. 'One Determinism'. *Essays on Freedom of Action*, 185–215.

HOSPERS, JOHN. 'Meaning and Free Will'. *Philosophy and Phenomenological Research*, x 1950, 313–30.

KENNY, A. J. P. 'Freedom, Spontaneity, and Indifference'. *Essays in Freedom of Action*, 87–104.

LAMB, JAMES W. 'On a Proof of Incompatibilism'. *Philosophical Review*, 1977, 20–35.

LEHRER, KEITH. 'An Empirical Disproof of Determinism?' In *Freedom and Determinism*. Ed. Keith Lehrer, 175–202.

——. '"Can" in Theory and Practice: A Possible Worlds Analysis'. In *Action Theory*, 241–70.

LOCKE, D. 'Three Concepts of Free Action'. *Proceedings of the Aristotelian Society*, supplementary volume, 1975, 95–112.

MACINTYRE, A. C. 'Determinism'. *Mind*, 1957, 28–41.

Melden, A. I. 'Philosophy and the Understanding of Human Fact'. In *Epistemology*. Ed. A. Stroll. New York: Harper and Row, 1967, 229–49.

Narveson, J. 'Compatibilism Defended'. *Philosophical Studies*, 1977, 83–7.

Neely, Wright. 'Freedom and Desire'. *Philosophical Review*, 1974, 32–54.

Schiffer, Steven. 'A Paradox of Desire'. *American Philosophical Quarterly*, 1976, 195–203.

Slote, Michael A. 'Free Will, Determinism, and the Theory of Important Criteria'. *Inquiry*, 1969, 317–38.

——. 'Understanding Free Will'. *Journal of Philosophy*, 1980, 136–51.

Stern, Lawrence. 'Freedom, Blame, and Moral Community'. *Journal of Philosophy*, 1974, 72–84.

Van Inwagen, Peter. 'Reply to Narveson'. *Philosophical Studies*, 1977, 89–98.

——. 'Reply to Gallois'. *Philosophical Studies*, 1977, 107–11.

——. 'Ability and Responsibility'. *Philosophical Review*, 1978, 201–24.

——. 'The Incompatibility of Responsibility and Determinism'. Proceedings of the Bowling Green Conference on Action and Responsibility. Forthcoming.

Watson, Gary. 'Skepticism about Weakness of Will'. *Philosophical Review*, 1977, 316–39.

Wiggins, David. 'Towards a Reasonable Libertarianism'. *Essays on Freedom of Action*, 31–6.

Wolf, S. 'Asymmetrical Freedom'. *Journal of Philosophy*, 1980, 151–66.

——. 'The Importance of Free Will'. *Mind*, 1981, 386–405.

Young, Robert. 'Compatibilism and Conditioning'. *Nous*, 1979, 361–78.

——. 'Autonomy and the "Inner Self"'. *American Philosophical Quarterly*, 1980, 35–43.

INDEX OF NAMES

(not including authors mentioned only in the Bibliography)